Colonial America Almanac

Colonial America Almanac

Volume 2

PEGGY SAARI

Julie L. Carnagie, Editor

AN IMPRINT OF THE GALE GROUP
DETROIT · NEW YORK · SAN FRANCISCO
LONDON · BOSTON · WOODBRIDGE, CT

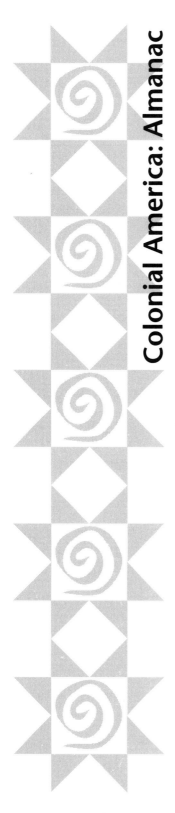

Colonial America: Almanac

Peggy Saari

Staff

Julie L. Carangie, *U•X•L Editor*
Carol DeKane Nagel, *U•X•L Managing Editor*
Thomas L. Romig, *U•X•L Publisher*

Shalice Shah-Caldwell, *Permissions Associate (Pictures)*
Maria Franklin, *Permissions Manager*

Rita Wimberley, *Senior Buyer*
Evi Seoud, *Assistant Production Manager*
Dorothy Maki, *Manufacturing Manager*

Pamela A. E. Galbreath, *Senior Art Director*
Cynthia Baldwin, *Product Design Manager*

LM Design, *Typesetting*

Cover photographs (top to bottom): The *Mayflower* reproduced with permission of The Library of Congress; Christopher Columbus landing in the New World reproduced by permission of The Bettmann Archive; The cultivation of tobacco reproduced by permission of The Granger Collection Ltd.

Library of Congress Cataloging-in-Publication Data

Saari, Peggy
    Colonial America: almanac / Peggy Saari.
        p. cm.
    Includes bibliographical references and index.
    Summary: Examines the colonial period in America, discussing both the Native American culture before the arrival of Europeans and the exploration and settlement of different parts of the New World.
    ISBN 0-7876-3763-7 (set). — ISBN 0-7876-3764-5 (v. 1). — ISBN 0-7876-3765-3 (v. 2).
    1. United States—History—Colonial period, ca. 1600-1775 Juvenile literature. 2. Almanacs,   American Juvenile literature. [1. United States—History—Colonial period, ca. 1600-1775.] I. Title.
E188.S12 2000
973.2-dc21   99-39081
                                                                  CIP

Contents

Volume 2

Advisory Board

Special thanks are due for the invaluable comments and suggestions provided by U•X•L's Colonial America Reference Library advisors:

- Katherine L. Bailey, Library Media Specialist, Seabreeze High School, Daytona Beach, Florida.

- Jonathan Betz-Zall, Children's Librarian, Sno-Isle Regional Library System, Edmonds, Washington.

- Deborah Hammer, Manager of Social Sciences Division, Queens Borough Public Library, New Hyde Park, New York.

- Fannie Louden, Fifth Grade History Teacher, B. F. Yancey Elementary School, Esmont, Virginia.

Reader's Guide

Colonial America: Almanac provides a wide range of historical information on the period in United States history between 1565 and 1760. The two-volume set describes the attempts made by European explorers and settlers to establish permanent communities on the North American continent in areas that are now part of the United States. Arranged in fifteen subject chapters, *Colonial America: Almanac* explores topics such as Native American life before the arrival of European colonists; European exploration, settlement, and colonization of the New World; the history of Africans in America during the colonial period; government and law; arts and culture; and science and medicine.

Additional features

Colonial America: Almanac includes numerous sidebars, some focusing on people associated with the colonial era, others taking a closer look at pivotal events. More than one hundred black-and-white illustrations enliven the text, while cross-references are made to people or events discussed in other chapters. Both volumes contain a timeline, a glossary, research and activity ideas, a bibliography, and a cumulative index providing access to the subjects discussed in *Colonial America: Almanac*.

Comments and suggestions

We welcome your comments on this work as well as your suggestions for topics to be featured in future editions of *Colonial America: Almanac*. Please write: Editors, *Colonial America: Almanac,* U•X•L, 27500 Drake Rd., Farmington Hills, MI 48331-3535; call toll-free: 1-800-877-4253; fax: 248-699-8097; or send e-mail via www.galegroup.com.

Introduction

Colonial America: Almanac tells the story of the period in American history when European explorers and settlers established colonies in territory that is now the United States. Presenting the story requires first answering the question: When did the colonial period begin and when did it end? According to many historians, the era started either with failed English attempts to settle on Roanoke Island (1584–87) or their successful founding of Jamestown in 1607. The conclusion is placed either before or after the French and Indian War (1754–60) or at the beginning of the revolutionary period (1775–76). These time frames, regardless of dates, put the thirteen English colonies at the center of American history. Yet the Spanish had been exploring North America since the early 1500s and had founded the first permanent European settlement at Saint Augustine, Florida, in 1565. The French were operating a thriving colony at Quebec in present-day Canada when the English arrived at Jamestown. Similarly, the Dutch established New Netherland around the time the English were colonizing New England. Although England dominated the Atlantic seaboard after taking New Netherland in 1664, Spain and France still held border regions that hemmed in the emerging English colonies.

The story of the colonial period is not confined to the European struggle for power in North America, however. By the time the Europeans stepped onto the continent, Native Americans had been developing complex civilizations since at least 30,000 B.C. Therefore, native peoples are equally significant players in the drama that began unfolding in the late 1500s. For this reason *Colonial America: Almanac* opens with a brief survey of Native American history prior to the arrival of Europeans. The narrative moves on to Spanish, French, and Dutch settlement, then finally to the founding of the "original" English colonies. Yet these groups—Native Americans, Spanish, French, Dutch, and English—did not exist in isolation from one another. They were always interacting as they competed for land, trade routes, and alliances. Colonial society became even more complex as immigrants from other European nations flooded into North America during the 1600s and 1700s.

Thus the history of the colonial period was shaped mainly by interaction among the original colonizing nations and Native Americans. The French and their native allies, in particular, had a profound impact through their continued presence on the western frontier along the Mississippi River. In fact, the English colonies' ongoing conflicts with Native Americans led to the French and Indian War. Many scholars regard the end of the war as the close of the colonial period as well, because colonists felt less militarily dependent on the British after the victory over France. It was also an important event for Native Americans, who lost their allies when the French were driven out of North America. Taking this perspective, *Colonial America: Almanac* concludes the story at the end of the war, in 1760. Although the conflict was not officially over (the Treaty of Paris was signed three years later), the hostilities had ceased and America had reached a turning point: Colonists felt newly empowered, and whatever was left of the Native American way of life began to disappear forever.

Timeline of Events in Colonial America

30,000 B.C. Native Americans arrive in North America via the Bering Sea Land Bridge.

1500 B.C. Eastern Woodland era begins in Mississippi River valley.

500 B.C.-A.D. 700 Mayans develop advanced civilizations in Mexico.

A.D. 1 Pueblo culture emerges in Southwest.

A.D. 986 The Thule Inuit encounter an expedition led by Eric the Red, who founds a settlement in Greenland.

c.1325 Aztecs build their capital, Tenochtitlán, in the Valley of Mexico.

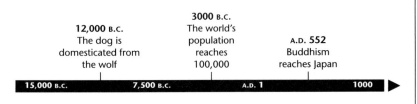

12,000 B.C.
The dog is domesticated from the wolf

3000 B.C.
The world's population reaches 100,000

A.D. 552
Buddhism reaches Japan

| 15,000 B.C. | 7,500 B.C. | A.D. 1 | 1000 |

1492	Italian sea captain Christopher Columbus, sailing for Spain, arrives in the Caribbean and founds Hispaniola, but reports that he has reached Asia.
1498	Italian navigator Sebastian Cabot, sailing for England, explores North America in search of the Northwest Passage.
1513	Seeking a mythical "fountain of youth," Juan Ponce de León of Spain lands in a part of North America he names Florida.
1519	Spanish explorer Hernando Cortes lands in Mexico; within two years, he and his expedition defeat the rich and powerful Aztec empire and claim Mexico for Spain.
1525	Giovanni da Verrazano, an Italian employed by France, reaches the North American coast; sailing north from the Carolinas, he discovers New York Harbor and the Hudson River, named at a later date for explorer Henry Hudson.
1525	Pedro de Quexco explores a huge bay on the North American coast, later known as Chesapeake Bay.
1527	Spanish explorer Panfilo de Narvaez lands on the Gulf Coast of North America with 400 explorers. The expedition is a disaster; all but a handful of members die of disease, in Indian attacks, or trying to return to Mexico by sea.
1527	The English ship *Mary Guilford* sails south along North America's Atlantic coast, from Canada to Florida.
1533	Francisco Pizarro, a Spanish explorer, conquers the great Inca empire in South America.
1534	Jacques Cartier of France lands at the mouth of the St. Lawrence River and claims the surrounding land for France.

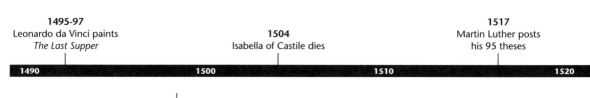

1495-97
Leonardo da Vinci paints
The Last Supper

1504
Isabella of Castile dies

1517
Martin Luther posts
his 95 theses

1490   1500   1510   1520

1535 Antonio de Mendoza arrives in Mexico as the first viceroy (governor) of New Spain, the name given to Spain's empire in the New World.

1539 Franciscan monk Marcos de Niza reports seeing the fabled "Seven Cities of Cíbola" while traveling in the American Southwest.

1539 Hernando de Soto, along with 600 men, sets out to explore the region that becomes the southwestern United States.

1539 Several Spanish expeditions claim the California coast for Spain, although no permanent settlements are attempted.

1540 A large expedition, commanded by Francisco Vásquez de Coronado, leaves Mexico and heads north through the Southwest. The expedition travels through the present-day states of Arizona, Kansas, New Mexico, Oklahoma, and Texas.

1540 Hernando de Alvarado travels along the Rio Grande into New Mexico.

1541 Jacques Cartier makes has last voyage to North America and explores the country around the Ottawa River.

1541 Hernando de Soto's expedition discovers the Mississippi River, near the present site of Memphis, Tennessee.

1542 A Spanish naval expedition under Juan Rodriguez Cabrillo reaches San Diego Bay, California; after Cabrillo's death, Bartolome Ferillo leads the expedition farther along the coast to San Francisco Bay.

1543 The Hernando de Soto expedition (minus its leader, who dies in 1542) returns to Mexico.

1559 Tristan de Luna y Arellano leads a Spanish expedition to Pensacola, Florida, to establish a settlement; the colony fails and the survivors leave two years later.

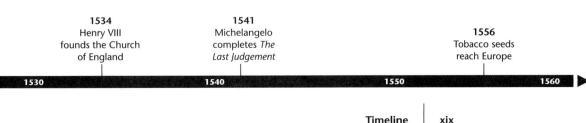

1534
Henry VIII
founds the Church
of England

1541
Michelangelo
completes *The
Last Judgement*

1556
Tobacco seeds
reach Europe

1530   1540   1550   1560

1562 Jean Ribault of France leads 150 settlers to the coast of what is now South Carolina in an attempt to found a refuge for French Protestants (Huguenots); the colony is abandoned soon after.

1564 A second French colonizing expedition commanded by Rene de Laudonniere lands in what is today Florida.

1565 Alarmed at the French presence close to Spanish Florida, a force under Pedro Menendez de Áviles attacks the colony, destroying it and killing almost all the settlers.

1565 Spain establishes Saint Augustine, its chief outpost in Florida and the oldest permanent settlement in what is now the United States.

1571 Spanish attempts to colonize northern Florida (now part of Virginia) fail when Indians overrun a Jesuit mission on the southern portion of the Chesapeake Bay.

1576 Elizabeth I of England grants Humphrey Gilbert a patent (royal authority) to colonize the New World for England and the crown.

1579 English captain Francis Drake's round-the-world expedition reaches San Francisco Bay, California; he claims the area for England, naming it New Albion. (Albion is another name for England.)

1583 Humphrey Gilbert founds a colony on the island of Newfoundland off the coast of Canada. Gilbert is lost at sea while returning to England and his patent passes to his half brother, Walter Raleigh.

1584 Captains Philip Amadas and Arthur Barlowe, sailing for Walter Raleigh, sail to the New World to pave the way for an English colony in the Chesapeake Bay region.

1585 Walter Raleigh names the land explored by his expedition "Virginia," in honor of England's unmarried queen, Elizabeth I.

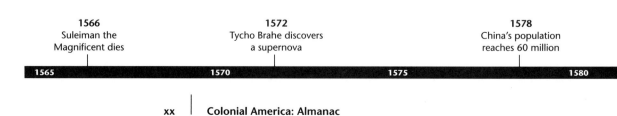

1566
Suleiman the
Magnificent dies

1572
Tycho Brahe discovers
a supernova

1578
China's population
reaches 60 million

| 1565 | 1570 | 1575 | 1580 |

1585   More then 100 colonists under Richard Grenville establish a colony in Virginia, on Roanoke Island off the coast of modern-day North Carolina.

1586   The first Roanoke colony fails; those colonists who survive are taken back to England by Francis Drake, who arrives at Roanoke after burning the Spanish fort at Saint Augustine.

1587   Another colonizing expedition arrives at Roanoke, bringing more than 100 settlers led by John White, who sails back to England for more supplies.

1587   Virginia Dare is born to Ananias and Eleanor Dare of the Roanoke Colony; she is the first child born of English parents in North America.

1602   After exploring and naming Cape Cod and Martha's Vineyard, Bartholomew Gosnold returns from America to England with a cargo of furs and lumber, fueling the movement to colonize North America.

1602   Sebastian Vizcaino explores a bay on the coast of central California and names it Monterey after the Count of Monte Rey, viceroy of Mexico.

1603   Samuel de Champlain embarks on the first of eleven exploratory voyages along the St. Lawrence River and the northeastern Atlantic coast of North America.

1604   Samuel de Champlain and Pierre de Monts establish the first French settlement in Acadia (Nova Scotia), on an island in Passamaquoddy Bay, along the present-day United States-Canada border.

1606   The London and Plymouth companies receive charters from James I of England to establish colonies in the New World.

1607   Under the charter granted to the Virginia Company of London, an expedition led by Bartholomew Gosnold, John Smith, and Christopher Newport founds

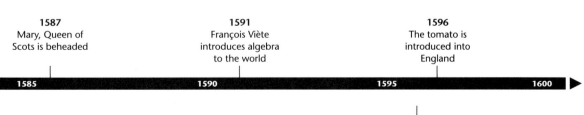

1587	1591	1596
Mary, Queen of Scots is beheaded	François Viète introduces algebra to the world	The tomato is introduced into England

1585   1590   1595   1600

Jamestown, the first permanent English settlement in North America.

1608 After five years of exploring the coast and rivers of North America, Samuel de Champlain founds Quebec, the first permanent French settlement on the mainland of North America.

1609 Henry Hudson, an English navigator sailing for the Dutch East India Company, explores Chesapeake and Delaware Bays, discovers the Hudson River, and claims all the land along its banks for the Netherlands.

1610 Spanish settlers under governor Don Pedro de Peralta found Villa Real de la Santa Fe de San Francisco de Asis (now Santa Fe, New Mexico).

1612 John Rolfe establishes what will be the most important cash crop of the southern colonies by cultivating new varieties of tobacco.

1612 The Virginia Company sends sixty English settlers to the Bermuda Islands.

1613 English colonists sail north from Virginia to destroy Port Royal and other French settlements in Acadia and Maine, beginning 150 years of armed struggle between the two countries for control of eastern North America.

1614 On his second voyage to America, John Smith explores an area he names New England and maps the coast from Maine to Cape Cod.

1615 Samuel de Champlain joins the Huron Indians in attacking the Iroquois near Lake Ontario, establishing for New France both an alliance and an enemy that will continue for the rest of the century.

1615 The first Franciscan friars arrive in Quebec to begin French missionary activity in Canada.

1619 The Virginia House of Burgesses, the first elected legislature in the colonies, meets for the first time.

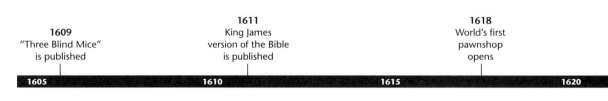

1609
"Three Blind Mice"
is published

1611
King James
version of the Bible
is published

1618
World's first
pawnshop
opens

1605   1610   1615   1620

1619   A Dutch ship arrives in Jamestown carrying the first
        Africans to arrive in the colony; they are put to work as
        indentured servants. Another ship brings women from
        London as wives for the settlers.

1620   Seeking religious freedom, the Pilgrims head for Vir-
        ginia on the *Mayflower* but go off course, landing on
        Cape Cod and later founding a colony at Plymouth,
        Massachusetts.

1620   Peregrine White becomes the first child born among
        the New England colonists.

1621   The Plymouth settlers establish a peace treaty with
        Massasoit, chief of the local Wampanoag Indians, who
        help the Pilgrims survive the winter.

1621   James I of England grants the Acadian lands already
        claimed by France to William Alexander for the pur-
        pose of founding the colony of Nova Scotia (New
        Scotland).

1622   One-fourth of the Jamestown colonists, 357 people,
        die in an attack by the Powhatan Indians, which
        begins two years of war.

1623   The Council for New England, which succeeded the
        Plymouth Company, establishes fishing and trading
        settlements in Portsmouth and Dover, New Hampshire.

1623   Thomas Warner establishes a settlement on St. Kitts
        (St. Christopher), the first successful English colony in
        the West Indies.

1624   On behalf of the Dutch West India Company, Dutch
        colonists establish fur-trading settlements at Fort
        Orange (Albany, New York) and New Amsterdam
        (Manhattan Island).

1624   James I revokes the Virginia Company's charter and
        takes control of the settlement, making it a royal colony.

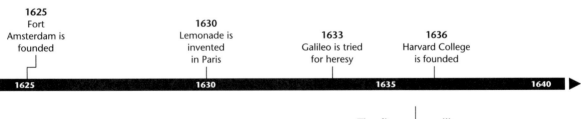

1625
Fort
Amsterdam is
founded

1630
Lemonade is
invented
in Paris

1633
Galileo is tried
for heresy

1636
Harvard College
is founded

1625   1630   1635   1640

1626	By the end of the summer, the Dutch construct over thirty wooden frame houses on the southern tip of Manhattan.
1627	A Swedish company receives a charter for that nation's first colony in the New World, although the colony (New Sweden, on the Delaware River) will not be founded for another decade.
1628	John Endecott, leading a group of about sixty Puritans fleeing religious persecution in England, founds Salem, Massachusetts, for the New England Company.
1629	The Massachusetts Bay Company receives a royal charter granting the company rights to establish settlements between the Charles and Merrimack Rivers in New England.
1630	John Winthrop and 900 Puritans found a self-governing settlement at Boston in the name of the Massachusetts Bay Company.
1631	The Council for New England, with Englishman Fernando Gorges as president, establishes a single plantation settlement at Saco Bay, Maine.
1632	The English return Quebec and Acadia to French control by a treaty under which each nation recognizes the other's established North American colonies.
1634	Under a charter granted to Cecilius Calvert, the second Lord Baltimore founds Maryland as a refuge for English Catholics who are seeking religious tolerance and civil rights.
1635	Seeking greater freedom than the Massachusetts Bay Colony offered, Thomas Hooker and sixty followers found Hartford, the first permanent settlement in Connecticut.
1635	English Puritans build the settlement of Fort Saybrook at the mouth of the Connecticut River, beginning competition with the Dutch for control of the river valley.

1646
England's civil
war ends

1648
Europe's Thirty Years'
War ends

1650
England's first
coffeehouse opens

1645   1647   1649   1651

1635   French colonists under Pierre Belaine, sieur d'Esnam-
        buc, establish a settlement on Martinique and seize the
        island of Guadaloupe, the first permanent French
        colony in the West Indies.

1636   Banished from Massachusetts for his religious and
        political views, Roger Williams founds Providence
        Plantation (later the colony of Rhode Island) on land
        he purchases from the Narragansett Indians.

1637   Colonial forces in Connecticut and Massachusetts,
        allied with the Mohegan and Narragansett Indians,
        destroy Pequot Indian villages, kill 500 to 600 Pequots,
        and scatter or enslave the surviving members of the
        tribe to avenge the murders of several colonists.

1638   Banished from Massachusetts for challenging the Puri-
        tan clergy, Anne Hutchinson moves to Pocasset (later
        known as Portsmouth), the second settlement in
        Rhode Island.

1638   Swedish colonists led by Peter Minuit establish Fort
        Christina (Wilmington, Delaware), the oldest perma-
        nent settlement in the Delaware River Valley.

1639   The Hartford and New Haven colonies establish a
        democratic, representative system of self-government
        under the Fundamental Orders of Connecticut.

1639   The charter for Maine grants the territory already
        claimed by the French as part of Acadia to aristocratic
        English proprietor Fernando Gorges.

1641   The colonial government of Massachusetts takes con-
        trol of the region known as New Hampshire.

1642   Paul de Chomedey, sieur de Maisonneuve, founds the
        settlement of Montreal, expanding New France's fur
        trade south and west.

1643   Four New England settlements (Plymouth, Massachu-
        setts Bay, Connecticut, and New Haven) form the

1653
Thomas Bartholin
describes lymphatic
system

1655
Sweden invades
Poland

1657
First fountain pens
manufactured

1653   1655   1657   1659

United Colonies of New England, joining in defense against both Indians and the Dutch.

1644 Roger Williams returns from England after obtaining a royal patent for the colony of Rhode Island.

1647 Four Rhode Island settlements (Providence, Portsmouth, Newport, and Warwick) join in a loose confederacy, drafting a code of civil law that expressly separates church and state.

1652 The Massachusetts Bay Colony takes over the territory of Maine and declares itself independent of the English Parliament.

1653 The Dutch West India Company allows New Amsterdam, with more than 800 residents, to incorporate as a self-governing city.

1654 Ships carrying Dutch settlers from Brazil, where they had been expelled, bring the first Jews to New Amsterdam.

1654 In their continuing effort to monopolize the northern fishing and fur trade, English colonists capture Acadia from the French.

1655 Led by Peter Stuyvesant, the Dutch capture Fort Christina and take control of all of the Delaware Valley.

1664 The English capture New Amsterdam, which they rename New York, and England's King Charles II grants to his brother, the Duke of York, all land from Maine to Delaware not already settled by English colonists.

1665 The colony of New Jersey, presented by the Duke of York to his friends George Carteret and John Berkeley, is founded.

1668 Jesuit priest Jacques Marquette founds a mission at Sault Ste. Marie in present-day Michigan.

1669 French fur trader Louis Jolliet begins his exploration of the Great Lakes region.

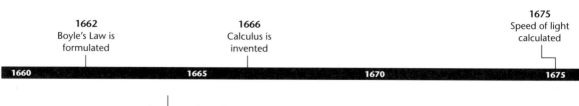

1662
Boyle's Law is formulated

1666
Calculus is invented

1675
Speed of light calculated

1660   1665   1670   1675

1673   Dutch forces recapture New York and the colonies along the Delaware River from the English, only to be forced to give them back again a year later.

1673   Louis Jolliet and Jacques Marquette, hoping to find a river route to the Pacific, explore the Mississippi River as far south as the Arkansas River.

1675   King Philip's War, between English colonists and Native American tribes in Massachusetts, Rhode Island, and Connecticut, causes damage or destruction in sixty-four colonial towns and destroys Indian villages and food supplies.

1682   After almost two years of traveling the Mississippi River, René-Robert Cavalier de la Salle reaches the river's mouth and claims for France all the land along its banks, a territory he names Louisiana.

1682   William Penn founds Philadelphia and the Pennsylvania colony as a refuge for Quakers and other persecuted religious minorities.

1698   Eusebio Francisco Kino leads a three-year expedition that charts a land course from Mexico to California, disproving the previous belief that California was an island.

1699   Brothers Pierre and Jean Baptiste Le Moyne establish Old Biloxi (present-day Ocean Springs, Mississippi), the first of several French settlements along the coast of the Gulf of Mexico.

1700   French settlers begin to construct forts, settlements, fur-trading posts, and Jesuit missions in the Illinois Territory.

1702   Queen Anne's War, the second war between England and France for control of North America, begins. Most of the fighting over the next twelve years will take place in the outlying settlements on the New England-Canada frontier.

1681
France annexes
Strasbourg

1687
The University of
Bologna is founded

1692
Aesop's Fables
is published

1680   1685   1690   1695

1710 British and New England troops capture Port Royal, which they rename Annapolis Royal, and the region now known as Nova Scotia, from the French.

1711 Almost 200 North Carolina settlers are massacred by the local Tuscarora Indians, initiating the year-long Tuscarora War, which results in the deaths of hundreds of Tuscaroras and the migration of the survivors to New York, where they join the Iroquois Confederation.

1716 Virginia governor Alexander Spotswood leads an expedition into the westernmost Virginia territory, crossing the Blue Ridge Mountains into the Shenandoah River Valley.

1718 On behalf of the French Company of the West, Jean Baptiste Le Moyne founds a city (New Orleans) at the mouth of the Mississippi that becomes the capital of the Louisiana territory four years later.

1718 Spanish settlers found the military post and mission of San Antonio, the first of several missions established in an attempt to counter French settlements along the western Gulf coast.

1720 France's treasury is bankrupted after the Mississippi Company is revealed to be a sham in a financially disastrous settlement plan known as the Mississippi Bubble.

1722 The Six Nations of the Iroquois Confederation (Mohawk, Oneida, Onondaga, Cayuga, Seneca, and Tuscarora), under a treaty with Virginia colonists, agree not to cross the Potomac River or move west of the Blue Ridge Mountains.

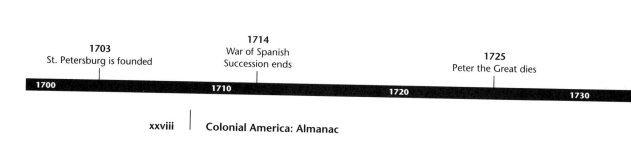

1703
St. Petersburg is founded

1714
War of Spanish
Succession ends

1725
Peter the Great dies

1700   1710   1720   1730

1729 French soldiers in the Louisiana territory massacre Natchez Indians. A ten-year war begins between the French and Indians.

1733 James Edward Oglethorpe founds the city of Savannah and the colony of Georgia, the last of the original thirteen English colonies, as a haven for the poor.

1747 Settlers from Virginia and Pennsylvania move onto land granted to the Ohio Company, prompting French settlers to construct a line of forts across western Pennsylvania.

1749 Georgia permits large landholdings and slavery, leading to economic prosperity for plantation owners. Following five years of war between French and British colonies (King George's War) in which little territory changes hands, the British found Halifax to strengthen their hold on Nova Scotia.

1750 German craftspeople in Pennsylvania develop the Conestoga wagon, soon to become the standard vehicle on the frontier.

1752 A year before their original charter is due to expire, the trustees of Georgia give all administrative power to the British government.

1754 Competing British, French, and Native claims to territory from the Appalachians west to the Mississippi River lead to the nine years of fighting known as the French and Indian War.

1755 Britain banishes defeated French colonists from Acadia, some of whom travel to Louisiana, where they become known as Acadians (Cajuns).

1760 The English capture Montreal from the French, essentially ending the French and Indian War.

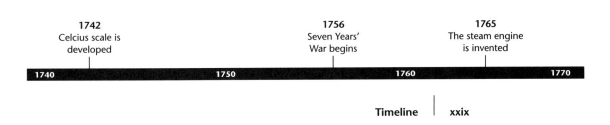

1742
Celcius scale is developed

1756
Seven Years' War begins

1765
The steam engine is invented

| 1740 | 1750 | 1760 | 1770 |

Words to Know

A

American Revolution: A conflict lasting from 1775 to 1783 in which American colonists gained independence from British rule.

Anabaptists: Those who oppose the baptism of infants; also know as Baptists.

Anglican Church: The official religion of England; also know as the Church of England.

Antinomianism: The belief that God has predetermined who would be saved from sin.

Apprentice: A person who learns by practical experience under skilled workers.

Archaeologists: Scientists who study ancient cultures.

Aristocrat: A member of the nobility, or ruling class.

B

Banished: The forced removal of someone from a colony.

Baptism: The initiation into Christianity through anointment with water.

Borough: An area under the jurisdiction of a local government.

C

Calvinists: Followers of French Protestant reformer John Calvin.

Capital: Money used for business purposes.

Capital offenses: Crimes requiring the death penalty.

Catechism: Religious instruction that involves questions and answers.

Charters: Land grants and governing contracts.

Common law: The body of law determined by custom and precedent.

Commons: A grassy area in the middle of the village.

Communion: The ritual in which bread and wine represent the body and blood of Jesus of Nazareth, the founder of Christianity.

Congregations: Separate groups of church members.

Conquistadors: Conquerors.

Constitution: A document that establishes an independent government.

Covenants: Solemn and binding agreements.

D

Deeds: Legal contracts.

Democracy: Government by the people exercised directly or by elected representatives.

Deported: Forcibly sent.

Dissenters: Those who oppose the church.

Doctrine: Policy and teachings.

Duties: Taxes.

Dysentery: A disease characterized by severe diarrhea.

E

Emigrated: To leave one country or region and settle in another.

Encomienda: A land grant.

English Civil War: A conflict lasting from 1642 to 1648 that pitted Parliament and the Puritans against Charles I and the Church of England.

Evangelicals: Those who emphasize salvation by faith, the authority of the scripture, and the importance of preaching.

F

Fords: Part of a body of water that may be crossed by wading.

Franciscan friars: Priests belonging to the order of Saint Francis of Assisi.

Freedom dues: Items given to a servant at the end of service.

Freedom of the press: The right of newspapers to print truthful information.

Freemen: Men with the full rights of citizens; women had no rights.

Free will: The idea that all people can make voluntary choices or decisions independently from God.

G

Gallows: A structure used for hanging people for execution.

Gentry: The upper or ruling class.

Glorious Revolution: The name given to the ascension of Protestant monarchs William III and Mary II.

H

Head right: A grant from the colony to a settler who paid his own way to North America.

Heresy: A violation of church teachings.

Huguenots: Members of a Protestant religious group.

Hydrography: The science of charting bodies of water.

I

Immigration: To come into a foreign country to live.

Indentured servants: Laborers who worked for a specific number of years.

Indigo: A plant used to make blue dye.

J

Jesuits: Members of the Society of Jesus, a Roman Catholic religious order.

M

Malaria: A disease transmitted by mosquitoes.

Magistrates: Judges.

Mass: The Catholic Eucharist, or holy communion service.

Matrilineal: Relating to a family headed by a woman

May Day: A celebration held in England on May 1 honoring the tradition of spring fertility rights in Egypt and India.

Maypole: A flower-wreathed pole that is the center of dancing and games during a May Day celebration.

Mercantilism: A system that advocates government intervention in the economy to increase the power of the state.

Mestizos: People having mixed Native American and white parentage.

Midwife: A person who assists women in childbirth.

Militia: Citizens' army.

Missionaries: People sent to do religious or charitable work in a foreign country.

Monopoly: An exclusive ownership through legal privilege, command of supply, or action.

Mulattos: People of mixed white and black ancestry.

N

New World: European term for North and South America.

Notaries: Officials who process legal documents.

P

Pacifists: People who do not believe in bearing arms.

Paganism: Having little or no religion.

Palisade: A fence of stakes for defense.

Parishes: Areas of church jurisdiction.

Parliament: England's lawmaking body.

Patent: A contract granting specific rights.

Patrilineal: Relating to a family headed by a man.

Patroons: Proprietors of large estates.

Pelts: Animal skins.

Penal colony: A settlement for convicted criminals.

Penance: The confession and punishment of sins.

Persecuted: Being punished or discriminated against because of religious beliefs.

Pig iron: Crude iron that has been made in a blast furnace.

Pirates: Bandits who robbed ships at sea.

Pope: The head of the Roman Catholic Church.

Pounds: The name of British currency.

Presbyterianism: A democratic system of church organization in which ministers and elders formed the governing body in a district.

Priest: An ordained clergyman of the Roman Catholic Church.

Privateer: A pirate licensed by the government.

Privy Council: The king's council.

Proprietary grant: A contract giving an individual or group the right to organize and govern a colony.

Proprietors: Individuals granted ownership of a colony and full authority to establish a government and distribute land.

Protestantism: A branch of Christianity formed in opposition to Catholicism; its consists of many denominations, or separate organized churches.

Provinces: Local regions.

Puritans: A Protestant group that advocates strict moral conduct and reform of the Church of England.

Q

Quakers: Members of the Society of Friends.

Quitrents: Fixed taxes on land.

Quorum: A minimum number of members required to approve legislation.

R

Revival meetings: Religious events based on spontaneous spiritual awakening.

Rickets: A disease that affects the young during the period of skeletal growth.

Roman Catholicism: A branch of Christianity based in Rome, Italy, and headed by a pope who has supreme authority in all church affairs.

Royal colony: Colony under direct rule of the king.

Royal council: A committee appointed by the governor, with the approval of the king, that helped administer the colony.

Royal governor: The highest colonial official, appointed by the king.

S

Salvation: The forgiveness of sins.

Scurvy: A disease caused by a lack of vitamin C.

Seditious libel: Making a false statement that exposes another person to public contempt.

Shilling: An early American coin.

Slaves: Permanent servants regarded as property.

Smallpox: A deadly skin disease caused by a virus.

Stocks: A wooden frame with holes for the hands, feet, and head used to punish people.

Surveying: A branch of mathematics that involves taking measurements of the Earth's surface.

Syndic: Representative.

T

Tariffs: Trade fees.

Tenant farmers: People who pay rent for farmland with cash or with a share of the crops they produce.

Theocratic state: Government ruled by the church.

Treason: Betrayal of one's country.

Tribute: Payment.

Trust: A property interest held by one person for the benefit of another.

Typhus: A disease transmitted by lice.

V

Vestryment: Members elected to make decisions regarding the church.

Veto power: The authority to prohibit.

Viceroy: Representative of the king.

W

Wampum: Woven belts of shells often used as currency by the Native Americans.

Whiskey treaties: Agreements signed while Native Americans were under the influence of alcohol.

Research and Activity Ideas

The following list of research and activity ideas is intended to offer suggestions for complementing social studies and history curricula, to trigger additional ideas for enhancing learning, and to suggest cross-disciplinary projects for library and classroom use.

Activity 1: Teen life in colonial America

Assignment: Imagine that you and two of your friends are living in colonial America and you possess the power of time-travel. The three of you have been invited by a present-day social studies class to tell about colonial American life from a teenager's perspective. You accept the invitation, promising to make your presentation both informative and entertaining.

Preparation: First you must select your roles. For instance, you could be Puritan teenagers living in a small town or on neighboring farms. You might be African slaves working together on a southern plantation. Or you could be Native Americans living in a village near one of the colonies. Next, using *Colonial America: Almanac* as a starting point, gather information about the daily life of the teenagers you have chosen to portray. Consult the library and Internet Web sites for additional material, including illustrations and other graphics. As you conduct your research, focus on food, clothing, shelter, community and family life, recreation, religion, education, and other relevant topics. You can facilitate this stage of the project by making specific assignments. For instance, each team member can gather information on two or three areas such as community and family life or food, shelter, and clothing.

Presentation: After you have gathered information, prepare a twenty-minute team presentation. Keep in mind that your goal is to tell about life in colonial America, but you also want to engage your audience. Use various strategies to bring your colonial teenagers to life: Wear colonial-style clothing, prepare a colonial recipe and share the food with the class, or distribute handouts that feature interesting facts. Explore other possibilities to draw upon the knowledge and talents of each team member.

Activity 2: A trip to the colonies

Assignment: Your teacher has asked you to start a travel service that specializes in planning family vacations to historic sites in the United States. To launch your venture, you must prepare a promotional brochure that features a one-week "trip through colonial America." The teacher has chosen you for this assignment because you know about colonial-period sites that are uncommon tourist attractions.

Preparation: You must first decide on a destination for the trip, so you need to gather more information. As an expert on the colonial era, you know there are several possible itineraries for a trip to colonial America—New England, the middle colonies, the southern colonies, the Southeast, and the Southwest. Using *Colonial America: Almanac* as a starting point, check the library and Internet Web sites for more information. In addition to obtaining facts, you want to find photos and illustrations of colonial sites.

You will probably discover that well-known places such as Plymouth Rock or Williamsburg, Virginia, will have to be included on your itinerary. But you can also guide travelers to less familiar sites. Examples are John Bartram's gardens outside Philadelphia, Pennsylvania; the oldest French building in the United States, at Cahokia, Illinois; and the statue of Jacques Marquette in Rotunda Hall in Washington, D.C. Once you have decided on a destination, select several sites that can be visited within a seven-day period, including as many lesser-known locations as possible.

Presentation: Now that you have completed the information-gathering phase, you are ready to create the brochure. One approach is to write a three-page paper in which you describe the itinerary of the trip to colonial America. Include the following information: (1) historical background on the region, (2) a detailed description of each site, and (3) an explanation of its significance. Then provide a trip map along with photos and illustrations of the sites. If you feel especially creative, you can use a computer to produce an actual brochure, then distribute copies to your classmates.

Activity 3: A "live" historical event

Assignment: For a school assembly program, your class has been asked to dramatize an important event in colonial American history. You are expected to base your dramatization on historical facts, although you are free to use your own dialogue and interpretation when necessary. Your goal is both to inform and entertain your audience. You must also involve each member of the class in the project.

Preparation: The first task is to choose an historical event. Possibilities include the Pilgrims' first winter at Plymouth, Bacon's Rebellion, or the Salem witch trials. To make a decision you might put the question to a class vote. Once you have chosen the event, you need to gather information for a script and other aspects of the dramatization. One approach is to form teams that will do research on a particular aspect of the event. For instance, if you are dramatizing a Salem witch trial, one team can find information about the accusations brought against so-called witches. Other teams could locate transcripts of accused witches' trial testimony, do research on how the judges made their decisions, and find out how the Salem community reacted to the trials.

Using *Colonial America: Almanac* as a starting point, the teams must find information at the library and on Internet Web sites. Look for historians' accounts of the event, which can provide a narrative frame for your dramatization. Also look for documents from the period, which can be used as the basis of speaking parts. For instance, William Bradford wrote about the Pilgrims' landing and first winter at Plymouth. Nathaniel Bacon issued a manifesto during his rebellion, and there are eyewitness accounts of the Salem witch trials.

Presentation: When all the teams have gathered their information, assign roles and responsibilities, such as script writers, a director, a narrator, major and minor speakers, "extras" for crowd scenes—perhaps even a publicity team, costume and prop crews, and lighting and sound crews, depending on the complexity of your production. Be sure everyone in the class is involved, and concentrate on making the dramatization both informative and entertaining.

Community Life

When the first European colonists arrived in North America, they brought with them their own cultural values and traditions. Confronted with a strange new world, they poured their energies into re-creating familiar ways of life. Inevitably, they found it necessary to adapt their lifestyles to their new environment. In addition, they came into contact with settlers from different parts of Europe and Native Americans. These experiences led to a gradual process of adaptation and exchange among very different cultures.

One way early European colonists sought to feel more at home was to attach familiar words to their strange surroundings. They exchanged exotic Native American place names for English, German, Dutch, or Spanish ones. They gave their towns familiar names such as Plymouth, Boston, and Ipswich. Settlers displayed loyalty to their kings by giving important towns names such as Jamestown, Charlestown, and Williamsburg. They clustered their homes in European village patterns, and they worked hard to duplicate the life they had known in the Old World.

Yet life in the colonies was very different from life in Europe, especially in the early colonial period. North America had climates, crops, and sources of food that the settlers had never before encountered. There was an unfamiliar abundance of land and materials. In addition, interaction with Native Americans demanded a variety of adaptations. The colonists not only learned from Native Americans but also had to learn about them. As time went on, great changes in European commerce, philosophical and scientific inquiry, technology, and warfare reached across the Atlantic to shape the new American society. All of these factors, plus the daily needs of the settlers, resulted in a wide range of changes. The colonies gradually evolved from struggling outposts in the early seventeenth century to productive farming communities and bustling cities by the middle of the eighteenth century.

New England and the middle colonies societies

As successive waves of European immigrants arrived in the colonies, the combination of old and new ways of life produced strikingly different regional societies (see Chapter 4). New England became a remarkably stable society of small family farms and villages distributed among the colonies that eventually became Massachusetts, Connecticut, New Hampshire, and Rhode Island. In the process of settlement, colonists spread slowly and methodically across the countryside, establishing towns in which families remained for generations. The middle colonies—New York, New Jersey, Pennsylvania, and Delaware—were home to a diverse population and different cultural patterns.

Although the English took New Netherland from the Dutch in 1664 and renamed it New York, the Dutch population continued to shape the colony. The Swedes were the first Europeans to settle along the mouth of the Delaware River. Later settlers from Scotland, Northern Ireland, England, and the Netherlands created ethnic and religious diversity in the colony that became New Jersey. When William Penn (1644–1718) established Pennsylvania in 1681, he welcomed settlers from all over Europe as well as Quakers from England; this colony, too, became quite diverse (see Chapter 4). During the eighteenth century the population of this region became increasingly mobile, each year pressing farther west toward the backcountry and south along the Appalachian Mountains.

The Chesapeake and the Carolinas societies

In the Chesapeake region, society was shaped largely by the cultivation of tobacco, the main export crop of Virginia and Maryland. Chesapeake planters established their farms along navigable rivers where ships could easily dock and take on each year's crop. Those who wanted to grow rich through tobacco cultivation needed large tracts

A wood engraving of family life among the Dutch settlers of the Middle Atlantic colonies.
Reproduced by permission of The Granger Collection.

of land and a substantial labor force. A comparatively small group of wealthy planting families came to occupy the top positions in society and to control the bulk of Chesapeake wealth and property. The bottom rungs of the social ladder were occupied by unfree laborers: English indentured servants for much of the seventeenth century, and African slaves after the 1680s.

North Carolina remained largely undeveloped until late in the colonial period, but South Carolina emerged as a second plantation society. Planters in this region specialized in rice and indigo, which produced a deep blue dye. By 1760 slaves of African descent made up 60 percent of the total population of South Carolina. As in the Chesapeake region, the large number of unfree laborers had a profound effect on the evolving society.

The Spanish colonies of the American Southwest and Southeast were organized fairly systematically to advance Spain's interests and control (see Chapter 2). The *encomienda* system created a society of Spanish soldier-settlers whose conquest of Native American populations gained them vast land grants from the Spanish Crown. These colonists also had the right to collect tribute from the Native Americans in the form of food, products, and labor. Spanish colonial society came to be organized as a racial hierarchy, which included members with Spanish, Native American, African, or mixed blood.

Settlers on the haciendas (large estates) of the Spanish borderlands used the *encomienda* system to control the land and the native people. French settlers along the Mississippi and Saint Lawrence River valleys created entirely new cultures to suit their environment, their small numbers, and the constant interaction with a large Native American population.

Social classes

European colonists had been accustomed to a distinct system of social ranks and roles. Their ideas of a class system came with them to the colonies, but, especially during the early 1600s, class lines and divisions were more easily changed than in Europe. In certain respects the American colonies provided greater opportunities for settlers who wanted to improve their social and economic status.

Life in the English colonies disrupted the traditional class system for several reasons. Neither the highest classes of English society nor the lowest came to America in large numbers. Many immigrants came from the ranks of urban artisans (skilled craftspeople) and shopkeepers, while others were farmers. So instead of a mix of classes, there was essentially a majority of midlevel citizens with a few people at the bottom or the top. In addition, the widespread availability of land made it theoretically possible for many ordinary people to become landowners; in Europe, this opportunity was virtually nonexistent. Land ownership raised social rank, wealth, and status.

Loss of social rank was also possible—just as the opportunities were greater in the colonies, so was the potential for failure. Settlement in the Americas was risky, and some members of established families were financially ruined. The fortunes of many were rising while others' were falling.

Yet the composition of the classes was more unstable than it had been in Europe. In Virginia, families such as the Byrds, Madisons, Randolphs, Washingtons, Lees, and Carters were not well known in the seventeenth century, but after a few generations they had become the leaders of their province. Benjamin Franklin (1706–1790), who began life as a poor , candle-maker's son in Boston Massachusetts made a fortune in publishing and assumed the place of a gentleman in Philadelphia, Pennsylvania. He spent his life pursuing philanthropy, governmental service, and scientific investigation (see Chapter 14). Ambitious young men were not content, as their fathers had been, to remain in the station to which they were born. They insisted on their right to make their own place in the world according to their character and abilities.

The Spanish borderlands and New France likewise experienced some shifting of social ranks. The *encomienda* system in the Spanish Southwest rewarded enterprising soldiers with land and the right to collect tribute from conquered peoples. This made it possible for some men to rise in status to a position similar to that of a feudal lord. New France emerged as a trading society along the Saint Lawrence and Mississippi River valleys, loosely organized at first but beginning to reproduce the social hierarchy of France as towns such as Quebec, Montreal, and New Orleans grew (see Chapter 3). The rank of *seigneur* was granted to many colonial families that had achieved wealth through trading or other enterprises.

 Titles Reflect Status

In English colonial society, social rank was important. People wished to have their rank acknowledged in the way others addressed them. Members of a provincial council had the title "honorable," while judges were called "esquire." An esquire's wife was referred to as "madam." Town officials of lower rank, as well as male property owners, were addressed as "mister" and their wives as "mistress." Especially in New England, a farmer was known as "goodman," and a farmer's wife was "goodwife" or "goody."

Social classes stay in place

Although the lines separating the classes had blurred, the class structure itself did not disappear. The inequalities the colonists saw around them seemed natural, and many people accepted differences in status as God's will. Massachusetts Bay leader John Winthrop (1588–1649) probably expressed a common view in 1630 when he said, "God Almighty, in his most holy and wise providence, has so disposed the condition of Mankind . . . [that] some must be rich, some poor, some high and eminent in power and dignity, others mean and in subjection." Consequently, few European colonists in North America challenged the social structures that originated in their homelands. Indeed, most of them regarded a class system as a mark of civilization. They wanted not to destroy the structure but to move up within it. In America, many saw their first opportunity to do so.

Labor needs shape society

The shortage of labor had a significant impact on the structure of colonial societies, especially in the early period. Settlers filled their needs for labor in various ways (see Chapter 7). In New England and the middle colonies and along the western frontier, families—usually with six or more members—supplied most of the labor on farms. The need for large families produced a steady increase in the population. These colonies also experienced a growing population density as farmers divided their lands among their male heirs, who themselves had families, and the settlements steadily expanded.

In contrast, early Chesapeake planters relied on the labor of indentured workers. Young, single Englishmen who could not find work in England would sign a contract called an "indenture" that committed them to work for up to seven years for a colonist in exchange for paid passage to the New World (an European term used for North and South America). Often the men worked on tobacco plantations. During the early colonial period few women came to the Chesapeake region, so indentured men did not often marry or start families. Once they had served their terms, the free

immigrants, who lacked the resources to establish their own plantations, eventually formed a large, unstable class of landless poor.

Northern colonists largely relied on indentured servants to meet the demand for skilled labor in the growing cities, domestic help in wealthy households, field hands on farms, and manual labor in such enterprises as iron foundries. Some northern colonists met these needs with African American slaves, but the north never came to depend upon slavery as did the Chesapeake and lower south, and the slave population in the middle colonies and New England remained relatively small. In New France, early colonists imported contract laborers (similar to English indentured servants), who worked for a stated number of years and then returned home. The Spanish, on the other hand, generally harnessed the labor of Native Americans. Slavery was technically illegal, but many Spanish settlers found ways around the law by using the *encomienda* system to exploit the labor of Native American farmers and cattle herders.

The necessities of life

Early after their arrival in the New World, many of the colonists realized that they lacked the skills vital to surviving in a land. Necessities were not as easily obtainable as they had been in Europe. As a result, the earliest settlers had to quickly learn to farm, make clothes, and build shelters in order to make the colonies livable places.

Food

The availability of food varied dramatically among the earliest colonists in North America: some found plenty to eat, while others starved to death. Depending upon their agricultural skills and attitudes, where they landed, and their relations with the Native Americans, early settlers experienced feast or famine. While in most areas there were abundant sources of wild food, some colonists lacked the skills necessary to catch or harvest it. In addition, most settlers arrived in the Northeast weakened by the long sea voyage and the poor rations onboard ship. Depending upon when they reached the American shore, they might have had to begin building houses immediately to protect themselves from the winter cold. Frequently they could spare little time or energy on hunting, gathering, or planting gardens and fields. Sometimes supplies of food brought over on ships were ruined by rats or spoilage. Colonists who depended on these supplies to feed themselves through the winter suffered greatly.

Some colonists were lucky enough to receive assistance from Native Americans. In the earliest days of settlement, native people brought gifts of food and taught settlers how to grow crops and harvest wild foods. The colonists sampled many new foods as a result of contact with Native Americans. Some of the foods that were staples of the Native American diet—corn, for example—became indispensable additions to colonists' meals. Indeed, many of the first colonists would not

 English Suspicions of Water

The English of the early colonial period believed that water was unhealthy. Of course, contaminated water was dangerous to drink, and they were probably justified in avoiding water as a beverage. But they also believed that bathing was usually unnecessary or even dangerous to the health. Washing was limited to a few parts of the body, and taking a real bath was virtually unknown. These prejudices were brought over to the New World. In 1630, for example, an English ship was readied for the trip to Massachusetts with three months' worth of provisions. Beverages for the passengers included 2 casks of Malaga and Canary wine, 20 gallons of "aqua vitae" (strong liquor), and 45 tuns of beer. (A tun is a large cask that equals 252 gallons.) In contrast, only 6 tuns of fresh water were placed onboard. This supply would have had to serve for cooking, drinking, washing, and bathing during the entire journey. While seawater might have been used for some purposes, this supply of freshwater seems completely inadequate by today's standards. With space a precious commodity onboard, alcohol was deemed more of a necessity.

have survived without the aid of Native Americans. The stories of Jamestown and Plymouth provide vivid examples of the settlers' dependence on native agricultural methods for survival.

In his *History of the Dividing Line* William Byrd II wrote that many of the Jamestown colonists were not prepared or willing to do the work needed to survive in the colony.
Reproduced by permission of Archive Photos, Inc.

Jamestown colonists ill-prepared The original settlers of the Virginia Colony at Jamestown died from starvation in great numbers (see Chapter 4). They had heard about the abundant natural resources of North America, which promoters in England had described as a "paradise," so they thought food would be readily available. Besides, many of the settlers were gentlemen who disliked farmwork and lacked the skills necessary for survival. So they were not prepared for the task of build-

ing a settlement. In *History of the Dividing Line* (1728), William Byrd II (1674–1744) of Virginia described the colonists as "idle and extravagant," adding that those who were not constantly quarreling "detested Work more than Famine." Captain John Smith (c. 1580–1631), Byrd wrote, "took some pains to persuade the men to plant Indian corn, but they lookt upon all Labor as a Curse. They chose rather to depend upon the Musty Provisions that were sent from England: and when [these] fail'd they were forct to take more pains to Seek for Wild Fruits in the Woods, than they would have taken in tilling Ground."

Before long, many of the men at Jamestown were too sick and weak to do much work anyway. In *The Generall Historie of Virginia* (1624), Smith explained the difficulty of killing animals for food: "Though there be fish in the seas, fowles in the ayre and Beasts in the woods, their bounds are so large, they so wild and we so weake and ignorant, we cannot much trouble them." By the end of 1607, only 38 of the 105 original colonists were alive. They were saved by Pocahontas (c. 1595–1617), daughter of Chief Powhatan (1550–1618), who brought corn, fish, venison (deer meat), squash, and other provisions (see Chapter 9). But just a few years later the English colony would once again face famine.

Hardships of the Pilgrims A few years later, in 1620, the Pilgrims (a Puritan group; also called Nonconformists) landed in Massachusetts, where they found conditions as grim as Jamestown (see Chapter 4). They had spent ninety-seven days onboard their ship, the *Mayflower,* eating a monotonous diet consisting mostly of "salt horse" (dried beef), smoked bacon, dried fish, cheese, and "ship's biscuit," which was made by mixing flour and water and allowing it to dry into something like a cracker. On the deck of the ship was a fire pit over which a large stew pot hung. The stew they ate every day was made of dried meat or fish and ship's biscuit. For drinking the passengers had beer, gin, and brandy. This diet was not very nutritious, and the lack of fresh vegetables and fruits caused many to suffer from scurvy (a disease caused by a lack of vitamin C). The hardships of the crossing itself further weakened them.

The Pilgrims reached Massachusetts in November, so the weather was extremely cold. They faced a winter filled with hardship. In *Of Plymouth Plantation* (1630), William Bradford (1590–1657), the future governor of the Plymouth Colony, described their arrival on the cold shores: There were "no friends to wellcome them, nor inns to entertaine or refresh their weatherbeaten bodys, no houses or much less townes to repaire too, to seeke for succoure [comfort]." The houses they hastily put up could not keep them warm. Many settlers died from a combination of illness, cold, and poor diet. Fortunately for the Pilgrims, during the following spring a Native American named Squanto (d. 1622?) arrived and gave them help. Squanto spoke English

The "starving time" at Jamestown

Most of the settlers of Jamestown starved to death during the winter of 1609 to 1610. John Smith had been wounded and had returned to England, and the Native Americans seemed to have decided to eliminate the colony. They stopped trading with the settlers and used armed warriors to keep them inside their stockade. The English became so afraid of the Native Americans that they would not venture out to hunt or fish. They had also run out of the corn the Powhatans had provided them. After every bit of food inside the stockade had been consumed, colonists ate rats, mice, snakes, and even shoes. Some colonists resorted to digging up corpses to feed themselves. They also had to burn most of their buildings to keep warm. The famine wiped out most of the colony: its numbers fell from almost five hundred people down to sixty. In May 1610 two English ships arrived to bring help to the colony. What they found was more like a ghost town peopled by skeletons.

because he had been kidnaped by an Englishman when he was a teenager and had lived for a few years in England. He knew how to raise crops and gather food from the wilderness, and he taught the Pilgrims many skills they needed. They regarded him as a blessing sent by God.

Squanto teaching the Pilgrims how to plant corn. Many of the Pilgrims would have died if Squanto had not taught them how to raise crops. *Reproduced by permission of The Granger Collection. Illustration by C. W. Jeffreys.*

Land of plenty Ironically, both colonies—Jamestown in Virginia and Plymouth in Massachusetts—were located in regions filled with food. There were all sorts of game birds, deer, rabbits, and other animals in the forests. Fish, lobsters, and mollusks could be plucked from the sea, and fish filled the rivers and streams. The land itself also proved fertile for growing crops, and berries, nuts, and other wild foods could be collected in the forest. After the first few years of adjustment,

the colonists of these regions did not have to worry about famine. Their food may often have been simple and dull, but they did not go hungry.

As early as 1607, John Smith found fish teeming in the James River. He wrote in *The Generall Historie of Virginia* that the river had "an abundance of fish, lying so thick with their heads above the water, as for want of nets we attempted to catch them with a frying pan . . . neither better fish, more plentie; nor more variety, had any of us ever seene so swimming in the water. . . . We tooke more in one houre than we could eate in a day." Other members of Smith's colony described finding mussels and oysters, "which lay on the ground as thick as stones," and of eating oysters "very large and delicate in taste" that had been roasted by the Native Americans. The Virginia explorers saw the vigorous cornfields planted by the Native Americans, who entertained the Englishmen with dances and feasts at which they served corn bread, berries, fish, "and other Countrie Provisions." The Native Americans also gave them tobacco and held dances in their honor. These observations were made in the year 1607, just a few years before the English colonists at Jamestown began dying of hunger.

In Massachusetts, likewise, the land was rich with things to eat. John Winthrop (1588–1649), the first governor of the Massachusetts Bay Colony, reported that there were great numbers of eels and lobsters in the bay. Francis Higginson, who became the first minister of Salem, wrote in *New England Plantation* (1630): "Fowles of the Aire are plentifull here, and all sorts as we have in England. . . . Here are likewise abundance of Turkies, exceeding fat, sweet and fleshy. . . . in Summer all places are full of [strawberries] and all maner of berries and fruits. This Country doth abound with Wild Geese, wild Duckes and other Sea Fowle. . . . Here is good living."

Colonial food and cooking As the colonists adapted to their environment and established their fields, they began to eat better. They had learned methods for farming and cooking unfamiliar foods. Native Americans introduced them to the staples of their own diet, such as beans, pumpkins and other squashes, and corn, which was ground into cornmeal. Soon the settlers were using the corn every day to make bread. Native Americans also showed the colonists wild foods, such as ground nuts, wild rice, cranberries, black walnuts, pecans, and the syrup of the maple tree. They introduced new ways to cook fish and shellfish. They showed settlers how to cook beans in clay pots and to make a stew of beans and corn called succotash.

Deprivation became uncommon, and the colonial diet settled into a predictable cycle that mirrored the seasons of various foods. Wealthier colonists had more variety in their diets, but the average family probably ate the same foods again and again until something new became available. In most households, a large stew pot

 "Pumpkins at morning and pumpkins at noon"

Native Americans introduced English colonists to pumpkins, a healthful food that could be grown easily and abundantly. Apparently this vegetable became a familiar sight on colonial tables. A wistful rhyme conveys the colonists' thankfulness for this food but also their desire for something else to eat:

> For pottage [stew], and puddings, and custards, and pies,
> Our pumpkins and parsnips are common supplies.
> We have pumpkins at morning and pumpkins at noon;
> If it were not for pumpkins, we should be undoon.

Source: Thomas, Gertrude Ida. *Food of Our Forefathers. Philadelphia: Davis Company, 1941, pp. 169–70.*

hung over the fire. Whatever available foods were cooked together in the pot. Salt-cured meat or fish, beans, vegetables—the combination and taste were not as important as feeding everyone adequately and efficiently. Some kind of bread, often corn bread, was served with the stew. If there was fresh meat, it could be roasted on a spit over the fire. The drippings of roasting meat, collected in a pan, were an important addition to gravy or bread.

Many colonists drank alcohol with meals whenever it was available.

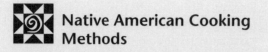

Native American Cooking Methods

Colonists recorded and sometimes adopted the cooking methods they saw Native Americans using. Lacking metal utensils and pots, the Native Americans had developed different ways to cook. They knew how to roast many types of seafood, such as eels and oysters, using an open fire. Native Americans taught the colonists a simple way to bake a gutted fish in the ashes of a fire. After the fish was cooked, its skin was slipped off and discarded before the flesh was eaten. Native Americans also introduced colonists to the clambake. Secotan women made huge clay stew pots that were designed to be partly buried in the ground. A fire was then built around the pot, and a stew of corn, meat, and fish was cooked by the heat of the surrounding fire. With this method, the Secotans did not need a hearth.

"Grog," a mixture of rum and water, was a popular beverage. Colonists also drank wine, beer, ale, whiskey, hard cider, or whatever kind of alcohol they could manufacture. Children might be given a small amount of wine to drink on special occasions, and some colonists believed that warm beer was a healthful beverage for children.

Native and imported foods As the colonies grew, so did the variety in their diet. Livestock was brought over from Europe, as well as the seeds to grow familiar garden vegetables and fruits. Trade with England also began to bring more variety to the colonists' diet. Sugar, rum, spices, sweets, and other imported foods slowly became available. As more land was cleared and successive generations built upon the work of earlier farmers, growing and preserving a greater variety of foods became possible.

But foods that were native to America retained their place in the colonists' diet. Corn, for example, remained a vital food that was used to make many dishes the colonists depended upon. Cornmeal mush (also called "samp," from the Algonquian word *nasaump*) was made from cornmeal that was boiled with milk or water until thick and then served with maple syrup, molasses, gravy, or meat drippings. Native Americans made baked cakes of cornmeal called appone or ponop, and the English soon began to make their own varieties of corn bread. One kind, called ashcake, was made of corn-bread batter wrapped in corn husks or cabbage leaves and baked in the hot ashes of the cooking fire. Corn puddings, cooked in a bag or in the dripping pan, were often served to accompany or follow a stew. In the summer, colonists ate corn on the cob. Other foods made from corn were hominy, grits, parched corn, and popcorn.

Colonists at the table Everyday meals in colonial America were simple and hearty. The food was not elegant, and neither were the manners and table settings of the settlers. They took most of their meals from the iron pot that always hung over the fire. It might contain a stew of beans, turnips, carrots, parsnips, pumpkin, onions, or corn, all cooked together, along with meat, if it was available. Often the pot was simply lifted onto the middle of the table at mealtime. Diners might eat directly from the pot, or they might spoon out a portion onto a wooden dish called a trencher. Individual dishes were rare; usually two diners shared a trencher.

Forks were extremely uncommon in the colonies until late in the period, but everyone had spoons, since stews and porridges were their constant meals. Spoons were made of wood or pewter. Dishes, even those made of wood, were so valued that they were often mentioned in wills and other formal lists of possessions. Individual drinking cups were also unusual. Two diners might share a cup, or one large vessel would be passed around the entire table for everyone to drink from. This practice was common even in inns, where strangers ate together.

In the homes of the gentry (upper class), meals were often more elaborate and might consist of several separate dishes. Travelers who described the diet of the colonists often reported what sounds like a delicious variety of foods, such as poultry, pork, venison, fish, oysters, vegetables, and fruits, among the dishes served by their hosts. Yet these meals were spe-cial ones intended to impress and satisfy visitors. Except among the wealthier colonists, the primary purpose of eating was to sustain the body, not to please the palate.

Fashions in clothing

Clothing served several purposes in the colonial period, as it does today: it provided warmth, preserved modesty, adorned the wearer, and reflected one's social station. The first generation of European settlers brought with them the fashions of their day. Portraits of early English colonists depict men and women in fashionable garments adorned with showy lace collars and cuffs. These pictures reveal that the wealthier colonists of Massachusetts Bay had a taste for fashionable clothing, as did some early settlers in Virginia. Puritan ministers urged people to give up the vanity of fashionable dress for the inner beauty of a pious (holy) life. New England magistrates (judges) tried to enforce their ministers' teachings through laws that regulated dress. In 1634, for example, the General Court of Massachusetts made it illegal to wear high fashion. The fact that such laws were considered necessary suggests that Puritan men and women were fond of fashion and sometimes wore fancy styles. Puritans were not limited to somber clothing in black or gray, however. The laws were mainly a way to prevent ordinary farmers or artisans from dressing "above their station" in clothing regarded as appropriate only for the wealthy. In general, Puritans were free to dress in a range of colors and styles regarded as suitable for their individual rank in society.

Mingling of styles The availability of materials and the requirements of environment influenced colonial fashions in the middle and late seventeenth century. In some regions, elements of Native American dress crept into colonists' clothing. For example, French settlers in New France often dressed in buckskin (soft, tanned deerskin). In winter men commonly wore hooded wool coats known as capotes to shield themselves from the icy winds. Native Americans, too, adopted some elements of dress from the Europeans. Sometimes they traded for European items; other times they added European touches to their own designs. For example, in the Denver Art Museum in Colorado, there is a coat made by the Cree Indians of Canada about 1750. The design of the coat is distinctly European, but the material is buckskin and the decorations are made from porcupine quills. Europeans were not always tolerant of Native American influences in clothing, however. In New Spain, a law passed in 1582 prohibited mestizo women (those of mixed Spanish and Indian heritage) from wearing Native American dresses. Instead, these women began to wear a shawl known as a rebozo, which over time came to be finely crafted and decorated.

English colonists brought with them a knowledge of spinning and weaving, but they never developed a large textile (fabric) industry. Imported cloth was scarce and expensive, so homespun woolens and linens became the common materials for ordinary citizens' clothing. Yet portraits of prominent colonists of the time, including Puritan ministers such as Cotton Mather (1663–1728), continued to imitate the fashionable styles in England. In spite of obstacles, many colonists maintained links to their European roots through the clothing they wore.

Eighteenth-century changes After 1700 a growing variety of textiles imported from England began flowing into colonial ports. Prices for imported fabrics dropped so low that colonial producers could not compete, and some households no longer found it worthwhile to invest the time and labor needed to make homespun cloth. A wide variety of English and Dutch fabrics, including silks, linens, velvets, and laces, were advertised in newspapers. Accessories such as gloves, stockings, and buttons were also available. Tailors placed their own advertisements, enticing customers with their ability to cut and sew the latest London fashions.

European fashion popular Writers of the time commented on the widespread imitation of European fashion in America. In 1740 the Anglican preacher George Whitefield (1714–1770) remarked on the fashionable dress of audiences he spoke to from Massachusetts to Georgia. He declared

A man and a woman in typical Puritan clothing. *Reproduced by permission of Corbis-Bettmann.*

Fancy Dress for Young Colonists

Colonial-era portraits depict the children of wealthy colonists wearing amazingly elaborate and expensive outfits, at least on special occasions. Young boys also wore wigs when they became fashionable. In 1750, a father in Portland, Maine, recorded among his expenses the cost of shaving his three sons' heads several times during the year so that they could wear wigs. He also recorded the considerable expense of the wigs he bought for his boys, who were aged eleven, nine, and seven years. Despite the cost of such items, wealthy families ordered wigs and fancy clothes from England for their children. Sometimes detailed orders for what seem to be entire wardrobes for children were sent to London or other European cities. Clothing made of silk, satin, and other fine fabrics was sent across the ocean, along with dress shoes, stockings, ribbons, gloves, hats, and fans.

that the people who came to hear him in Charleston, South Carolina, dressed more extravagantly than gentry from the most fashionable districts of London. Again, portraits from this period demonstrate that European styles were widely worn. Even ordinary colonists began to buy fancy items, and many colonial leaders worried that class distinctions were being erased as more and more people added fashionable wigs, fancy dresses, handsome waistcoats, silk stockings, and silver buckles to their wardrobes. From newspaper notices describing runaways, we learn that even slaves and indentured servants often wore fashionable cast-off clothing.

Clothing on the frontier On the frontier, however, fashion was influenced by factors other than the latest European fads. Traders and settlers in the backcountry adopted certain elements of Native American clothing, such as buckskin garments, moccasins, and snowshoes, because these items were better adapted to the environment. Dressing this way also helped to establish cultural ties with the native people, whom colonists in the backcountry encountered more frequently. In fact, the Indian commissioner William Johnson (1715–1774) adopted Iroquois dress to help him gain their trust and understanding as he pursued diplomacy (skill dealing with people) among the Six Nations of upstate New York.

Farther south in the Carolina backcountry, the Anglican missionary Charles Woodmason expressed shock at European women who went barefoot and wore thin, tight-fitting garments that exposed their lower legs. This was considered immodest dress for women at the time. Such clothing was partly the result of poverty and partly an adaptation to the hot southern climate. Gradually, as eastern fashions became affordable, frontier colonists also began to wear them.

Housing

The size and structure of colonial houses varied widely throughout North America and changed over the course of the colonial period (see "Architecture" in Chapter 13). The first settlers brought the construction methods they had known in Europe and adapted them to the materials and conditions of the land in which they settled.

Early two-room houses Homes of the first few generations of English settlers followed the pattern of houses in England. These consisted of two equal-sized main rooms separated by a wall containing a single fireplace, which heated both rooms. These rooms were called the hall and the parlor, and both had to serve multiple purposes. The parlor usually served as a bedroom. In English and French households the hall was for cooking, eating, and work. It was usually the core of the home and was used for entertaining guests as well as for cooking and working. English, Dutch, and French farmhouses shared this same basic form, although the houses of each group differed in external appearance according to custom. In Dutch houses, the parlor was called a *groot kamer,* or "best room," and served for social occasions as well as for sleeping. Often colonists would add lofts to their rooms for storage or sleeping space, and as a family grew, they might add rooms for a separate kitchen, bedroom, or storeroom.

The floor plan of the English colonial dwelling kept family members

Average Wardrobe, 1740

Like most aspects of colonial life, dress varied according to social class. Slaves received only one or two changes of clothing per year, while wealthy colonists possessed large wardrobes tailored for every occasion in a variety of fine imported textiles. But what about the average family? According to one historian, a man might have one good suit, two fine shirts, three coarse shirts, two pairs of work pants, two pairs of breeches, one waistcoat, one coat, and one hat. A woman might have one good gown, one petticoat, one good cloak, two bodices or short gowns, two aprons, two shifts [nightgowns], and a coarse cloak.

Source: Hawke, David Freeman. Everyday Life in Early America. *New York: Harper & Row, 1988.*

close to one another. Whole families commonly slept in the same room, with the parents in a large bed and the children in a smaller one or on mats by the hearth. Infants slept with their parents or in cradles. Even when family members slept in separate rooms, they had to pass through one room to reach another. There was little privacy, and all daily activities in the home were carried out in close quarters. When overnight guests came, they often shared the family bed with their hosts.

Adapting to local conditions In the southeastern colonies, builders placed

Sharing Rooms and Beds

People staying overnight in colonial inns or private houses often found themselves sharing their rooms and even their beds with total strangers. A traveling doctor, Alexander Hamilton, spent one night in a New York country inn. When he woke up in the morning he found "two beds in the room, besides that in which I lay, in one of which lay two great hulking fellows, with long black beards, having their own hair, and not so much as half a nightcap betwixt both of them. I took them for weavers, not only from their greasy appearance, but because I observed a weaver's loom at each side of the room. In the other bed was a raw-boned boy, who, with the two lubbers, huddled on his clothes, and went reeling downstairs, making as much noise as three horses."

Source: Hamilton, Alexander. Itinerarium, *edited by Robert M. Goldwyn. New York: Arno, 1971.*

---

fireplaces at the ends of houses, rather than in the center, so that heat would be more easily carried away. Summers in the South were so hot that some houses had separate "summer kitchens" so that daily cooking would not make the main house intolerably warm.

Houses in the Spanish borderlands varied considerably from region to region, depending upon available building materials and the climate. In Saint Augustine, Florida, for instance, a distinctive long, rectangular style of house emerged, and in New Mexico, colonists constructed long adobe (a sun-dried brick of clay and straw) houses only one room deep.

Building materials Timber, which had been scarce in England, was plentiful in the colonies. Builders took advantage of this by siding homes entirely in wood and roofing them with wooden shingles rather than with thatch (reeds) or slate (a type of rock). The log-cabin design was introduced to America by Swedish settlers, and by 1700 colonists in frontier New Hampshire and in the middle colonies were building homes in this style. Dwellings in the Spanish Southwest were built of adobe (or stone, where available). These houses had to be constructed to provide protection from attack by hostile neighboring tribes. People who lived in towns commonly built their homes close together around a central plaza so that the outer walls of the houses could double as the walls of a fort. Haciendas were structured the same way, with dwellings and outbuildings arranged in a square around a central patio.

More spacious houses By 1700 wealthy English colonists began to build reproductions of larger houses in Europe. The gentry wanted to display their wealth and taste by constructing larger, more formal houses made of brick. Some of these elegant homes were even designed by professional architects. Built in the symmetrical

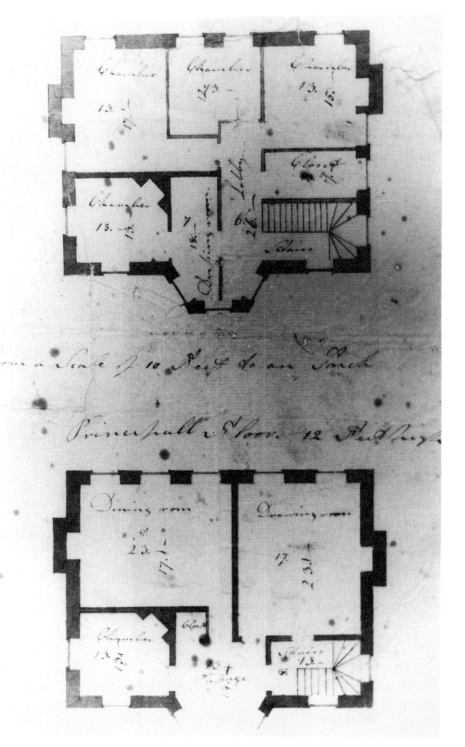

A floor plan of a colonial home. *Reproduced by permission of Swem Library, The College of William and Mary.*

style fashionable in Europe, houses of well-to-do colonists included ornamental exterior woodwork and beautifully finished interiors. The new floor plans included many rooms, each with specialized uses and separated by corridors for greater privacy. Children and parents began to sleep in separate rooms, and bedchambers were often located on the second floor, away from the parlors and halls where guests were entertained.

Gradually, less privileged colonists began to build homes with some of the same features, not only in external style but also in interior layout. These homes reflected a newfound desire for privacy, with multiple rooms designed for distinct purposes and separated by corridors or partitions. As farmers became more prosperous, they not only built larger houses, but they also located them farther away from barns. A separate laundry might be added, as well as a smokehouse for curing meats.

Imported goods

In the seventeenth century, most colonists depended to some degree on goods imported from Europe (see Chapter 7). In fact, English settlement followed the paths blazed by traders who acquired furs from Native Americans in exchange for European manufactured goods, which rapidly transformed Native American ways of life. Early colonists in New England and the Chesapeake sustained a steady trade by introducing items such as metal goods, firearms, and woolen fabrics. Established settlers relied on obtaining materials from new immigrants, who brought such goods as nails, gunpowder, lead shot, glass, cooking utensils, books, and cloth to trade for lumber and food. A modest flow of English products arrived in colonial ports throughout the century. Some of the items were purchased by wealthier colonists for resale to their neighbors. For instance, seventeenth-century farmers traded tobacco to Dutch and English merchants for European-made products, while farmers in Massachusetts traded grain and salt pork for West Indian sugar, molasses, and rum.

In the early eighteenth century, the flow of European goods began to increase, and by the 1740s colonists were experiencing a consumer revolution. In Britain, artisans were producing goods at lower prices, making it possible for more people to buy them. In addition, merchants learned how to create demand for their products with appealing newspaper advertisements, shop-window displays, and other techniques. By 1740 ceramics, glass products, textiles, paper, metal items, and teas were becoming available at lower prices than American producers could match—and their quality was often superior.

Shopping

Colonists could obtain imported products in several ways. Northern port cities boasted specialty shops where colonists could buy items such as fabrics, pins, tools, and building supplies. Elsewhere people sold consumer goods mainly to supplement their primary incomes as farmers or artisans. Some colonists, such as Long Island whale-oil exporter Samuel Mumford, kept small stores of English goods that he could sell for cash or barter for products such as grain or tobacco, which he might in turn sell on the international market. Many southern planters kept supplies of imported materials to sell to their neighbors. Virginian Ralph Wormeley, for example, kept a trunk full of trade items under his bed. Throughout the colonies traveling peddlers carried wares to smaller communities and isolated farmhouses, where imported goods were harder to come by.

As the volume of imported goods increased in the eighteenth century, retail shops began springing up throughout the colonies. Many were locally owned, but in the South there were some that were virtually chain stores, owned by merchants based in Glasgow, Scotland. Shopkeepers learned to arrange their goods in attractive displays, encouraging shoppers to browse and compare.

Buying tastes and habits

The new abundance of imported products meant significant changes in the self-perceptions, tastes, and habits of American colonists. By the middle of the eighteenth century, items that were once luxuries enjoyed only by the upper class became expected needs of everyday life. In

"Unnecessary" Finery in a Colonial Cottage

Many colonial families adorned their homes with imported goods if they could afford them. Members of the upper classes often found such decoration to be pretentious. The Scottish physician and traveler Alexander Hamilton illustrated this attitude in an account of his visit to a household in New York. Hamilton's companion on the visit was a man named "Mr. M—s," who was quite critical of items owned by their host: "This cottage was very clean and neat, but poorly furnished, yet Mr. M—s observed several superfluous things which showed an inclination to finery in these poor people; such as a looking-glass with a painted frame, half a dozen pewter spoons, and as many plates, old and wore out, but bright and clean, a set of stone tea dishes and a teapot. These Mr. M—s said were superfluous, and too splendid for such a cottage, and therefore they ought to be sold to buy wool to make yarn; that a little water in a wooden pail might serve for a looking-glass, and wooden plates and spoons would be as good for use, and when clean would be almost as ornamental. As for the tea equippage it was quite unnecessary."

Source: Hamilton, Alexander. Itinerarium, *edited by Robert M. Goldwyn. New York: Arno, 1971.*

1700, for example, tea was rarely seen outside the homes of the wealthiest colonists, whose servants poured the drink as refreshment for honored guests. Teapots, teacups, and even sugar to sweeten the drink were expensive luxuries. By 1750, however, many ordinary families of farmers and artisans enjoyed tea every day. It was served from inexpensive delftware (Dutch ceramic tableware), and adding a lump or two of sugar was not uncommon.

Imported items were changing table manners as well. Family members no longer shared meals from a single pot that sat in the middle of the table. Now people ate from individual ceramic plates or bowls and used forks and knives as well as spoons and fingers. Women and men adorned their clothes with English lace and buttons, brightened their parlors with brassware, and covered their beds with linen. Wealthy families decorated their homes with fine rugs imported from Turkey, rich Oriental tapestries, and elegant Dutch fabrics.

Expanding awareness

As the colonies gradually changed from isolated outposts to prosperous provinces, travel, communication, and trade enabled colonists to keep abreast of the dramatic developments that were transforming life on both sides of the Atlantic (see "Communications" in Chapter 7). These forces enabled people in once-isolated colonies to learn more about events in America as well as in Europe. Ships sailed along the coast and across the Atlantic with increasing frequency, distributing news from Europe and from other colonies. News spread from

colonial ports inland along trade routes to the increasingly interconnected settlements. Educated colonists bought European books and journals to keep up with the latest advances in scientific knowledge, theology (the study of religion), law, and politics. Colonial newspapers began appearing, keeping readers informed of the latest developments in European affairs as well as matters of interest from other colonies. Wealthy families cultivated transatlantic friendships with persons of influence in European society, and the richest sent their sons to Europe for education in the liberal arts and law (see Chapter 12). As 1750 approached, colonists exhibited an increasing awareness of their place in a world of exciting possibilities.

Colonial identity

Colonists gradually came to think of themselves as inhabitants of civilized provinces rather than rustic colonies. As British Americans, they shared with the people in England a common identity, an enjoyment of finery, and loyalty to their king. The growing availability of English imported goods during the eighteenth century, along with the desire of colonists to attain a lifestyle modeled on English customs, resulted in an increased similarity among colonial societies that had been strikingly diverse in 1700. Earlier settlers could not have imagined uniting with other American colonies to form a nation independent of Britain. They still regarded themselves as part of the most independent and enlightened empire the world had ever known. They looked to Britain as the source of products that they believed would make their lives decent, respectable, and civilized.

African slaves

In the late seventeenth century fewer and fewer indentured servants arrived from England to supply labor to the southern colonies. As a result, Virginia and Maryland planters began to purchase large numbers of African slaves (see "Slave laborers" in Chapter 7). South Carolinians likewise relied on slave labor beginning in the 1670s. Many planters from Barbados brought their African slaves with them to South Carolina to carve out new settlements there. By 1700 the Chesapeake and South Carolina had become slave societies, where the economy depended almost completely on forced labor and the great numbers of slaves shaped the social system.

Strive to preserve identity

The variety of societies and conditions in colonial America resulted in diverse experiences for people of African descent. African captives brought with them a range of languages, beliefs, and practices. They had to adapt their traditions to the new environment and to other African cultures they encountered, combining them with selected European elements to produce the first African American

cultures. These emerged in several different patterns.

In the South Carolina and Georgia rice-growing country, slaves worked on a "task system": completion of their assigned tasks freed them to devote time to other pursuits. In these regions, plantation owners preferred to spend the hot summers on the seacoast, away from their plantations. In addition, slaves outnumbered Europeans. Because of these factors, the slaves in South Carolina and Georgia were able to form communities and shape a culture with a rich mixture of African customs.

In contrast, the lives and work of slaves in the Chesapeake region were much more regulated and supervised. Slaves worked in a "gang system" that kept them in the tobacco fields all day. Planter families outnumbered slaves and remained on their plantations year-round. Nevertheless, Chesapeake slaves formed supportive communities with a distinctive African American culture they passed down to later generations.

Farther north the conditions of slavery were often milder, but the much smaller slave population made it difficult to create the kind of communities that could preserve African traditions. In the eighteenth century, free African American communities began to emerge in parts of New England, the middle colonies, and South Carolina. People living in these communities often faced discrimination from whites, finding themselves pushed into separate neighborhoods

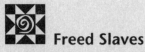

Freed Slaves

By 1720 a majority of slaves in the Chesapeake region were American-born. Some had even gained their freedom. In 1760, for instance, there were two thousand freed slaves (2 percent to 3 percent of the African American population) in Virginia, and in the North about 10 percent of the total African American population were freedmen. Many former slaves owned farms. For instance, freedman Anthony Johnson began acquiring his own plantation in Virginia during the 1640s. By 1651 he owned 250 acres of land, and he became known as the "black patriarch" of Pungoteague Creek, the area of Virginia where his estate was located. Gracia Real de Santa Teresa de Mose was founded as a town for freed blacks in 1738. Located in Spanish Florida 2 miles north of Saint Augustine, Mose was the only town of its kind in what would become the United States. The earliest settlers were escaped slaves from South Carolina. English attacks forced evacuation of the town from 1740 to 1752, and its inhabitants moved to Saint Augustine.

and onto poorer lands. In addition, they were denied rights that their English neighbors enjoyed. Yet African Americans developed tightly knit communities held together by culture, kinship, and faith.

African American dwellings

The vast majority of African Americans were slaves, and their dwellings were nothing like the great houses of the gentry. In the eighteenth century many slaves built their houses from materials provided by their masters. Whether they used English or African construction methods, slaves often organized their buildings in patterns that supported the communal ways of life of Africa. Single-room houses were often built around a common central area where the residents could interact, share household work, and hold social gatherings when time and tasks permitted. Free African Americans tended to adopt European designs, and their homes were probably similar to those of poorer whites.

Native Americans

Native Americans in all regions of colonial America lived in tribes or clans, forming societies based on agriculture and hunting. They generally grew corn, squash, beans, and tobacco. Women tended to the crops while men hunted and fished, and communities produced only enough food for their own needs. Living in stockaded (fenced) villages, Native Americans built houses made of saplings (small trees) that were often occupied by several people. Later in the colonial period these dwellings were replaced by log cabins. Many native groups had a

Reconstructed slave quarters at Carter's Grove Plantation in Virginia. These residences were mostly small, one-room houses made of logs. *Reproduced by permission of The Granger Collection.*

strong warrior class and established alliances with neighboring native groups to protect their towns and land from European colonists and hostile tribes. Most Native American societies were matrilineal (headed by a woman), but this tradition began to change after increasing encounters with European colonists (see Chapter 9). The fur trade in particular had a profound impact on native culture, producing a dependence on European-made goods that gradually brought an end to the native way of life. Equally disruptive were European diseases, wars, and the reservations system.

Native American hunting techniques

Native Americans used ingenious techniques for hunting animals. For instance, they drove deer or other animals into fenced areas where they could be kept alive until meat was needed. Others drove huge buffalo, which might otherwise be difficult to kill, over cliffs. Native Americans also had interesting ways of deceiving their prey when they hunted. Hunters in some tribes could imitate the calls of the animals very accurately. They also used disguise. For example, the Timucua dressed in whole deerskins when they were hunting deer in order to blend in with the herd when they crept up on their prey. Native Americans hunting turkeys used masks of feathers to hide their faces. (See Chapter 1 for a more detailed description of Native American life during the colonial period.)

Family Life | 9

European colonists in North America had varying family patterns, especially during the 1600s. In the New England colonies, the early settlers immigrated in whole family units (now called nuclear families) composed of a father, mother, and children. They formed communities based on these nuclear families, which provided valuable stability for British colonial society. The climate of New England proved to be remarkably healthful, and the land supported numerous crops that made a relatively nutritious diet possible. As a result, family members in these colonies were on average healthier than people back home in England and in other colonies. The number of infant deaths was relatively low, and people lived longer lives.

The situation was quite different in other colonies. For instance, family life in New Netherland was unstable until Peter Stuyvesant (1610–1672) became leader of the colony in 1647 (see Chapter 4). He established policies to promote the immigration of nuclear families, which brought new stability to the colony. In early Virginia and Maryland, deadly diseases and different social conditions produced less stable communities. In the early seventeenth century, far more men than

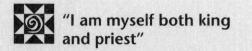

"I am myself both king and priest"

A letter published in the *Spectator,* an English magazine, in 1712 illustrates the patriarchal beliefs common in the colonial period. The writer stated: "Nothing is more gratifying to the mind of man than power or dominion: and this I think myself amply possessed of, as I am the father of a family. I am perpetually taken up giving out orders, in prescribing duties, in hearing parties [disputes], in administering justice, and in distributing rewards and punishments. . . . In short, Sir, I look upon my family as a patriarchal sovereign, in which I am myself both king and priest."

Reprinted in: Middleton, Richard, ed. Colonial America: A History, 1585–1776, *second edition. Malden, Mass.: Blackwell Publishers, 1996, p. 252.*

women came to the region, most of them unmarried indentured servants (people bound by signed documents to work as laborers for a specified time) who worked in tobacco fields. The few young women who did arrive during this period often found prospective husbands who paid off their terms of service so they could marry sooner. Plantation owners sometimes brought wives with them, but the overall ratio of men to women remained unbalanced, and there were not enough families to sustain the population until the 1680s (see Chapter 7).

The unhealthy climate also took a heavy toll on families in these colonies. Many people died of diseases such as malaria (a disease transmitted by mosquitoes), typhus (a disease transmitted by lice), and dysentery (a disease characterized by severe diarrhea). Few seventeenth-century families in the Chesapeake region survived intact until the children reached adulthood. For this reason, households and kinship extended beyond the nuclear family to include children from multiple marriages, children from households of relatives, and other relations.

Men's work, women's work

Family life in colonial America was based on the division of labor between men and women. Most English colonists lived and worked on farms, where men and women shared the responsibility of managing the household and making a living. Both might have participated in plowing and planting a field, harvesting and processing the crops, and caring for farm animals and livestock. Englishmen, however, tended to avoid domestic tasks such as food preparation and the care of young children. As their farms became established, husbands and wives tended to divide their tasks more clearly into housework and farmwork. Men might have herded and sheared sheep, for example, while the women carded, spun, and wove or knitted the wool into fabric. Vegetable gardening was also done by women, assisted by older children, especially girls. From an early age all children had simple chores to do around the house or in the garden.

Relations between men and women differed by region, according to their ethnic background and particular circumstances. Men and women in effect led separate lives. In most colonial societies, however, women were expected to respect their husbands' authority. A man was considered the head of the household and the family, while women were seen as totally dependent on men. Men dominated the world outside the household as well, since only they could vote and hold public office.

Marriage customs

Like other social patterns in colonial America, marriage customs varied according to colony, ethnic background, and social rank. Love was only one reason for colonists to get married, and often it was not the most important factor. New England Puritans thought a happy marriage depended on love between prospective partners. Other colonists, however, did not think love was a necessity before marriage, although they expected it to follow the taking of vows. Throughout all of the European colonies, marriage served to create bonds between important families. For instance, Spanish American aristocrats (ruling class or nobility) worked hard to limit their children's marriages to persons of the same rank. In the English colonies marriage could sometimes provide a way for young men or women to climb

the social ladder. It could even strengthen the position of young gentlemen, as in the case of future U.S. president George Washington (1732–1799). By marrying the widow Martha Dandridge Curtis, he acquired the additional lands and wealth needed to make him one of the leading political figures in Virginia.

Different customs among English

For most English colonists marriage meant establishing a separate home and having children. Large families ensured that the family name would carry on, that the church and community would have a strong future, and that the household would have sufficient workers. Young colonists who wanted to marry could usually choose their partners themselves, although parents watched closely to make sure they made a suitable match. English colonists tended to marry later than people in other regions because fathers controlled the distribution of land to their sons and used this power to keep them at home until they were in their early to mid-twenties. Daughters generally waited until their twenties to marry as well. Marriage between teenagers was rare. In New England marriages were generally stable and long-lasting. Newlyweds usually formed a separate household and began to have children within the first nine to fifteen months of marriage.

In the Chesapeake region, in contrast, many young women were married before their sixteenth birthday, seven to ten years sooner than women in New England or England. In these colonies, the high death rate meant that only one in three early marriages lasted as long as ten years. Because of the scarcity of women, remarriage was common for widows. This pattern produced complex extended families with many stepchildren and gave women unusual control over their families and property. Husbands often willed their estates to their wives, so wealthy widows enjoyed a wide range of potential husbands.

New France and Spanish borderlands

New France (present-day Canada) achieved an even balance in the ratio of men to women only after 1710, but the healthful climate contributed to stable nuclear families. Beginning in the early years of colonization, French trappers or traders often married or formed partnerships with Native American women, who could serve as interpreters and guides. The wilderness survival skills of these women were valuable to immigrant men. Relationships between native women and Europeans in New France remained common throughout the colonial period.

Similarly, the small number of Spanish women in the borderlands settled by Spain prompted the earliest soldier-settlers in that region to marry Native American women. (The Spanish borderlands were the Southeast, Southwest, and parts of present-day South

west.) Carolina and Alabama.) The Spanish government worked hard to promote the immigration of Spanish women, whose marriages helped create an upper class of mostly Spanish descent. In a society composed of both Spanish and mixed-race families, there was significant diversity in customs, and extended families became quite common in the Spanish borderlands.

Weddings as celebrations

Weddings in colonial North America were not universally considered religious occasions, but they were often celebrated with community festivities. Anglicans in Virginia and elsewhere considered weddings sacred rites. Anglican weddings were conducted by a minister, either in a church or in the bride's home, and were sealed with an exchange of rings and elaborate vows. Virginians commonly celebrated a wedding with feasting, dancing, and gift giving that involved the whole community and could last for days. Puritans, in contrast, considered weddings to be civil rather than religious occasions. They were usually conducted at home by a local justice of the peace. No rings were exchanged; the Puritans regarded this custom as superstition. A Puritan wedding often consisted of both partners answering a single question concerning their commitment and fidelity (faithfulness) to each other. Seventeenth-century New Englanders celebrated weddings with modest dinners (sometimes with large feasts by the eighteenth century), and wedding guests often completed the

A newly married couple dance at their wedding. Colonial weddings were festive events .

festivities with a noisy celebration called a "charivari," in which they banged on pots, rang bells, and cheered outside the couple's honeymoon bedroom. Pennsylvania Quakers observed an elaborate, sixteen-stage process to complete a wedding, mixing celebration with religious ritual.

Children's lives

The way children were brought up in colonial America depended in part on where they lived. In regions where nuclear families were the norm, children commonly grew up in large families with seven or more siblings, though family size declined in the eighteenth-century coastal settlements. Typically the carefree childhood was short: children were expected to help the family with daily work at an early age. Ninety percent of colonial Americans lived on family farms, where children's labor was needed. Boys over the age of six worked as field hands and were trained to perform various farm chores as soon as they could handle them. Girls learned to help with domestic tasks. In many regions children also learned to

A Wedding in the Spanish Borderlands

Couples in areas controlled by the Spanish had very different weddings from those held in New England. In Spanish colonies a wedding was both a community celebration and a solemn religious ceremony. The celebration began with a great procession in which the veiled bride, with her father at her side, walked from her home to the church and up the aisle to the altar, preceded by her bridesmaids, family, and friends. At the altar the father literally gave the bridegroom his daughter's hand. The priest read a passage from the Bible and then stepped down in front of the couple, where he explained to them and the community the meaning of marriage. He concluded his remarks with the Latin statement *"ergo vos in matrimonium conjugo"* ("Therefore I unite you in marriage"). The groom then gave a ring to the bride, slipping it on her thumb first with the words "In the name of the Father," then on her index finger while saying "and of the Son," next on the middle finger with "and of the Holy Spirit," and finally on the fourth finger with "Amen." Wealthy grooms gave their brides gold rings, while commoners gave bands of wood or leather. After the ring was given, the couple was often wound with a large rosary or rope to symbolize their union. If he had not already done so, the groom then gave the bride an *arras,* a symbolic gift of thirteen coins in a pouch. The priest often rented this item to grooms who might not otherwise be able to afford the custom. The wedding concluded with a mass, and then the priest gave the kiss of peace to the groom, who then gave it to the bride. Afterward the couple left the church amid music, gun salutes, and loud celebration, which served both to congratulate the couple and to ward off evil spirits.

Reprinted in: Gutierrez, Ramon A. When Jesus Came, the Corn Mothers Went Away: Marriage, Sexuality, and Power in New Mexico, 1500–1846. *Stanford, Calif.: Stanford University Press, 1991.*

read and write, although boys usually received more education than girls (see Chapter 12). As boys grew into teenagers, they assumed more responsibility at home or became apprentices in order to learn a trade. Teenage girls often served their own sort of apprenticeships by working as domestic servants in other households.

Loss, hardship, and faith

Early colonists led hard lives, and the lives of their children were equally difficult. Although the birthrate in colonial families was higher than the European norm, only a fraction of the children who were born survived to adulthood. Many died at a young age, most from illness and dis-

A colonial family harvesting wheat. As this illustration shows, children were expected to help with chores at an early age. *Reproduced by permission of Corbis.*

ease. Their parents mourned their deaths but probably viewed these losses as inevitable. Parents needed large families in order to protect themselves from poverty, and they had many children in order to ensure that some survived to work on their farms and to take care of them when they became too old to provide for themselves.

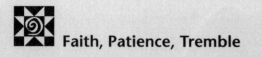

Faith, Patience, Tremble

The names many early English colonists gave to their children seem to reflect the parents' perceptions of the danger and hardship of their lives—and their hopes and fears. One infant whose father died was named Fathergone; another fatherless child was named Abiel ("God is my father"). Many names were taken from the Bible: Joseph, Abigail, Sarah, Hannah, Zurishaddai ("the Almighty is my rock"), and Gershom ("I have been in a strange land"). Others reflected virtues or hopes: Comfort, Deliverance, Hope, Patience, Faith, Endurance, Submit, Silence, Joy, Hoped For, Temperance, Preserved, Waitstill, Hopestill, Wait, Thanks, Experience, More Mercy, Return, Believe, Tremble. Most of these names sound strange to modern ears, but they convey some of the values the early colonists hoped to instill in their children.

Puritan notions of children

The early colonists of New England did not conceive of childhood as a carefree time of play. Nor did they think of children as generally innocent. Beliefs about the nature of childhood varied according to the religious backgrounds of the colonists, but many believed that children were born with potentially evil qualities. Their natures had to be changed before they could become good. Among the northern colonists, only the Quakers believed that children were inherently good and could be taught by example. Others felt that strict discipline was necessary to civilize children. In *Child Life in Colonial Days,* historian Alice Morse Earle quoted John Robinson, a Pilgrim minister, who expressed the general view of childhood when he wrote, "Surely there is in all children (though not alike) a stubbernes and stoutnes of minde arising from naturall pride which must in the first place be broken and beaten down that so the foundation of their education being layd in humilitie and tractablenes other virtues may in their time be built thereon." So the first step in bringing up a child was to "break and beat down" his or her stubborn and rebellious nature. Idleness and play were viewed as foolishness.

Early childhood

Most infants were baptized soon after birth to protect their souls if they should die. Even during the coldest days of winter, newborns were taken to the church to be baptized. The water in the christening bowl might be covered with ice, which had to be broken. Samuel Sewall (1652–1730), a Boston, Massachusetts, judge described such baptisms of his children in chilly water. On January 22, 1694, he wrote in his diary, "A very extraordinary storm [today] by reason of the falling and driving of Snow. Few women could get to Meeting. A Child named Alexander was baptized in the afternoon."

Beginning in infancy, children were molded, physically and emotionally. Many infants wore swaddling clothes, long cloths wrapped snugly around the baby's body in an effort to make it grow straight. Crawling and sleeping in the fetal position (the position of an unborn child in the womb) were considered signs of children's tendency to behave like animals, so parents tried to discourage these habits. Colonial parents encouraged babies to skip over the crawling stage by placing them at an early age in "go-carts," or walkers, which held the baby in an upright position with its feet on the ground. A similar device was the "standing stool," a frame with a toy tray, which supported the baby in an upright position but did not roll.

In their first few years of life, colonial children probably did not receive much attention from their families. Every able-bodied person was busy with work, and children were not thought to need much beyond the necessities of food and warmth. Besides, it was believed that a child who received too much affection would be spoiled. Usually, older children or servants kept an eye on the youngest ones.

Most colonial children had few if any toys; instead they probably invented ways to play with whatever they could find. Older children could play games like leapfrog, hide-and-seek, blindman's buff, marbles, or similar games that did not require much equipment. Some children had a simple doll or other toys, usually homemade. Young children of both sexes

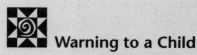

Warning to a Child

A verse in a child's schoolbook makes clear the consequences for misconduct:

My child and scholar take good heed
unto the words that here are set,
And see thou do accordingly
or else be sure thou shalt be beat.

Reprinted in: Earle, Alice Morse. Child Life in Colonial Days. *New York: Macmillan, 1899; reprinted Stockbridge, Mass.: Berkshire House Publishers, 1993, p. 191.*

wore the same gowns of homespun fabric during their early years, especially if they lived on a farm. Boys graduated to wearing pants at about age six. The children of the gentry had much more elaborate and fine-textured clothing, at least for special occasions.

Beginning responsibilities

At about age six most children moved to a new stage of childhood, in which they were expected to assume more responsibility. They were given chores to do around the farm or in the home. In many regions they might also begin to receive some education. Whether they were studying or doing chores, children were expected to work diligently. Often they were busy for most of their waking hours, for many colonial parents believed that "the devil finds work for idle hands." In the early eighteenth century, the

A child's doll from the colonial period. Dolls like this were probably one of the few toys that colonial children might have. *Reproduced by permission of Corbis.*

Brainerds, a Puritan family in Connecticut, kept their sons constantly busy as this excerpt from *Child Life in Colonial Days* shows:

The boy was taught that laziness was the worst form of original sin. Hence he must rise early and make himself useful before he went to school, must be diligent there to study, and promptly come home to do "chores" at evening. His whole time out of school must be filled up with some service, such as bringing in fuel for the day, cutting potatoes for the sheep, feeding the swine, watering the horses, picking the berries, gathering the vegetables, spooling the yarn. He was expected never to be reluctant and not often tired.

Even before they reached their teen years, children knew that life meant hard work and responsibility. And although parents recognized that adolescents could not handle all the responsibilities of the adult world, society hurried them toward maturity as quickly as possible. They believed that an individual's spiritual salvation, as well as their success in the adult world, depended upon avoiding the pitfalls of childishness and reaching a sober maturity.

In order to learn a trade, some boys were sent to work for a master at about the age of ten in an arrangement called an apprenticeship (see "Apprentices" in Chapter 7). Usually they lived with and worked for their masters for about nine years. The master took over the shaping of the young man and had a relationship with him much like that of a father—strict but kind. Sometimes boys were sent to live with a master because they had been orphaned or their own families were too poor to feed them. Some of these boys were abused or exploited, but most were probably treated much as they had been at home. If a family was poor, girls might be sent to work as servants in

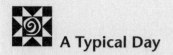

A Typical Day

Maria Carter was the young daughter of Landon Carter, owner of the Stuart Hall plantation in Virginia. She wrote the following letter to her cousin—also named Maria Carter—who lived at Cleve plantation. The writer described a typical day in her life as a girl in an aristocratic family.

March 25th 1756

My Dear Cousin

You have really imposed a Task upon me which I can [by] no means perform, viz [namely] that of writing a merry & comical letter; how shou'd [I] . . . my dear that I am ever confined either at School or with my Grand-mama[.] [You?] know how the World goes on. Now . . . I will give you the history of one Day, the Repetition of which without variation carries me through the Three hundred & sixty five Days which you

know compleats the year. Well then first to begin, I am awakened out of a sound Sleep with some croaking voice either Patty's, Milly's, or some other of our Domestics with Miss Polly Miss Polly get up, tis time to rise, Mr. Price [her tutor?] is downstairs, & tho' I hear them I lie quite snug till my Grand-mamma raises her Voice, then up I get, huddle on my Cloathes & down to the Book [lessons], and then to Breakfast, then to School again & may be I have an hour to my self before Diner & then the same Story over again till twi-Light, & then a small portion of time before I go to rest, and so you must expect nothing from me but that I am

Dear Cousin

Most Affectionately Your's

Maria Carter

Source: Manuscript. The College of William and Mary, Earl Gregg Swem Library, Manuscript and Rare Books Department.

the homes of wealthier colonists.

Children as miniature adults

It has often been noted that portraits from the colonial period depict children as miniature adults—in their dress, their poses, and their expressions. Sometimes even the proportions of their bodies are more like those of adults than of children. Such distortions reflect the conceptions of children of those times. While colonial portraits of children of the gentry

may have reflected the artist's idealized version of these subjects, it is also true that at an early age, colonial children were expected to behave in a mature and sober fashion, to take work and studies seriously, and above all, to honor and obey their parents, teachers, and ministers.

The serious minds of New England children can be found reflected in their journals. Some made entries about daily activities, but most of the surviving books are devoted to religious subjects. Children's journals dis-

A depiction of a child being punished with a beating by his teacher. This form of punishment was not uncommon during the colonial period. *Reproduced by permission of The Granger Collection.*

ken, they could be prepared not only for religious salvation but also for functioning well in Puritan society. Some parents tried gentle methods to teach a child to obey, but whipping was commonplace, at home and at school. Other times children might be made to wear painful devices on their noses or in their mouths and to wear signs that announced their offense. Disobedient students might be yoked together with a device similar to an ox yoke, or labeled with signs such as "Tell-Tale," "Bite-Finger-Baby," "Lying Ananias," "Idle-Boy," or "Pert-Miss-Prat-a-Pace." Not learning one's lesson might be punished by beating or by having to stand on a stool wearing a dunce cap (a conical cap used as punishment for slow learners at school).

Colonial parents and schoolteachers did not always use harsh punishments. For example, it seems that Dutch schoolmasters were much less likely to beat their students. Some schoolmasters were quite progressive in their ideas about teaching and discipline.

Sewall's diary only occasionally referred to having punished his children. Once he whipped his son for lying; on another occasion, in 1692, he wrote that "Joseph threw a knob of Brass, and hit his sister Betty upon the forehead so as to make it bleed; upon which, and for his playing at Prayer-time, and eating when Return Thanks [during the blessing] I whipped him pretty smartly." But Sewall also described how sad he was when his son's behavior reminded him of

play a preoccupation with Puritan ideas of the importance of self-improvement, as well as with topics like sin, punishment, and hell. These diaries give us some idea of the things parents, ministers, and teachers discussed with children.

Conduct and manners

Children growing up in New England farming and artisan families were viewed as naturally inclined to being bad. If their wills could be bro-

Adam's disobedience in the Garden of Eden (according to the Christian Bible, Adam was the first man on Earth who committed the first sin): "When I first went in . . . he sought to shadow and hide himself from me behind the head of the Cradle, which gave me the sorrowful remembrance of Adam's carriage." This incident illustrates the way Puritans saw evidence of people's inescapable sinfulness everywhere. When they perceived it in children, they sought to destroy it for the good of the child.

Families outside New England may not have used the strict methods of the Puritans to correct their children, but they did resort to spankings, deprivation, and other means of punishment to make their children conform to the demands of the community. Children of Chesapeake and Carolina planters were instilled with the community's values of competitiveness and assertiveness, but they were also taught to observe the elaborate social rules that governed planter society. They learned to bow or curtsy, to address their parents and social superiors respectfully, to show courtesy to their equals, and to be kind to their social inferiors.

Behavior at the table

Expectations for the table manners of children in the colonies were apparently intended to reinforce their subordinate position in the family. In some colonial homes, children never ate sitting at the table with adults—they either stood at the table throughout the

 The Advantages of the Rod

Samuel Johnson, the eighteenth-century English lexicographer (a person who studies vocabulary), held a view on whipping that was probably shared by many American colonists: he endorsed the beating of children even though he himself had suffered under the correction of an unusually severe schoolteacher. According to Johnson, his teacher would shout as he beat his students, "This I do to save you from the gallows [a structure used to hang criminals]." Johnson said that his beatings were probably the reason for his having learned Latin. He argued that the rod was a better motivator for children than the promise of parental approval for good behavior:

I would rather have the rod to be the general terror to all, to make them learn, than to tell a child, if you do this, or thus, you will be more esteemed than your brothers and sisters. The rod produces an effect which terminates in itself. A child is afraid of being whipped, and gets his task, and there's an end on't. Whereas, by exciting emulation [imitation] and comparisons of superiority, you lay the foundation of lasting mischief; you make brothers and sisters hate each other.

Reprinted in: Earle, Alice Morse. Child Life in Colonial Days. New York: Macmillan, 1899; reprinted Stockbridge, Mass.: Berkshire House Publishers, 1993, p. 194.

meal or stood behind the adults, who passed food to them. Some ate at a side table. In *Child Life in Colonial Days,* historian Alice Morse Earle quoted from a widely circulated book on manners for colonial children, which sternly spelled out rules for behavior at mealtimes:

Never sit down at the table till asked, and [only] after the blessing. Ask for nothing; tarry [wait] till it be offered thee. Speak not. Bite not thy bread but break it. Take salt only with a clean knife. Dip not the meat in the same. Hold not thy knife upright but sloping, and lay it down at right hand of plate with blade on plate. Look not earnestly at any other that is eating. When moderately satisfied leave the table. Sing not, hum not, wriggle not. Spit no where in the room but in the corner. . .

Other bad habits of the day are brought vividly to light in the following instructions: "Eat not too fast nor with Greedy Behavior. Eat not vastly but moderately. Make not a noise with thy Tongue, Mouth, Lips, or Breath in Thy Eating and Drinking. Smell not of thy Meat; nor put it to Thy Nose. . ."

Courtesy, respect, and obedience

Children in the colonies had to display respect toward adults at all times. For instance, Earle mentioned this: "When any speak to thee, stand up. Say not I have heard it before. Never endeavor to help him out if he tell it not right. Snigger not; never question the Truth of it." Standing and bowing was expected when any adult entered the room. Etiquette books even addressed the issue of how to walk to school:

Run not Hastily in the Street, nor go too Slowly. Wag not to and fro, nor use any Antick Postures either of thy Head, Hands, Feet or Body. Throw not aught on the street, as Dirt or Stones. If thou meetest the scholars of any other School jeer not nor affront them, but show them love and respect and quietly let them pass along.

Standards for children's public behavior seem designed to suppress all playful, silly, or rebellious urges.

The missionaries (people who do religious work in foreign lands) David and John Brainerd were brothers who were born in Connecticut in the early 1700s and grew up in a Puritan family of humble means. Earle quoted from their biography, which gave a description of the upbringing of boys at the time:

A boy was early taught a profound respect for his parents, teachers, and guardians, and implicit prompt obedience. If he undertook to rebel his will was broken by persistent and adequate punishment. He was taught that it was a sin to find fault with his meals, his apparel, his tasks or his lot in life. Courtesy was enjoined as a duty. He must be silent among his superiors. If addressed by older persons he must respond with a bow. He was to bow as he entered and left the school, and to every man and woman, old or young, rich or poor, black or white, whom he met on the road. Special punishment was visited on him if he failed to show respect for the aged, the poor, the colored, or to any persons whatever whom God had visited with infirmities.

The care of children

During the colonial period people had no understanding of the role that bacteria and germs play in spreading disease or infection. Many of their daily habits created opportunities for illness. Washing the body, or even the hands, was not considered necessary. In most early households, all family members ate from shared dishes or even out of the same large pot set in the middle of the table. Often one large drinking vessel was passed around the table and each person drank from it in turn. Toilet facilities were primitive, usually consisting of an outhouse or "privy" in the yard.

Colonists did realize that some diseases could be spread from one person to another, but they did not always know how. Some used vinegar as a disinfectant. Sometimes a sick person was isolated, but many communicable (contagious) diseases were not thought to be spread by contact. At any rate, the everyday habits of the colonists meant that these efforts were probably useless. It is fortunate that in North America they did not encounter many new diseases, at least in the northern colonies. (Native Americans had the opposite experience: contact with Europeans brought them many fatal epidemics; see Chapter 1.) However, harsh environments—bitterly cold in the North, hot and humid in the South—combined with the unsanitary practices of the colonists meant that many people died of illness and infection.

Colonists who fell ill often had to endure strange medical practices and unpleasant medicines. Seventeenth-century colonists still believed that the position of the planets and even weather conditions could affect health, one's fate, and the effectiveness of medicines, which gives us some idea of how limited their medical knowledge was. Throughout the colonial period, useless or even harmful practices such as bloodletting (draining "bad" blood from the body), sweating, dipping in cold water, and purging (giving laxatives) were used.

Colonial home cures Today the cures and medicines used in colonial times seem worse than the diseases themselves. One popular medicine was a liquid called "Venice treacle." This tonic contained white wine, "vipers" (venomous snakes), opium, "spices from both the Indies," licorice, red roses, juice from the sour black fruit of the blackthorn shrub, honey, and many herbs, including germander and Saint-John's-Wort. Recipes for medicines were circulated among the colonies. Another potion commonly used was "snail water," which was believed to cure rickets (a disease that affects the young during the period of skeletal growth), which many children suffered from in the colonies. *The Servants Directory* (1682), a book instructing nursemaids in the care of children, gave the following cure for rickets:

> First give the child three doses of gentle physic [medicine]; then get a peck of garden snails, bruise them in a marble mortar, then throw them into a flannel bag, and let [the liquid] drop into a bason, which liquor you are to save. Then take the child, the first thing in the morning and the last at night, before the fire whether in summer or winter, and with a piece of new flannel in your hand rub the child all over the back and joints; then dip it in the snail liquor, and rub the child well with it on every joint and the back bone . . . after

this practice, give it one dip with the head foremost into water every morning, then put on it a flannel shift immediately, and let it run about and play for an hour to exercise it, and stir its blood; then dress it, and by God's Blessing, this will cure any ricketty child.

Unpleasant as this sounds, it could not have been as bad as having to drink it: snail water was also recommended as a tonic!

Another cure for rickets appeared in a 1769 letter written to Joseph Perry, a Connecticut minister reprinted in Alice Earle's book. The author asserted that a syrup made of black cherries and molasses, given several times a day, would cure rickets. He also advised:

If you Dip your Child, Do it in this manner: viz [namely]: naked, in ye morning, head foremost in Cold Water, don't dress it Immediately, but let it be made warm in ye Cradle & sweat at least half an Hour moderately. Do this 3 mornings going & if one or both feet are Cold while other Parts sweat (which is sometimes ye Case) Let a little blood be taken out of ye feet ye 2nd Morning and yt [it] will cause them to sweat afterwards. Before ye dips of ye Child give it some Snakeroot and Saffern Steep'd in Rum & Water, give this Immediately before Diping and after you have dipt ye Child 3 Mornings Give it several times a Day ye following Syrup made of Comfry, Hartshorn, Red Roses, Hog-brake roots, knot-grass, petty-moral roots, sweeten ye Syrup with Melosses. . . . I have found in a multitude of Instances of diping is most effectual means to break a Rickety Fever. These Directions are agreable to what I have practiced for many years.

Dipping children's heads or feet into cold water was often recommended to cure illness or sustain health. Three-year-old Josiah Quincy, who lived in Massachusetts, was taken every morning from bed and dipped three times in a tub of freshly drawn cold water. English philosopher John Locke (1632–1704), whose ideas on child rearing were widely respected in the colonies, recommended that children's feet be washed daily in cold water. He also thought that having shoes that leaked enough to keep children's feet wet was healthy. Josiah recalled having cold, damp feet much of the time as a child but said it apparently did him no harm. Locke's idea of using cold water on the body was strange to colonists at first, but it may have been beneficial—at least some type of bathing was now considered healthy.

Changing attitudes about children

The belief that children were wayward gradually began to change during the eighteenth century, at least among the wealthier classes. There were several reasons for this new understanding. As families became more prosperous, they stopped having to worry about day-to-day survival and had more time to spend with their children. People were living longer, and this meant grandparents could become involved in the lives of their grandchildren. Life was less of a struggle for every member of the family. Parents could step back and look at their lives and think about their children's future. As life became easier, there may also have been more reason to see God as a benevolent [good natured] protector rather than a harsh judge, which must in turn have softened parents' ideas of their role in their children's lives.

Another reason for the change was Locke's influence. Many of Locke's ideas about children sound quite modern. He believed that it was better to teach children by setting a good example than by using harsh discipline. He also thought that the environment influenced children more than the character they were born with. These ideas caused people to see children as more innocent. They also persuaded many parents to discipline their children with more affection and guidance than punishment. By the end of the colonial period, many parents were more likely to show affection to their children, to see play as an innocent pastime, and to give them more toys. In fact, attitudes toward childhood by the middle of the eighteenth century were starting to resemble the modern understanding of children.

John Locke's ideas on raising children were widely respected in the colonies.
Reproduced by permission of The Library of Congress

Approaching modern family patterns

By the end of the colonial period, family patterns and concepts had changed in several ways. Attitudes toward childhood had moved in a modern direction, with children seen as more innocent beings in need of guidance instead of breaking and remolding. There was more emphasis on the importance of the individual and the uniqueness of each person. For children, there was more affection and more time for play, and for adults, the pursuit of personal fulfillment began to be valued. The nuclear family and the home

became the focal point of people's lives, rather than the wider community. Colonists also developed a need for privacy in family life that had previously been unknown. There may even have been a new questioning of patriarchy and the authority of fathers in the home, reflecting the trend toward freedom from autocratic (single-person government with total power) authority that was preparing the way for the American Revolution (1775–83). Women and children may not have had equal rights under the law, but the emphasis on individual happiness meant that relations within the family probably changed in their favor. Colonial society was beginning to resemble our own.

African American families

Slaves in the American colonies adapted traditional African family arrangements to the constraints of slavery as best they could, but attaining any kind of stable family life was difficult. The first Africans who came to the colonies faced so many physical and psychological challenges that few formed relationships that led to the birth of children. Besides deprivation and disease, slaves were impeded by an imbalanced ratio between men and women, since far more African men were brought to the colonies than women. In addition, groups of slaves were isolated from one another and individuals had few, if any, choices for partners. It is believed that in South Carolina some African men formed relationships with Native American women, who were also kept as slaves.

Slave owners initially believed that importing new slaves was the best way to supply their needs, rather than encouraging their own slaves to reproduce. Some slave owners supported the formation of nuclear families among their slaves, but as slavery became a profitable business, more families were broken up.

Gradually, as slaves managed to find partners, the first generations of African Americans were born. Since girls and boys were born in roughly equal numbers, a better balance of sexes was gradually achieved, and the African population began to grow. A number of factors contributed to the fertility of later generations: the more balanced numbers of men and women, the natural immunity to American diseases, and the fact that the new generations had been born into slavery.

A broader concept of family

Although African Americans began to form relationships and have more children, the development of the nuclear family did not follow. Partners could be separated through death or sale; children could be taken from parents the same way. White colonists did not acknowledge the validity of African American marriages. Family members could be sold or separated if money was needed or when the owner died and his estate was broken up. Planters also might send slaves to new plantations they were establishing or give them to sons and daughters who operated other plantations.

For African American slaves, the extended family became the important social structure, providing vital support for adults and a safety net for children. The extended family was important even when individual families remained intact because mothers were often put back to work soon after childbirth. It was even more important when family members were separated through death or sale. Kinship provided slaves with a survival system: companionship, love, sympathy, and

Engraving showing a family being sold at a slave auction. This was rare since most families were broken up rather than being sold together. *Reproduced by permission of Archive Photos, Inc.*

understanding, as well as with lessons on how to avoid punishment, cooperate with other slaves, and maintain a sense of self-worth.

Matrilineal family emerges Families in West Africa were generally patrilineal (headed by a male), but this tradition did not survive under the conditions of slavery. The African American family moved toward a matrilineal (headed by a woman) form for several reasons. A young child was more likely to be kept with the mother if the family was separated. Fathers usually worked farther away, outside the domestic world where mothers cared for children. In addition, during her lifetime a woman might have several partners, from whom she could be separated by death or sale. Therefore a child's identity and sense of kinship was more likely to be associated with the mother.

In the North, where slaves did not usually live in groups but in the attics, sheds, and cellars of their owners, family life was even harder to

"very naughty children"

Europeans were alarmed by numerous Native American customs, such as their "heathen" worship of nature, their "lascivious" sexual behavior, and their "enslavement" of women (native women did most of the physical labor). Europeans were also shocked by the child-rearing practices they found in the New World. In 1632 Father Gabriel Sagard, a French Franciscan monk, lamented that Native American parents did not believe in discipline:

> *Nevertheless they love their children dearly, in spite of . . . the fact that they are very naughty children, paying them little respect, and hardly more obedience; for*

unhappily in these lands the young have no respect for the old, nor are children obedient to their parents, and moreover there is no punishment [such as spanking] for any fault. For this reason everybody lives in complete freedom and does what he thinks fit; and parents, for failure to punish their children, are often compelled to suffer wrongdoing at their hands, sometimes being beaten and flouted [disregarded] to their face. This is conduct too shocking and smacks of nothing less than the brute beast. Bad example, and bad bringing up, without punishment or correction, are the causes of all this lack of decency.

Source: Axtell, James, ed. The Indian Peoples of Eastern America: A Documentary History of the Sexes. *New York: Oxford University Press, 1995.*

maintain. Husbands and wives tended not to live with each other, and children were often sold at an early age because they absorbed time their mothers could spend working. Once children were nine or ten years old, they were given chores to do. At about sixteen they started doing regular agricultural or domestic work. As adolescents and young adults, they were often sold or sent to work on another plantation. Again, the extended family often eased this separation, since a half-brother might also be sent to the same plantation or a cousin might be rediscovered there after many years of separation.

Native American family patterns

Native American life changed dramatically after the arrival of Europeans (see Chapter 1). Some groups were more immediately affected than others, but as colonialism expanded, Native American groups displaced by or interacting with Europeans faced great upheavals in their ways of life. Family patterns were but one area where they had to adapt. Although each Native American group was unique, generalizations can be made about the structure of their society, both before and after the process of colonization. Generally a clan of related Native Americans lived together. The family network therefore included far more relatives than a nuclear family. The decision to marry was made by the individuals; divorce was acceptable and could be initiated by either partner. Marriage partners were usually chosen from outside the group, but fundamental loyalties and ties were to one's clan.

The Iroquois and Cherokee were two large tribes that functioned as matrilineal societies. This pattern was common among Native American groups. Property and sometimes family names were passed down through the females of the clan. In such tribes a married couple often lived with the wife's clan. This structure gave women a source of identity, support, and influence that women in the patrilineal societies of the colonists often lacked.

Transformation and destruction

As European settlers moved onto Native American land, the lives of the native peoples changed, often dramatically. Death from European diseases claimed many, destroying entire clans or reducing their numbers drastically. Wars against the Europeans also had a dramatic impact on clan and family life. Most of the men in a clan might be killed in battle, leaving a group of women, children, and elderly people. Other clans were displaced and had to restart their lives in new environments. Native Americans who interacted peacefully with the colonists found their ways of life transformed as they began to use imported goods and eventually rely on trade with Europeans. And some native women, especially in New France, formed relationships with white traders, leaving their clan and its way of life.

Finally, the arrival of European missionaries in North America brought more change, as Christian belief systems, which were clearly patriarchal, were substituted for native traditions. Native Americans who converted had to give up many aspects of their culture, including familiar concepts of the family and the role of women. As European influence expanded, Native American family life moved away from the clan-centered structure. Instead of loyalty to the larger group, the husband, wife, and children were regarded as the basic unit. The clan was not abandoned, but it began to have a lesser place in daily life as the nuclear family became central and families took on a patrilineal structure more like that of the European communities.

Colonial Women | 10

The story of the colonial era has usually been told as if white European males acted alone in settling North America. Prior to the mid-twentieth century, history books generally gave only slight attention to the lives of colonists who lacked access to power—servants, women, Native Americans, African slaves—thus creating wide gaps in the story of America. Yet without the efforts of these silent actors, the new country would never have been built. Scholars eventually recognized this fact, and during the 1970s they began collecting and publishing information about the daily existence and contributions of ordinary European settlers such as servants and other laborers. Anthropologists and ethnologists (scientists who study human culture) also retrieved a rich history of Native Americans dating back thousands of years (see Chapter 1). Efforts to piece together the story of African Americans were ongoing at the end of the twentieth century, producing a better understanding of slave culture (see Chapters 5, 7, 8, and 9). Similar efforts were being made to tell the story of colonial women—European, African, Native American—who worked hard to build their communities but remained essentially voiceless.

The idea that the New World (a European term for North and South America) was a place of unlimited growth, freedom, and opportunity did not necessarily apply to women. This chapter explores the context in which colonial women lived and highlights those who made their mark on American history. Not surprisingly, most of the documents from the period deal primarily with women of European descent because Europeans kept written records, whereas Native Americans and African Americans relied on oral traditions (stories handed down from generation to generation in spoken form). Few accounts remain of the lives of Native American women or female African slaves, and for that reason they are underrepresented here.

The first colonial women

In the early 1600s, before any European women came the New World, Native American women were experiencing profound changes as their communities increasingly came into contact with both hostile and peaceful European settlers, who would eventually displace or eradicate the native inhabitants of the country that became the United States. Native American women found themselves living in two worlds as the boundaries between outsiders and themselves increasingly disappeared. Many became translators and traded goods with these foreign people, often providing a financial and diplomatic service to both communities.

Cultural translators and resisters

Native women were adaptive and resourceful in dealing with the colonists. In times of peace they increased their production of goods for trade with the settlers and enhanced the sustenance and trading capabilities of their people. In times of aggression and violence, native women were also involved in the struggle against colonial forces. Many were sexually assaulted or captured by European colonizers who sought to destroy native culture and enslave native people.

Although most Native Americans initially welcomed Europeans, they eventually began to resist colonization in order to protect their own culture and traditions. This was particularly true in the case of religious conversion. Accounts written by Jesuit missionary priests (members of the Society of Jesus, a Roman Catholic religious order) in New France (present-day Canada; see Chapter 3) show that native women actively resisted Jesuit attempts to convert them to Christianity. The women openly mocked the priests, passing this attitude on to their children, who had to struggle even harder to retain an independent identity. Historical records show that native women tried to adapt to colonization without compromising their cultural, spiritual, and physical integrity.

The "village world, forest world"

Prior to the arrival of Europeans, most Native American groups

Pocahontas and Rebecca

The story of Pocahontas (c. 1595–1617) is one of the most frequently retold accounts of the early days of colonization. The Native American "princess," who was the daughter of Powhatan, the powerful chief of the Powhatan nation, became famous at the age of eleven. According to legend, in 1607 Pocahontas begged her father not to execute John Smith, one of the founders of the nearby Jamestown settlement, who was feared by the Powhatans. Chief Powhatan listened to his daughter's pleas and set Smith free, starting a new relationship with the settlers in which Pocahontas played a key role as a translator and sort of ambassador between cultures. Through the centuries many historians have cast doubt on the accuracy of this story, which Smith told in various versions. Nevertheless the legend of Pocahontas remains a favorite tale of the struggle between Native Americans and Europeans.

In 1613, after renewed local tensions, Pocahontas was kidnaped by the English and converted to Christianity. She took the English name Rebecca and, soon after her release, married an English tobacco planter named John Rolfe (1585–1622). Pocahontas traveled with her

Pocahontas. *Reproduced by permission of the International Portrait Gallery.*

husband and son to England, where she was celebrated by the queen in the royal court as a heroine. She died in 1617 at age twenty-one from tuberculosis and pneumonia while onboard the ship that was taking her back to her native land. Her story gives us an idea of how strange and difficult it must have been to stand between two opposing cultures. One reason Pocahontas is so well remembered is that she renounced her native culture in favor of European life—which is also what killed her.

divided the work of men and women along similar lines. Men generally did the hunting and fishing, while women gathered foods like berries and nuts. But women also took charge of planting, caring for, and harvesting food in gardens and fields. In many tribes, women were also responsible for cutting fire-

In addition to preparing food, many Native American women were also responsible for cutting firewood and other physically demanding work.
Reproduced by permission of Corbis-Bettmann.

wood and other physically demanding work. Some even took charge of building houses, like the Pueblo women in the Southwest. Native American women did these jobs in addition to making pottery and clothing and performing other daily necessities. The Iroquois considered that women controlled what they called the "village world," while men were responsible for duties in the "forest world"—hunting, fishing, and defense.

Seeing native women working in the fields caused many Europeans to believe that Native American men treated their women like slaves. It is likely, however, that women enjoyed considerable authority because of the variety and importance of their roles. At the beginning of the eighteenth century, a missionary visiting the Iroquois wrote, "it is they [the women] who really maintain the tribe. . . . In them resides all the real authority" (John Demos, *The Tried and the True,* pp. 48–49).

Loss of status and support

The arrival of Europeans in the Americas changed life for Native Americans in many ways. One result of colonization was that Native American society moved from a clan structure to a nuclear-family orientation. In societies based on nuclear families (those composed of father, mother, and children), women lost the support of their clan and had to depend more on their husbands. And while clan life had been matrilineal (headed by women) for many tribes, within the new family structure it was the father who assumed control of property and made decisions for the family.

Relations between the sexes therefore changed in Native American society. The position of women began to resemble that of European women as patriarchal (male-dominated) habits and values were adopted. Decision-making power, for example, was one area where women began to have less influence than before. While clan governance had always been largely a man's arena, Native American women had often played an official role in tribal matters. For example, women elders (leaders) in each Iroquois clan had been responsible for selecting the chief, who represented the clan at tribal councils. After the arrival of Europeans, the new Native American systems of governance usually excluded women from political life entirely.

Finally, as trade with the Europeans became a more important source of income and goods for Native Americans, women's work in the village as artisans (skilled craftspeople) and gardeners was no longer as important. As life began to revolve around obtaining furs and other materials to trade for European-made goods, many traditional responsibilities of women—such as the making of baskets, clothing, and other articles for daily use, as well as the tending of gardens—gave way to a role as a helper in trade.

Earliest European women

The first European women who came to the colonies also faced a dual existence, leaving behind familiar traditions for what they hoped would be better lives in an unknown land. No women are known to have been in the so-called "First Supply" of settlers to Jamestown, Virginia, in 1607, and only two are believed to have been in the "Second Supply" a year later. The first group of settlers were men who came to explore a new world considered too rugged and wild for women. This would change as soon as the men realized the need to reproduce and the need for more laborers.

The first real wave of European women arrived in 1619 as indentured servants who worked on tobacco plantations in Virginia. Indentured servants were men and women from the working classes of Europe, mainly England (see Chapter 7). The 150 women who came to Virginia were mainly young urban women. They had signed contracts to work for an employer in the colonies for a specified length of time in exchange for free ship passage to North America and a few benefits when they completed their term of service.

The cost of passage was very high, and it took most of a woman's

Women arriving at Jamestown, Virginia, in 1619. Initially employed as indentured servants, many of these women became wives of the male settlers.
Reproduced by permission of The Granger Collection.

youth to pay off. Until they had fulfilled their contracts, indentured servants were "owned" and forced to labor under the same conditions as African slaves. By 1625, three-fourths of the original group of women had died from the hardships of the journey or the unending toil on the plantations.

Conditions improved slightly after critics in England charged that the servants were actually slaves. Laws were passed to make distinctions between white female servants, who were given mostly domestic tasks, and black female slaves, whose plight remained the same (see Chapter 6).

This strange new world

Women who came to the South as indentured servants found their new homes very different from those they had left behind. Many were used to living with their extended families on small plots of land. Suddenly they found themselves scattered throughout a vast colony among strangers under extreme living conditions. The roles that had neatly divided women from men at home were blurred by necessity in the plantation colonies. The intensity of cultivating tobacco required everyone to work long, grueling days in the fields. Housing was usually much cruder than what the women had known. Homes were typically 25 by 18 feet with dirt floors and offered none of the luxuries or accommodations that aided sanitation or comfort. Women had to make do with what little they had, sewing clothes out of coarse linen and wool and surviving on ground corn soup. They worked from morning until night for years, and few survived their indentures. Physical hardships made them more susceptible to diseases such as malaria (a disease transmitted by mosquitoes), pellagra (a disease characterized by dermatitis, gastrointestinal disorders, and central nervous symptoms), dysentery (a disease marked by severe diarrhea), and deadly fevers, for which there were no real cures at the time.

Having followed the promise of better lives, the women found themselves alone and completely responsible for their own welfare. In addition to enduring hard labor, they had to obtain food, attend to daily and long-term survival, and struggle to purchase their freedom. They survived, when they could, by any means available. Those who managed to do so carried their hard-earned independence into their new lives as free people. By the mid-1600s women were working as indentured servants throughout the colonies. Although conditions may not have been so grim in the north, women nevertheless

"unremitting hardships"

A letter written by Judith Giton records the conditions many women found when they arrived in the New World. She was fleeing the persecution of Protestants in France when she came to South Carolina as an indentured servant in 1685. Her letters tell of "unremitting hardships" and describe her life as filled with "sickness, pestilence [fatal epidemic disease], famine, poverty, and the roughest labor."

Source: Kamensky, Jane. The Colonial Mosaic: American Women, 1600–1760. *New York: Oxford University Press, 1995, p. 25.*

encountered a difficult existence in their new home.

Slaves replace indentured servants

Several changes in the 1660s shifted the tide for indentured servants in the South and brought yet another kind of exploitation. There was a slump in tobacco prices, combined with rising wages in England and lower mortality (death) rates in the New World, just as women were starting to outlive their servitude and have families. In Virginia rebellions by the lower class against wealthy plantation owners were breaking out and threatening the entire social order (see "Bacon's Rebellion" in Chapter 5). These factors prompted plantation owners to begin using African slaves instead of white indentured servants and laborers. They had decided to rework the system rather than watch it crumble. The rich hoped that by giving freedom and small plots of land to the poorest white settlers they could stifle discontent without decreasing their profits. They also knew that importing slaves would create a new class distinction, elevating poor whites in status; slaves were now the permanent lowest class of workers, who had no hope of upward mobility. In a sense, plantation owners created a new solidarity based on whiteness, which turned poor whites against poor blacks rather than poor whites against rich whites.

A lifetime of servitude

The first African slaves, like the first European women servants, arrived in Virginia in 1619. Initially the slaves had an uncertain status and could eventually buy their freedom, just like indentured servants (see Chapter 7). By the turn of the century, however, their status had changed so dramatically that two-thirds of bound laborers in Maryland and Virginia were slaves doomed to a lifetime of servitude by laws called slave codes (see Chapter 6). Slaves experienced brutality and hardship on every level. They were forced to serve their owner's every need, working day and night to sustain the comfort and wealth of the ruling class. They barely had any time or energy left

for their own sustenance. They struggled to survive the slave system and keep themselves alive physically, culturally, and spiritually.

Most slaves worked in the fields regardless of their age or sex, but as the plantation economy grew men were more often diverted into skilled labor, leaving the majority of the intensive field work to the women. Only 20 percent of female slaves were considered "indoor slaves" who worked as personal servants to their masters' families. Often female domestic slaves worked even longer hours than outdoor slaves and were more vulnerable to the abuse from their owners that was prevalent during this time. By the late 1600s African families were almost always separated. Female slaves found themselves raising their children under the cruelest and most hopeless circumstances, often to watch them be sold to another owner and never see them again (see Chapters 6, 7, and 9). They lived in even cruder conditions than those of the indentured servants they were replacing. Exploitation and abuse were rampant, and many women fought back against the cruelties forced upon them.

A different life in northern colonies

In the South the main lure to attract immigration (moving from one country to another) was the promise of economic advancement. By contrast the northern colonies

Resisting Enslavement

Though few names and records exist of early slaves' lives, many performed courageous acts of resistance that made a mark in white colonial history. With the risks of sexual exploitation high, many African women rebelled against this type of abuse. Others used their survival skills to buy them some time or relief from their toil. "Mary" of Virginia faked fits to escape work. "Sarah" had an eleven-month pregnancy, which her owners viewed as a ploy to avoid working in the fields. Other nameless women went further and murdered their owners, set fire to their homes, and ran away in search of freedom. One woman was burned at the stake in 1755 for poisoning and killing the master who had raped her. "Hannah" ran away from the Stephen Dence plantation later in the eighteenth century. She was her master's illegitimate daughter, and her light skin helped her make it North. She used her long straight hair to hide the whipping scars on her back. Slave women survived against unthinkable odds, buying a little time here and there to sustain their children or plan their escapes. Most did not make it out alive, and many of their stories died with them.

Source: Kamensky, Jane. The Colonial Mosaic: American Women, 1600–1760. *New York: Oxford University Press, 1995, pp. 42–43.*

were mostly pious religious communities seeking independence from intolerance and persecution back home (see Chapter 4). Settlers in the northern colonies were more likely to duplicate their old lifestyles, bringing traditions and gender roles with them (see Chapter 8). Most colonizers were extended families who formed religious communities (see Chapter 9). This tendency had consequences for women. Despite major economic and social differences between the North and South, most women in both regions spent lives of continuous toil and hardship.

Life cycles of colonial women

Most women in the colonial era learned their roles and duties from their mothers at an early age. With no other form of education available, this was the primary guide for young women in all areas of life. Girls were expected to begin assuming some of their mothers' domestic duties at the age of twelve or thirteen. Although there were differences—between rural and city life, upper class and lower class, enslaved and free—certain general themes can be seen in women's life cycles throughout colonial society.

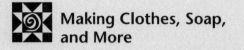

Making Clothes, Soap, and More

Making cheese, soap, clothing, and other essentials took a lot of time and energy. Making clothes, for example, required a spinning wheel and a loom, which were rare and expensive items. A loom was so large that it required its own room. Even if a housewife had these tools, she would spend long, tedious hours working for a small result. Yet there was still an advantage because she could produce necessities for her family and for trade. Before the barrel churn was invented in 1760, women had to make butter with a crude plunger and disk that required about three hours of constant agitation to produce a few pounds of butter. Soap and cheese were slightly easier to make, requiring only large vats or containers and some intensive labor. Soap was made by boiling potash and separating out the potassium carbonate, which was then mixed with animal fat. Cheese simply needed to be curdled and pressed to eliminate excess liquid before cutting it into blocks for consumption.

Daily toil

Women were kept busy from morning until night. Their responsibilities included cooking, baking, cleaning, sewing, preserving food, fermenting beverages (to make alcohol), spinning yarn, producing soap, making candles, raising children, and serving their husbands. In rural areas this list also included caring for livestock and poultry, milking cows, producing dairy products, and working in the fields or garden. If there was no mill nearby, they had to grind their own wheat or corn with a mortar and pestle to provide daily bread. All meals had to be cooked every day because there was no effective way to store leftovers. Laundry had to be done by hand two or three times a week. In addition to these everyday chores, women were responsible for seasonal work such as raising cattle (spring); making cheese, sausage, and bacon (summer); making preserves (fall); and sewing clothes (winter).

No relief in sight

Women's work was often tedious and repetitive, being both physically strenuous and boring. There was rarely a chance to break away from a life of toil unless a family became wealthy enough to hire a servant or buy a slave—in which case the woman's work would become managerial at the expense of another woman's toil. In bigger towns and cities, women could sometimes purchase some of the basic necessities, but they often had to work for a wealthy family on the side to obtain the cash to do so. Since women were always working, they had hardly any time to themselves. The few records from the colonial period indicate that women got little satisfaction from their work, and the general attitude was that women's work, like the pain of childbirth, was to be endured as a consequence of "Eve's curse." (According to the Old Testament of the Christian

Bible, Eve was the first woman on Earth, and she gave in to sin in the Garden of Eden. Church leaders used this story to explain why humans have to endure hardship.) In times of limited educational opportunity, women were fairly resigned to this reality.

Diaries speak of hard lives

Middle-class women who had been taught to write often kept diaries that provide historians with insight into their experiences and emotions. A passage from Mary Cooper's diary, written in the 1760s in Oyster Bay, New York, reprinted in Jane Kamensky's *The Colonial Mosaic* is a typical example: "This day is forty years since I left my father's house and come here and I have seen little but hard labor and much sorrow . . . I am dirty and tired almost to death."

Even wealthy women who had servants to help them wrote in detail about the intense labor of their daily lives. For instance, Elizabeth Sandwith of Philadelphia, Pennsylvania, was married to Henry Drinker, a prominent Quaker (member of the Society of Friends, a religious group). She gave birth to and raised nine children and kept extensive journals chronicling her life for more than five decades. Though she was aided by servants, her journals show that she was as busy and exhausted as women in the lower classes. Mary Vial Holyoke of Salem, Massachusetts, was a housewife whose diaries speak of her wealth and power as well as a life filled with chores. Even though she also had ser-

vants, Holyoke wrote extensively about butchering animals, churning butter, and planting and harvesting crops from her garden, all while leading a stylish social life. Accounts left behind by wealthy women only make more apparent the incredible hardships endured by the poorest white women and African women slaves, who had no hope of relief.

Literacy and education

For most of the colonial era, education was not available to girls, keeping female literacy rates extremely low until the latter part of the eighteenth century. When education was offered, it was usually for religious or domestic reasons (see Chapter 12). The Puritans (a religious group that believes in strict moral and spiritual codes) of New England, for example, taught all children basic reading skills so that they could read the Bible. Boys were required to learn reading, writing, and arithmetic, but girls were limited to needlework and reading. This prevented women from becoming involved in business or law. One exception was the Dutch colony of New Netherland (now New York), where both men and women were active in business and legal life. In this region 75 percent of the women could read and write by the late 1600s, in contrast to only 30 percent of women in New England and 1 percent of slave women in the South. Rural girls were not likely to receive schooling, and in the southern colonies the absence of a strong reli-

A depiction of a Puritan woman reading the Bible to her family. Although colonial women had little education, they were taught basic reading skills so they could read the Bible. *Reproduced by permission of The Granger Collection.*

gious motivation to read the Bible made schooling almost nonexistent for girls. Daughters of the gentry (nobility), however, received some education so they could perform social duties as the wives of planters.

Legal status

In an era when few women had the opportunity to support themselves, marriage was the only chance for economic survival. However, a woman's status changed upon marriage, from "free person" to a "femme couvert," which meant that her legal status and civil identity were "covered" and controlled by her husband (see Chapter 6). Women in general also could not vote, own property, run for office, serve in the militia (citizens' army), or become ministers.

Some families created a trust (a property interest held by one person for the benefit of another) in order to protect their daughters' property. Without this provision creditors could take a wife's land and holdings from her as collateral for her husband's unpaid debts. Without a trust a widow could also find herself left with absolutely nothing if her husband's will passed her property on to creditors or his family members.

Though the concept of a trust may at first glance seem to be a positive protection for married women, the real goal was to protect the rights of male children and heirs. If a woman remarried after her husband's death, she typically lost all rights to the trust and her

The 1695 wedding of Dr. Francis Le Baron and Mary Wilson in Plymouth. Marriage was the only chance for economic survival for colonial women.
Reproduced by permission of The Library of Congress.

property went to her children or her husband's family. Puritans did not permit the use of a trust because they viewed it as a corrupt device invented by the English aristocracy in order to have two separate households, allowing the husband to keep a mistress (a sexual partner who was not his wife). They believed that marriage itself was the only protection a woman needed. To protect a wife from the most extreme form of property loss, the Puritans did permit a jointure (a marriage settlement). In this case the bride's family contributed a sum of money or land that was matched by the groom's family and set aside. Although the property in a jointure was still under the husband's management, it could not be used to pay off his debts and thus remained insurance for the wife and their children, especially in the case of a husband's death.

Marriage for slaves and indentured servants

Indentured servants and slaves were not allowed to marry. As a consequence, in the southern colonies ser-

The Dilemma of Martha Cross

In 1664 a young woman named Martha Cross, from Ipswich, Massachusetts, became pregnant without being married. The predicament she found herself in was compounded by the fact that the father, William Durkee, had no interest in marrying her. Martha was uncertain about what to do, so she consulted her father. Against the tradition of the day, he decided he would rather keep his daughter at home and help raise the child than give her away to a man who openly professed his indifference to her. However, the county magistrates overruled him and forced the couple to marry before the child was born. Courts often took this action to prevent unwed mothers from becoming a burden on the community. Their actions also reflected a strict legal adherence to biblical moral codes.

vant women tended to marry later in life, after their indentures were worked off. A female servant could also get married if she found a partner who would pay off her indenture contract (see Chapter 7). Some poor women had greater freedom in choosing a mate because they had nothing to lose if their father or community disagreed (usually a woman's father and community members had to give their approval before she could marry). However, due to the shortage of women in the Chesapeake region, many were raped and impregnated during or after their indentures, which ruined their chances of a decent courtship or a choice of spouse. Between 1658 and 1705, one-fifth of all indentured maidservants in the Chesapeake region were officially charged with premarital pregnancies. With pregnancy outside marriage defined as a criminal act, women were frequently required to marry the men who had forced them into a sexual relationship or simply ostracized (cast out of society) and fined for their "crime." Similar laws existed in New England, where one out of ten women became pregnant prior to marriage for the same reasons. Slaves were not legally allowed to marry until 1705. Even then the unions were unofficial and unlikely to last because slave owners frequently split up married couples and sold them to different buyers.

Duties and status in marriage

A married woman's responsibilities were to please her husband, bear children, and manage the household. She was considered to be inferior and was expected to obey her husband without question. It was especially important for a woman to comply with her husband's sexual advances, and as a result women spent most of their lives pregnant. Double standards concerning sexual morality punished women for the same acts allowed men. According to the Bible, a married man caught having an affair with an unmarried woman was simply considered a fornicator (one who has sexual intercourse outside wedlock). A woman in the same situation was charged with adultery (having sexual relations with one man while married to another), regardless of the marital status of her lover. The Puritans enacted the Scarlet Letter Law for exactly this purpose: a woman caught in an adulterous relationship was forced to wear a badge of shame, a red "A" sewn to her clothes, for the rest of her life. Punishment was even severer for a woman who got pregnant as a result of adultery; public whippings and standing on a gallows were common punishments in this instance.

Childbirth is dangerous

During the colonial period childbirth was a serious threat to a woman's life. Each pregnancy was a sort of time bomb, largely because women were frequently pregnant and lived under such harsh conditions. A woman weakened by years of toil and malnourishment (lack of food) was usually ill-prepared for the rigors of birthing, particularly if there were serious complications. The worst circumstance occurred when the child was trapped in the womb, requiring a cesarean section, during which the child was cut out of the mother. Since medical knowledge was so primitive at the time (see Chapter 14), these operations were excruciatingly painful and nearly always fatal to the mother. According to historical records, one in three women died before the age of fifty, many in childbirth.

If a mother was fortunate enough to survive childbirth, she had hardly any opportunity to rest. Very wealthy women could take a few days off, but most went back to work right away. In the South many women used a female slave as a wet nurse (one who breast-feeds an infant in place of the mother), but generally women breast-fed their own babies. Children were usually weaned between a year and eighteen months of age. Since most women had several children, they did not have time to give individual attention to each child. In addition, mothers had so many other responsibilities that child care was usually a low priority.

Nevertheless the birth of a child was an occasion that brought women together. While midwives (women who aid during childbirth) took charge of delivering the baby, female neighbors and relatives gathered at the mother's home to help, offer support, and socialize. Depending on the outcome of the birth, they celebrated or mourned together as well.

Escaping a bad marriage

A man's duties to his wife were to support her economically, be sexually faithful, and not go beyond the bounds of "necessary correction" in "disciplining" her. Men were expected to teach their wives to obey and be submissive through whatever means necessary. The only exception was if a man inflicted serious bodily harm, in which case a woman could appeal to the courts for a divorce or separation. The

Elizabeth Montague: From Maidservant to Old Lady

Elizabeth Montague came from England to Virginia as an indentured servant in the 1650s and was twenty-five years old when she got married. She and her husband, Doodes, lived with his parents until they could save enough money to buy a few acres of their own. As soon as they moved, Elizabeth started giving birth to children, one after the other. She had six children, three of which survived. In contrast to her own experience, her daughter married in her early teens, surrounded by suitors, in a time when marriageable women were scarce. Elizabeth lost Doodes at an early age and remarried two times, outliving both her second and third husbands and all three of her children. She died at the age of fifty-two, which was considered extremely old at the time.

Puritans allowed divorce only on the grounds of adultery or desertion (the abandonment of a relationship without legal justification). Nevertheless this was a humiliating and expensive endeavor, requiring special acts of the legislature (governmental lawmaking body), that few women had access to. Some women ran away from abusive husbands to their families, or with another man, but in either case they lost all rights to their property and their children.

Mental cruelty was not legal grounds for divorce. Only if a woman feared for her life and showed some capacity for economic survival outside marriage would a court grant her a divorce. More often than not the courts viewed a divorced woman as such a burden on society that they refused divorce requests. Male legal authorities considered the moral, legal, and financial implications of a broken family much worse than an abused wife. Records show very few actual divorces were granted during the colonial period, on average there was one divorce a year during the entire seventeenth century.

Records also show that many women were abused. For instance, in 1736 Jane Pattison of Maryland begged authorities to grant her a divorce on the grounds that her husband beat her ferociously. Her claims were supported by her neighbors and family, all of whom were deeply concerned for her life, and she apparently received her divorce. Rachel Davenport of New Amsterdam (now New York City) was also beaten for several years until she could no longer bear it. Fearing she would be killed by her husband, she was granted a divorce in the 1670s. Also on the books are examples of women who "stepped out of line." They faced stiffer penalties than those given to men. Joan Miller of Plymouth, Massachusetts, was charged with beating and reviling (verbally abusing) her husband and encouraging her children to help her. She had to pay a fine. Goody Lawrence of Massachusetts was censured (criticized) in court for calling her husband a "bald-patted old rogue."

Widowhood

The only way in which a woman might escape direct male domination was through widowhood. Several consequences were possible if a woman was widowed, although laws differed slightly throughout the colonies. Often the death of the husband signified the end of the family unit. For example, if a man's wife died, he naturally gained access to all of her property. If a woman was widowed, however, she received just a small amount of her husband's property and the family was dissolved. At the beginning of the seventeenth century, a woman was legally entitled to one-third of her husband's property and lifetime use of one-third of his estate. By the eighteenth century a woman was entitled to one-third lifetime use of his estate, but access to his property was limited to his clothing. This shift reflected the increased use of British common law (the body of law developed in England that constituted the basis of the English legal system) in the colonies, which made much narrower provisions for women's rights.

Most inheritances were nowhere near a fortune, and a widow had to work any land or property herself to make any kind of a living. She was not able to sell the property because it never legally belonged to her. She occupied her husband's land as a temporary tenant until her own death or remarriage. Many men anticipated the difficulties of economic survival for widows, so they provided for their wives by stipulating that their eldest son was responsible for his mother.

Women who could not survive on their inheritance thus became dependent on their sons, essentially repeating the role they had with their husband. Frequently, out of true compassion for his spouse, a man redefined the legal terms of her inheritance and ensured she would get at least half of his property.

New Netherland the exception

The Dutch colony of New Netherland granted exceptional legal rights to widows. There a woman stood to inherit and own her husband's entire property for her own use or sale. In the event that she remarried she was still legally entitled to half of what had been his. This had profound implications because a widow could provide for herself, cash in on the land, or even start her own business. Even after the English takeover of New Netherland in 1664, Dutch custom governed social and legal norms for women in this region (see Chapter 6). Because of Dutch traditions that required women to be business partners with their husbands, women in New Netherland enjoyed more freedom than women in other colonies. Though still viewed as subordinate, a woman could own her own business, have an inheritance equal to that of her brothers, sue on her own behalf, and make a will leaving property to whomever she chose. In extreme cases she could even sue her own husband in court. Naturally, New Netherland women prospered at a much higher rate than their counterparts throughout the rest of the colonies.

Maria van Cortlandt van Rensselaer

Maria van Cortlandt van Rensselaer was an upper-class housewife who lived in the Dutch colony of New Amsterdam. When her husband died she became the overseer of his family's estate, Rensselaerswyck, so that her children would have an inheritance. Van Rensselaer was raised in the tradition of seventeenth-century women in the Netherlands, who were considered the freest in Europe. This freedom was the result of their being educated and trained to manage household accounts and to take over the family business if they were ever widowed. Dutch women in the New World were also expected to hold on to the family's wealth so that their children would have an inheritance. Van Rensselaer lived her life in accordance with these expectations and thus was able to keep one of the largest estates in New York secure for her children.

Women and religion

One crucial aspect of a colonial woman's life was her experience with religion. Regardless of the denomination, all religions had some effect on women's roles in society because religion was the basis for morality and law at the time. Stories in the Old Testament (the first part of the Christian Bible), for example, showed the dan-gers of allowing a woman too much freedom. In this case Eve, the first woman, was evicted from paradise because she could not resist the temptation to eat the forbidden apple, which represented sin. This simple story had an enormous impact on women's lives because women were considered sinful, even evil, by nature. Sermons, laws, and social opinion reflected the idea that women were living out some form of punishment for Eve's original sin and that they should never again have the freedom to repeat this sort of offense against God.

The Puritan way

New England was populated mostly by Puritans, who based all laws and customs on the Bible. One of the most popular topics of discussion in Puritan society was the nature of women. Between 1668 and 1735 at least seventy-five printed treatises (a formal, written account) were written on women's lives and roles. Many of these concentrated on Eve's original sin as the rationale for keeping women silent and submissive. Only a few Puritan leaders gave a different perspective in their sermons. As women became the majority of the congregations (groups of people gathered to worship) in most communities, sermons rejecting the inheritance of Eve's sin became popular among common people. One preacher, John Cotton (1585–1652), taught that in a godly society women were an asset rather than a necessary evil. He viewed women as joint heirs to salvation (forgiveness of sins) and saw marriage as a chance for both men and women to find sweet companionship. Cotton's sermons drew women to the church in such great numbers that by the mid-1670s they made up well over half of every Puritan congregation. Even though their status remained inferior, many women clung to the idea of moving on to a better place and waited out their time on Earth in hopes of going to heaven. One of Cotton's followers was Anne Hutchinson (1591–1643), who was excommunicated from the church and banished from Massachusetts as punishment for criticizing the Puritan power structure (see "Religious dissent: The Anne Hutchinson trial" in Chapter 5).

The Society of Friends

The Society of Friends, or Quakers, as they called themselves, were radically different from most other religious groups in colonial North America. They granted women autonomy and equality, believing that anyone who felt the "inner light" of God could become a lay minister. Out of the fifty-nine Quakers who arrived in America in 1656, twenty-three were female preachers. Margaret Fell, one of the early Quaker leaders, argued that the Eve story was irrelevant to godly people who had experienced "the light." The Quakers were quickly banned from New England and pushed south toward the middle colonies, where a diverse array of immigrants had created a more tolerant society. In 1681, King Charles II granted huge areas of land along the Delaware to

 **Religious Ecstasy**

Sarah Piedmont Edwards was the daughter of a prominent Puritan minister in New Haven, Connecticut. At age seventeen she married Jonathan Edwards, a Harvard-educated minister. She was known and respected for her intense religious fervor and piety, which her husband encouraged her to write about. Once she heard an extremely moving lecture by Puritan minister Samuel Buell, which gave her such a surge of joy that she stayed up the entire night experiencing a state of ecstasy and a "perfect union with god." Edwards became famous for her spirituality and preached widely until her death in 1758. This religious experience gave her a voice in a community that usually did not grant such freedom to women.

Quaker William Penn (1644–1718), and many Quakers moved en masse to what would become Pennsylvania (see Chapters 4 and 11). They started what they called "The Holy Experiment," and by 1715 they had gathered twenty-three thousand immigrants (people who move to another country) from many denominations to live in their new settlement, which spread from Pennsylvania to parts of Delaware and New Jersey. This area became known for the encouragement of female participation by preachers who claimed that "in souls there is no sex."

Mary Dyer Challenges Puritans

Mary Dyer (d. 1660), a former follower of Anne Hutchinson, traveled to England in 1652 and became a Quaker. She returned in 1657 to preach the Quaker doctrine in New England and was quickly hounded out by Puritan ministers. She went to New Haven but continued to return to Boston, Massachusetts, and attempt to convert the Puritan masses. Each time she returned she was forcibly removed until the Puritans decided she should be hanged in public for disobeying their authority. As she was being led to her execution the sentence was dropped and she was banished instead. She returned for the last time in May 1660 to protest the Puritans' outlawing of the Quaker faith. This time she was finally hanged for her crime of trespass, as ordered by Puritan

Mary Dyer. *Reproduced by permission of The Granger Collection.*

leader John Endecott. Today Dyer is considered a symbol of religious freedom.

Quaker women started holding their own meetings (religious services) so they could express themselves freely and take care of community business. Penn stated his opinion on the matter in his pamphlet *Just Measures* (1692): "Why should women meet apart? We think for very good reason . . . women whose bashfulness will not permit them to say or do much, as to church affairs before men, when by themselves, may exercise their gift of wisdom and understanding, in a direct care of their own sex."

Southern Anglicanism

Southern women enjoyed even less power to speak out in their communities than their Puritan sisters up north. Though high mortality rates made it difficult for the Anglican Church (the official religion of England; also known as the Church of England) to become established, it became more popular as the southern colonies began to prosper (see "Church of England [Anglicanism]" in Chapter 11). Southern Anglicanism was supported by taxes and gave power to elite laymen (unordained religious leaders) called vestrymen, thus allowing the church to grow virtually unchallenged. Governed by the instruction of Saint Paul (one of the prophets in the Bible), which ordered women to be silent, the Anglican Church offered women nothing but the role of quiet piety and obedience. They believed strongly in women's innate (inborn) inferiority and felt that women needed instruction from men on matters of life and religion.

Exceptional women

It is clear that certain aspects of colonial life reinforced the subordination of women. Marriage, religion, childbirth, the law, and social views served as powerful constraints to women's advancement as individuals. However, against these odds, women throughout the colonies led lives outside convention. They became merchants, innkeepers, teachers, plantation owners, and renowned poets. It is important to remember, however, that some of the women who made names for themselves did so because they took advantage of slave labor or independent wealth.

She-merchants

Wealthy urban businesswomen who were widowed or remained unmarried were referred to as "she-merchants." Some opened small grocery stores that sold tea, coffee, spices, salt, sugar, tobacco, and liquor. Others sold goods ranging from

Mary Taney's Plea

Mary Taney, the wife of the sheriff of Maryland, wrote a letter to the Archbishop of Canterbury, the spiritual leader of the Church of England. She felt her community was in great distress because of the corruption of local leaders and the lack of an official place of worship. Therefore she asked the archbishop for money and a minister to start a church. Her plea went before the king of England and was granted immediately. Although church authorities in her colony would have ordered her to be silent, Mary made her voice heard by a monarch all the way across the Atlantic Ocean.

fine clothing to farm equipment. In the eighteenth century several women ran bakeries or coffeehouses. These shops became quite fashionable in urban areas for the "entertainment of gentlemen," providing chocolates, newspapers, and coffee.

Elizabeth Murray Smith established what was called a millinery, or dry goods shop, in Boston, Massachusetts, before marrying a prominent local merchant. She returned to the business after her husband's death and drafted a prenuptial agreement before she married again, stipulating her right to stay in the trade. Her business did so well that she became one of the wealthiest people in Boston. Smith was dedicated to encouraging other women to sidestep traditional roles, and she funded small businesses and education to help them get started.

Rural businesswomen

In less urban settings women owned and operated taverns or inns, renting out rooms in plantation homes or in smaller houses on trade routes. Liquor licenses were easily acquired by women who showed some degree of managerial know-how. Many community leaders chose to give women some degree of financial independence rather than risk their becoming a burden on the community. In the southern colonies some women ran entire plantations without a husband or father. Margaret Brent (c. 1600–c. 1671) arrived in Maryland in 1638 as an independent heiress. She chose to remain single, thereby retaining her status as an independent person, or "femme sole." She developed several plantations and was so widely admired that Governor Leonard Calvert granted her power of attorney over his property while he was away and made her the executor of his will.

Elizabeth "Eliza" Lucas Pinckney (c. 1722–1793) also found success in the plantation economy. The daughter of army officer George Lucas of South Carolina, she was given many responsibilities while he was away on military service. She was only seventeen years old when she took over his three large plantations, which spanned more than 5,000 acres. She experimented with different crops and plants from the West Indies and was responsible for the importation and cultivation of indigo (a plant used to make dye) in the colonies. By 1748 she had spread the crop throughout the region and made it profitable not only for her plantations but for others as well. By the time Pinckney died of breast cancer in 1793, indigo had become the main export crop in South Carolina.

Some women found themselves thrust into their late husband's enterprises without warning. For instance, Dinah Nuthead inherited control of her husband's printing press. She took over St. Mary's Press in Maryland with such flair and dedication that she was appointed as the printer for the Maryland assembly. Elizabeth Timothy of South Carolina inherited a similar fate when her husband died and left her with the *South Carolina Gazette*. She successfully ran Charleston's first newspaper while raising seven children on her own.

Changing laws for women South Carolina was the only colony in which the issue of women in business was seriously addressed. In 1712 the assembly passed a law allowing women to sue and be sued as "femmes sole" in order to give them more equitable legal status and prevent them from escaping creditors. Although Pennsylvania enacted a similar provision, it was granted only temporarily to a woman whose husband was gone for long periods of time. The permission was withdrawn upon his return.

Teaching presented fewer commercial or legal difficulties for women than business. Many communities that could not afford a "qualified" instructor paid a local woman to educate their children. Though the women's schools at first were little more than nurseries or orphanages, they earned money and eventually some of them expanded into boarding schools for the elite. For instance, Sarah Kemble Knight (1666–1727) of Boston was able to pursue her career as a teacher and writer because she had only one child and a supportive husband. Literate and educated, Knight started out by teaching penmanship and reading to local children. After her husband's death she ran a boardinghouse in her home, opened a shop, and traveled extensively throughout the colonies on business. She then moved to Connecticut, buying property in Norwich and New London. From 1714 until her death, she operated a shop and a house of entertainment, managed many farms, and conducted business with Native Americans. When Knight died she left an estate worth 1,800 pounds—a sizable fortune in those days.

 Susannah Cooper Beats Odds, Bends Law

When Susannah Cooper was married in Virginia in 1717, she brought her husband a huge dowry. Within three years he had deserted her, leaving behind a massive collection of debts. She rose to the occasion and continued to run the plantation they had started, making it a success. Nevertheless, because she was still technically married to her husband, she could not sell any of her assets, sue trespassers on her property, or even make a will in favor of her children. This prompted the Virginia assembly to pass a private bill on her behalf, granting her status as a "femme sole" so she could operate her business as an independent person. Similar provisions were sometimes made in the colonies to enable other women to run their plantations and businesses. Yet for the most part the law created severe obstacles for women.

Poets and captives

Several women made their marks on colonial history by publishing poetry or writing accounts of their lives. Anne Bradstreet (1612–1672) remains one of the most famous women of the colonial era. Born in England and schooled by tutors, she had the advantage of an early childhood education. At the age of sixteen she met and married Simon Bradstreet, who would be her partner for life and the subject of many of her writings. They moved to Massachusetts together, and her poetry was eventually published. Some of her writings, ironically, reinforced the importance of women's domestic roles and subservience to their husbands. Bradstreet's poem "To Her Husband Absent on Public Employment" praises Simon as the ruler of her life and home. He was a supportive and financially stable husband, treating her as a partner in life. Her collection of

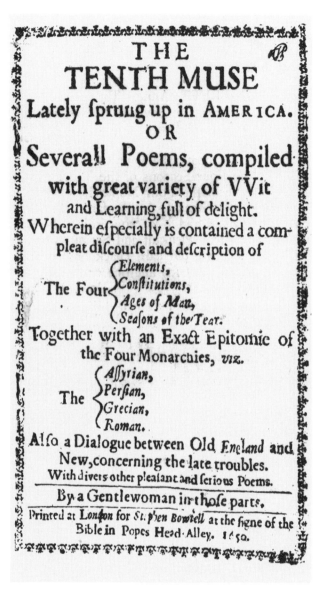

The title page from *The Tenth Muse Lately Sprung up in America,* Anne Bradstreet's collection of poems. It remains one of the most widely read works of the colonial era. *Reproduced by permission of Corbis-Bettmann.*

poems, *The Tenth Muse Lately Sprung up in America,* was published in 1650, receiving critical acclaim, and it remains one of the most widely read works from this era (see Chapter 13).

A few women lived to tell their stories after being taken captive by Native Americans during times of conflict. One of the most famous was Mary White Rowlandson (c. 1635–1711), who lived in rural Massachusetts at a time when tensions between English colonists and a confederacy of Native Americans were running high. In 1676 Rowlandson's tiny village was attacked while her husband was away. After one of her children was killed, Rowlandson and her other two children (all of whom had been wounded) were taken captive with twenty-one other towns-people and marched into present-day Vermont. Separated from her children, she lived with the Native Americans for eleven weeks before she was ransomed by her husband and returned home. Rowlandson's writing skills enabled her to put her story in print. With the publication of *The True History of the Captivity and Restauration of Mrs. Mary White Rowlandson* in 1677 and again in 1682, she became a popular heroine in the colonies and England.

Hannah Duston (1657–?1736) was another frontier woman who was taken captive by Native Americans. She was living near Haverhill, Massachusetts, with her husband, Thomas, a farmer and bricklayer, when warriors attacked the town on March 15, 1697. Duston had recently given birth to her twelfth child, and a neighbor, Mary Neff, was helping out during her recovery. Thomas witnessed the raid while he was working in the fields. As the war party approached the farm, he took his eleven older children to a safe hiding place. However, he could not rescue his wife, Neff, and his infant son. The captives were taken north toward Canada, and during the march the warriors killed the baby. Eventually they stopped at a Native American settlement on an island off the coast of New Hampshire. There Duston and Neff met Samuel Lennardson, an Englishman who was also a captive. When the three prisoners were told that harsh punishment was in store for them, they decided to fight for their lives. During the night of March 30, Duston and Lennardson attacked their sleeping captors with hatchets. Lennardson killed one Native American and Duston killed nine others. As Duston, Lennardson, and Neff started to run away, they realized the settlers at Haverhill might not believe their story. So they went back and scalped their victims. After they returned to Haverhill they took the scalps to the General Court in Boston as evidence of their daring feat. Duston received a cash reward and became an instant heroine in the region by writing and speaking about her story.

The people who chose to stay with Native Americans Both Mary Rowlandson and Hannah Duston became famous for something other than their piety (devotion to God and family) and silence, which was the usual acclaim given to women of their area. What is interesting, however, is that out of the many people who were kidnaped during these times of conflict, many chose

Mary Rowlandson being kidnaped by Native Americans. *Reproduced by permission of The Granger Collection.*

not to return at all. Most captives were women and children, and records show that one-third of them chose to stay with the Native Americans. This became so prevalent that several decades later French traveler J. Hector St. John Crévecouer wrote, "Thousands of Europeans are Indians but we have no examples of even one of those aborigines having from choice become Europeans."

Eunice Williams was kidnaped at the age of seven in 1704, along with her parents and four siblings. They were taken to Kahnawake, a Mohawk village near present-day Montreal, where they stayed for nearly three years until their release in 1707. When they were set free, Eunice chose to stay with the village. She grew up to marry a Mohican, changed her name to Marguerite A'Ongote Gannenstenhaw, and gave birth to three children. She remained in contact with her family, who pleaded with her to return throughout her life. She lived to be ninety-five years old and by all accounts never once regretted the choice she had made in her youth.

Is life better for women?

By the end of the colonial period the non-native population of the colonies reached 2,500,000 people, 65 percent of whom were slaves. The population boom of the eighteenth century had many repercussions on women's lives. For poor families the increase meant lower standards of living and having to make do with less. Up to five generations of one family could be crammed onto a tiny plot of land. The average size of a plot in 1650 was 150 acres; by 1750 this was reduced to 50 acres. Poor families could promise their children little in terms of future land or wealth. For daughters this also meant parents had less control over their marriage choices. By 1750 there was a 40 percent premarital pregnancy rate throughout the colonies, reflecting this shift in control. Though women had slightly more freedom to choose partners themselves, once married they had to survive on

fewer resources. They faced a harsher existence than women had experienced in the seventeenth century.

Rich versus poor

One of the factors that made a difference was the existence of the wealthy few in contrast to the expanded poverty. The well-to-do elite in urban centers stood out as bitter reminders to the poor. Wealth was flaunted as poverty spread, creating social unease. Diversity in the cities was marked by contrasts in power. Poor or rich, black or white, enslaved black or freed white—all lived side by side in cramped conditions. In the same way that plantation wealth suppressed servants and slaves, the social structure of cities exploited the poor. Even the freed slave or former indentured servant was reduced to virtual slavery by wages that provided little chance for survival. Many women ended up homeless, and cities were forced to open almshouses to care for them and others who could not support themselves.

Women on the eve of revolution

On the eve of a massive national struggle for freedom and independence from British control, colonial America still had little to offer women. Women watched men across the colonies proclaiming their struggles for emancipation (freedom) from tyranny while slaves continued to be shackled and women continued to lead hard and bitter lives. Although some women managed to claim a voice through preaching, writing, escaping abusive masters and husbands, or choosing not to marry, many were living in conditions very similar to those their grandmothers had faced. Women were still giving birth endlessly and spending every hour of the day doing backbreaking work. The people who ruled them continued to be male, and they still were not receiving expanded opportunities for education. Furthermore, the increased use of slavery throughout the colonies pushed a significant percentage of the female population back into their most domestic roles.

Religion

11

When Europeans began arriving in North America in the sixteenth century, they encountered Native American traditions that dated back thousands of years. Although native peoples observed a wide variety of religious practices, they all believed in a supreme creator who was present in every aspect of nature. For instance, Native Americans in eastern North America (known as the Eastern Woodland tribes) believed they were only a small part of a harmonious world created by the Great Spirit. All of nature contained this divine spirit and was to be respected. Thus they changed their environment as little as possible, taking only what they needed. They thanked a tree for dying and providing them with wood for a fire. They thanked an animal they had killed for giving up its flesh to feed them and its skin to clothe them. The European view— that humans dominated nature and could change it for their advantage—made no sense to these people. Access to the spirit world came through dreams, which shamans (priests) interpreted for them. Often these shamans were women, who seemed to be more in contact with the spiritual realm because of their role in the miraculous event of childbirth.

Europeans did not recognize the basic similarities between Native American beliefs and their own Christian religions. Therefore most European colonists attempted to convince native peoples that the Christian God was the one true god and only European religious practices were correct. They also promoted the European way of life, which made it easier to convert Native Americans to Christianity and suppress their traditional religious practices. (Conversion was also a way to acquire more land and expand European settlement.) Native Americans who did convert usually practiced their own religion as well, producing a blend of native traditions and Christianity.

Spanish introduce Roman Catholicism

Roman Catholicism (also known as Catholicism) was the first European religion in North America. The Spanish introduced it in the sixteenth century, after they had conquered wealthy empires in Peru and Mexico and moved north in search of more riches. One of their other main goals was to convert Native North Americans to Christianity. At that time, Catholicism was the only church in western Europe (the term *catholic* means universal), and leaders of nations were determined to spread their religion to non-Christian lands. Spain was especially dedicated to this goal, and the pope (the head of the church) granted so much power to the Spanish monarchs, King Ferdinand (1452–1516) and

Queen Isabella (1451–1504), that they virtually became "vice-popes." Seized by religious enthusiasm, they were determined to promote Catholicism in the New World (a European term for North and South America) after Italian explorer Christopher Columbus (1451–1506) discovered it in 1492 (see Chapter 2).

Roman Catholicism has undergone many changes since the sixteenth century, but its major characteristics have remained the same. The Catholic Church (officially titled the Holy Catholic and Apostolic Church) is a Christian religion based in Rome, Italy, and headed by the pope (the bishop of Rome), who is considered Jesus's representative on Earth. (Jesus of Nazareth, also called the Christ, was the founder of Christianity.) Catholic doctrine is based on the Bible (the Christian holy book), which the pope interprets with the advice of a council of bishops (leaders who govern church dioceses, or regions). The pope, either alone or in consultation with his bishops, determines matters of faith and morality, and Catholics must accept his word as absolute truth. Catholics honor the Virgin Mary (the mother of Jesus) and other saints (those who have been declared holy by the church), who each have a special day that is celebrated by the church.

Catholic worship services are based on the sacraments, or rituals through which God directly conveys forgiveness of sins. The principal sacraments are penance (confession and punishment of sins) and the Eucharist

"the blessings of being a Christian"

Spanish Franciscan friars (priests) eventually succeeded in converting the Pueblo to Christianity. Nevertheless they met resistance along the way, especially among the older generation. In 1634 Fray Alonso de Benavides wrote an account of the missionaries' efforts to Christianize the Native Americans. He told the story of one priest, Fray Martín de Arvide, who had been cruelly treated by an old Pueblo priest at the village of Picuries two years earlier:

[Fray Martín de Arvide] converted more than two hundred Indians, suffering great hardships and personal dangers, as these people are the most indomitable [hardest to subdue] of that kingdom. He founded a church and convent large enough to minister to all the baptized [those admitted into the church]. Among the newly converted, there was a young man, a son of one of the principal sorcerers [Pueblo priests]. On a certain occasion, the latter undertook to pervert his son and dissuade him from what the padre [Father Arvide] taught. When the father was informed of it, he left the convent with a crucifix [cross bearing the likeness of the crucified Jesus] in his hands and, filled with apostolic [missionary] spirit, he went to the place where the infernal minister [the Pueblo priest] was perverting that soul and began to remonstrate [express objections] with him, saying, "Is it not sufficient that you yourself want to go to hell without desiring to take your son also?" Addressing the young man, he said, "Son, I am more your father and I love you more than he, for he wants to take you with him to the suffering of hell, while I wish you to enjoy the blessings of being a Christian." With divine zeal, he advanced these and other arguments. The old sorcerer arose, grasped a large club near by, and struck the blessed father such a blow on the head that he felled him and then he and others dragged him around the plaza and ill-treated him cruelly. Miraculously he escaped from their hands; although very eager to offer his life to its Giver, God preserved him for a later occasion.

Reprinted in: Kupperman, Karen Ordahl, ed. Major Problems in American Colonial History. *Lexington, Mass.: D. C. Heath, 1993, pp. 42–43.*

(holy communion). In the sacrament of penance, the penitent (one who has sinned) is required to confess his or her mortal (serious) sins at least once a year to a priest (an ordained clergyman of the church). The priest determines penances (punishment), which usually involve the penitent saying certain prayers. The sacrament of the Eucharist involves church members consuming bread and wine, which are considered the body and blood of Christ. This central ritual of the Roman Catholic Church is performed during the mass (religious service).

Missionaries find easy converts

The first Spanish settlement in North America was a Catholic mission

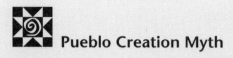

Pueblo Creation Myth

Like all major religions, the Pueblo's spiritual philosophy had at its center a creation myth to explain the phenomenon of life. They believed they had once lived in the center of the Earth (called the middle cosmos) with their mother and all other living creatures. When it was time to leave, she gave them corn to take the place of her nourishment and appointed a priest to take care of them. With aid from the birds, insects, and animals, the Pueblo and their gods climbed up to the surface of the Earth. They entered into the "White House," from which they could view the sky, the third level of the cosmos (universe). In the sky, two sisters were contending to see who was stronger. They fought to a draw. One sister then went east and became the mother of the white people, while the other went west and became the mother of the Native Americans. The Pueblo remained with their gods at the White House, where they were taught how to farm, how to honor the gods, and how to perform the sacred rituals and ceremonies that would integrate humans with the forces of the cosmos. Upon completing their instruction, the people left the White House and established their villages.

at present-day Saint Augustine, Florida, which prospered for many years after its founding in 1565. Jesuits and Franciscans (men who belong to Catholic religious orders) established missions, hospitals, and convents in Spanish territory, called La Florida, which extended north from Saint Augustine to present-day South Carolina and Alabama. After 1598 the Spanish ventured into New Mexico, Arizona, and Texas, where they slowly established the largest concentration of missions in North America. By 1634 there were thirty-four Franciscans maintaining forty-four missions and ministering to more than twenty-five thousand Native American converts. They conducted most of their mission work among the Pueblo, a group of tribes who lived in apartment-like structures. These farming people eagerly adapted the agricultural technology of the Spaniards and welcomed the Franciscans, showing great respect for the European spiritual leaders.

Pueblo observe ancient traditions

Like the Spanish, the Pueblo kept religion at the center of their culture. Pueblo rituals were performed by spiritual leaders (priests; also called medicine men); it was believed they were sent to Earth by the gods, who instructed them before their descent into this realm. The *kiva* was the most sacred place in all of the Pueblo villages, for it represented the hole in the Earth through which they came, a hole that extended into the underworld, the first level of the cosmos. It was through the *kiva* that they could communicate with their gods. The *kiva* was located at the center of each village, from which all else was measured—the apartments, fields, and boundaries of the village. In this circular area was a partially underground room where all the ceremonies that marked the phases of the year took place. This was the time during the ceremonies when it was necessary to enlist the help and advice of the gods and cosmic forces. Next to it was a room where sacred masks and other religious paraphernalia were stored. A chief priest cared for these objects and oversaw the rituals, aided by trained assistants.

Pueblo absorb Catholicism

At first the Pueblo had no difficulty incorporating Catholicism into their traditional religion because they considered the white friars the priests or assistants of the eastern sister (the mother of the white people). The Christian god therefore took his place among their own gods. The Pueblo added to their rituals such Catholic practices as kneeling in prayer and chanting. They included chalices (cups used for drinking wine during communion) among the objects in their sacred warehouse. In addition, they found similarities between Catholic crucifixes (crosses bearing the image of the crucified Jesus of Nazareth, also called Christ) and their own prayer sticks, and the use of incense (a material used to produce a fragrant odor when burned) in Catholic worship services resembled their own rituals in which they smoked pipes. The friars welcomed this blending of traditions and even formed Pueblo boys' choirs to perfect their chanting.

Catholics driven out of Southwest

However, the Pueblo became increasingly resentful of the missionaries. In 1680, after eighty-two years of Spanish occupation, the Pueblo revolutionary leader Popé (c. 1625–1690) led a revolt against Catholicism. Defying Spanish laws, Popé urged the Pueblo to return to their traditional religion and way of life. Organizing a massive force at Santa Fe, New Mexico, he led a siege in which four hundred Spanish missionaries and colonists were killed. The survivors fled hundreds of miles south, into Mexico. As the new leader of the Pueblo, Popé set about removing all traces of Spanish influence: he outlawed the Spanish language, destroyed Catholic churches, and cleansed people who had been baptized by missionaries. Within a decade, however, Popé's power was weakened by Apache raids, internal Pueblo dissension (discord), and his own harsh rule. In 1692, less than two years after Popé's death, the Spaniards once again conquered the Pueblo.

French bring Catholicism to Canada

While Spanish missionaries were spreading Christianity in the southeastern and southwestern regions of North America, the French were introducing Catholicism in New France (present-day Canada; see Chapter 3). French explorers were attracted to the New World by the promise of a profitable fur trade in the Great Lakes

A Jesuit missionary preaching to a group of Iroquois. Native Americans were initially resistant to Christianity. *Reproduced by permission of Archive Photos, Inc.*

eign cultures in a campaign to draw converts to Catholicism. Attired in distinctive black tunics, they were called the "Black Robes" by the Hurons. The Jesuits stayed in New France until the fall of Quebec, the main settlement, four years later. The French then moved south into territory that is now the United States. (The province of New France was restored in 1632.)

When the French ventured south, however, they encountered hostility from the Spanish and the English. Spreading Christianity therefore became less important than expanding French territory and protecting trade routes. The Jesuits also met resistance from several Huron and Iroquois groups who did not want to adopt European customs. In 1647 the Jesuits therefore relaxed their requirements for baptism (initiation into Christianity through anointment with water) and became more tolerant of traditional Native American religious practices. They also took advantage of the natives' belief in the supernatural. For instance, the priests claimed the Catholic crucifix had the power to heal simple diseases. They made a great show of their ability to read and write and predict solar eclipses (the total or partial obscuring of one celestial body by another), which seemed magical to the Native Americans. The Jesuits also capitalized on their own practical skills, their willingness to share belongings, and their ability to endure hardship—all characteristics that Native Americans admired and respected. The Jesuits ultimately had little impact on the culture of the Hurons, but they left

region of Canada and the present-day United States (territory bordering a chain of five lakes: Superior, Michigan, Huron, Erie, and Ontario). Like the Spanish, the French combined conquest with conversion. Leading the effort were members of the Society of Jesus, or Jesuits, who arrived in New France in 1615 to minister to the Hurons, a mighty nation of thirty thousand who inhabited the region around Lakes Huron, Erie, and Ontario. The Jesuits were known throughout the world for their ability to adapt to for-a legacy of Christian commitment among French settlers in Canada and along the northern boundaries of the present-day United States.

Catholics start Maryland colony

Catholics were also among the early English settlers in New York, Pennsylvania, and other colonies. They were often denied political rights and found the most freedom in Maryland. In 1632 King Charles I granted a proprietary charter (a privately held contract granting the right to form a self-governing colony) to George Calvert, first Lord Baltimore, to found the Maryland colony (named for Queen Henrietta Maria, the king's wife). Calvert died soon thereafter, so his son Cecilius Calvert, second Lord Baltimore, developed the colony as a place of refuge for his fellow Catholics. At that time England was embroiled in a conflict that culminated in the English Civil War (1642–48) and the execution of Charles I. The complex political situation was fueled by a religious struggle, primarily between Puritans (a religious group that believed in strict moral and spiritual codes) and Catholics. The Puritans had an intense hatred of Catholics, whom they persecuted, and they especially feared Charles because Queen Henrietta Maria was Catholic.

In 1634 a group of settlers—both Catholics and Protestants—arrived in Maryland. Calvert remained in England, but he told the Maryland governor not to offend the Protestants and advised the Catholics to worship privately. Such toleration of other denominations (organized religious groups) was the only way the Catholics could have any rights at all. A church building was immediately erected in Saint Mary's, the first settlement, and within five years at least four other Catholic parishes had been started. For the first decade the conduct of church affairs was in the hands of Jesuit priests, who converted both Protestants and Native Americans. However, their success provoked the growing numbers of Protestant settlers, and the Calverts quietly began to limit Jesuit activities and invite the ministries of other orders.

In 1649 the Catholic-dominated assembly (lawmaking body) passed an Act Concerning Religion, putting into law the long-practiced policy of toleration. Protestants briefly held power from 1689 to 1691, after Protestant monarchs King William III and Queen Mary II took the English throne during the Glorious Revolution. Maryland then became a royal colony (came under direct rule of the English Crown). The Calverts regained control in 1715, but by this time they had converted to Anglicanism (the official religion of England). Nevertheless, they maintained their earlier policy of toleration, and a small core of Catholics continued to practice their faith in spite of increasing Protestant threats. As moderately wealthy landowners, Catholics enjoyed sufficient social status to sustain their churches.

An illustration of a celebration of the first mass in the Maryland Colony.
Reproduced by permission of The Granger Collection.

Church of England

The Church of England (also called Anglicanism) was founded as the official religion of Great Britain in 1534. The church was indirectly a result of the Protestant Reformation. The Protestant movement began in England in 1531 when King Henry VIII decided to annul (make legally invalid or void) his marriage to Catherine of

Aragon. A staunch Roman Catholic, Henry wanted to marry again because Catherine had not borne him a son and he was determined to father a male heir to the throne. He encountered strong resistance from the Catholic pope, who had the final authority to nullify marriages. Since Catherine was a Spanish princess and the Catholic Church depended on Spain to fight Protestantism in Europe, the pope could not afford to alienate the Spanish by granting the annulment.

Henry formally broke with the Catholic Church in 1534 and declared himself head of the Church of England. But his quarrel with Catholicism was political, not religious. Although he closed monasteries (houses for monks, or men who take religious vows) and seized Catholic lands, he retained bishops and priests. Henry actually did not want to change the church because he loved the rituals, especially the elaborate ceremonies and fancy vestments (robes) worn by bishops and priests during the mass.

Anglicanism in the Chesapeake

With the English founding of Jamestown in 1607 (see Chapter 4), Anglicanism was possibly the first Protestant religion introduced in North America. It became a dominant force, especially after all of the colonies came under English control in the late 1600s and early 1700s. For many years, however, the church was mostly a social organization. The first Anglican churches were clustered around the Chesapeake Bay in Maryland and Virginia, where settlers lived far apart on plantations. They were under the jurisdiction of church authorities in London, who paid them little attention. Making matters worse, Anglican clergymen, who were educated and ordained (officially appointed) in England, did not want to exchange their comfortable positions at home for the poor pay and primitive conditions in the colonies. Most clergymen therefore came to the colonies because they were unable to find a parish (area served by a church) in England. They offered hardly any religious instruction and discipline and rarely bothered to provide a moral example to their parishioners.

Church serves gentry

In the seventeenth-century South, the Anglican Church supported the power of the gentry (upper class), who were the vestrymen of the parish (congregation members who administered the business of the church). These men handled church finances, determined who was to receive public assistance, investigated complaints against the minister, and generally conducted the day-to-day business of the parish. A vestry position was the first rung on the ladder to political power that members of the gentry climbed on their way to colony-wide offices. Taxpayers were assessed a fixed amount to pay for the minister and parish activities. Often the tax was figured in tobacco, which almost everyone grew (tobacco was the main crop of Virginia and Maryland) and which the ministers could sell to support themselves.

Anglican worship services consisted of prayers from the Book of Common Prayer (the official text for church rituals), reading of the Scriptures (the Bible, or Christian holy book), and the minister's sermon. Communion (a ritual in which bread and wine represent the body and blood of Christ; also known as the Lord's Supper) was served four times a year, and anyone who had been confirmed as a church member and seemed to be of sound moral character could participate. Clergymen benefitted from supporting the upper classes (mainly plantation owners), so they frequently used their sermons to remind the lower classes (servants and laborers) to pay proper respect to the gentry. Attending church was mainly an opportunity for colonists to exchange news and conduct business. Once the lower classes had settled down for worship, the gentry paraded into the church and took their seats in the best pews. Sometimes they did not even bother to enter at all.

Renewal of Anglicanism

The arrival of minister James Blair (1656–1743) in 1689 marked the beginning of improvements in the Anglican Church. He was the commissary, or personal representative, of the bishop of London, who supervised parishes in the colonies. Blair was determined to centralize all church authority and administration into his own hands and then mold the clergy into true spiritual leaders. Although vestrymen resisted his efforts, he managed to improve the conduct of exist-

ing clergymen and attract more educated ministers to the colonies. As a result of Blair's efforts, Maryland established Anglicanism as the main religion in 1702. Carolina followed suit in 1706, creating ten new parishes and building the elegant St. Philip's Church in Charleston.

African religions

Africans were among the earliest immigrant groups in North America, arriving as slaves in Virginia in 1619. Most came from the western areas of Africa and held a variety of religious beliefs. There were some common patterns, however. Africans believed in one High God, who created the world. He was often associated with the sky and remained somewhat uninvolved in the lives of humans. Lesser gods and ancestral spirits, however, were actively involved with people's daily lives. Groups of gods were associated with aspects of nature, such as thunder, the earth, and especially water. Gods of nature resided in trees, hills, and animals. They could be kind or cruel and had individual personalities.

Ancestral spirits honored

Humans had to maintain proper relationships with the gods by constructing shrines, wearing certain colors, eating certain foods, and conducting religious ceremonies that pleased them. Ancestral spirits were more varied and personal than gods. Whether they had lived long ago or recently, they were honored as founders of villages and kinship groups. The spirits served as custodians (one in charge) of culture and laws and as mediators between humans and gods. They could grant or deny fertility (the ability to bear children) and health. The spirits were reincarnated (reborn in another human form) in one of their descendants, but their souls returned to the High God after that human died.

Africans respected the elderly because they preserved the memory of the dead and because they were closer in age to the ancestors. Burial rites ensured that the dead entered the spirit world and did not linger in the natural world as restless and evil ghosts. Funerals were long affairs. After death the ancestors demanded offerings of food and drink in ceremonies that often became quite complex. Priests served as mediators, able to read the fates of individuals, to divine the wills of gods and ancestral spirits, and to identify witchcraft. They prescribed amulets, or charms, that contained magical powers to protect and help humans and knew of the natural herbs and roots that promoted healing. Priests also conducted the religious ceremonies devoted to individual gods and ancestral spirits. Interwoven with these rituals were music, dancing, drumming, and singing.

Islam and Catholicism merged with traditions

Some Africans who came to North America were Muslims. Trade

 Society for the Propagation of the Gospel

In 1701 the Anglican Church founded the Society for the Propagation of the Gospel in New England. The goal of the organization was to reverse the embarrassment that the colonial Anglican Church had become to the mother church in England. The society sent out missionaries to start congregations and convert Native Americans and African slaves. Although the missionaries had mixed success with the southern Yamasee and northern Iroquois tribes, they made more progress in converting and baptizing slaves. In New England the society spent much of its energy trying to weaken the dominance of Puritans. The middle colonies proved an exceptionally fertile ground, with their large population of recent immigrants who were hungry for religious services conducted by any Protestant minister.

networks in northwest Africa had brought the Islamic religion, which drew on Jewish and Christian history and scripture. The Muslims (followers of Islam) viewed Jesus of Nazareth as a minor figure, however, and they believed that Muhammad (the founder of Islam) was the true prophet. Muslims followed the teachings of the Koran (the holy book of Islam), observing dietary restrictions and praying in the direction of Mecca (their holiest city) five times a day. Africans had also been converted to Catholicism by Portuguese explorers.

During the early colonial period many Africans intermingled Islam and Catholicism with their own belief systems. To them, God (the Christian supreme spirit) and Allah (the Muslim supreme spirit) were just different names for the High God (God and Allah are actually the same deity). Mary (the mother of Jesus), Jesus, and Muhammad served the same purpose as lesser gods, and Catholic saints were similar to ancestral spirits. The importance of water in African religious ceremonies prepared them for the sacrament of baptism.

African Americans adapt Protestantism

White masters increasingly pressured their African slaves to accept Christianity—in most cases Protestantism (a branch of Christianity formed in opposition to Catholicism). Nevertheless the masters had no control over how the Africans practiced their new faith, so second- and third-generation African Americans began adapting Protestant teachings to their own traditional religions. They were drawn to Old Testament (the first part of the Bible) stories, such as the captivity of the Hebrews in Egypt, which mirrored their own experience. Africans also embraced the New Testament (the second part of the Bible) image of Christ as the savior of the oppressed. During the Great Awakening, a wide-spread revival of Protestantism in the mid-eighteenth century, a small percentage of African Americans were converted to Christianity. By this time black preachers were also spreading the Christian message among slaves.

Puritanism

From the earliest years of the colonial period, Puritans dominated all aspects of life in New England, the northeast region of the present-day United States (see Chapter 4). The Puritans were a Protestant Christian group that advocated reform of the Church of England and stressed strict moral and religious codes. They objected to elaborate church rituals that were derived from Roman Catholicism. Puritans adopted many of the teachings of sixteenth-century French reformer John Calvin (1509–1564), who elaborated on the Reform movement started by Martin Luther. Because of their efforts to reform the Anglican Church, the Puritans were subjected to extreme persecution in England. In the early 1600s they began leaving England in search of religious freedom. Many Puritans made their way to America and founded two colonies—Plymouth in 1620 and Massachusetts Bay in 1630—side by side in the southeastern part of New England. However, they held differing views about the Church of England. The Plymouth settlers were Nonconformists (also known as Separatists), who advocated complete separation from the church. The Massachusetts Bay colonists wanted to reform the church and saw no reason to declare total independence.

Puritans follow Calvin

The Puritans immediately put Calvin's teachings into practice. Towns were organized around Puritan congregations (separate groups of church members) that controlled all aspects of life in the colony. The Puritans adopted covenants (solemn and binding agreements), which were patterned on covenants God had made with humans. In the covenant of works, for instance, Adam and Eve (the first man and woman on Earth, according to the Christian Bible) agreed to achieve salvation (the state of being saved from sin) by their own good works (moral behavior). Adam and Eve broke this covenant by sinning, however, and lost God's grace (goodwill). Through the covenant of redemption, Jesus of Nazareth agreed to take upon himself the guilt and sins of all other human beings, thereby restoring them to God's grace. In the covenant of grace, God's spirit entered certain people, called the "elect," who had been predestined (chosen by God) for salvation.

According to the Puritans, God also made covenants with groups of people, such as Abraham (an important Hebrew leader in the Old Testament of the Christian Bible) and his descendants. He looked upon these people with special favor if they tried to obey his will. The Puritans believed they were one of these favored groups—they often referred to themselves as "saints"—so they created their

A portrait of religious reformer John Calvin.
Reproduced by permission of The Library of Congress.

own covenants that regulated every function of society. Taken together, these separate covenants formed society's covenant with God, who was quick to punish anyone who violated the agreement.

Simplicity stressed by Puritans

Puritan leaders were a few "elect" men who had achieved salvation, and church membership was limited to those who could prove they had been saved. The Puritans believed that people could be saved by hearing and understanding the word of God with the help of an ordained minister. A Puritan church (also called a meetinghouse) was a plain, square building without a steeple (a tall structure, or tower, on the roof), stained-glass windows, or ornaments of any kind. The Puritans rejected these features, which could be found in Anglican churches, as being too much like the elaborate cathedrals built by the Roman Catholic Church. Worshipers sat on hard, wooden benches (pews) facing the minister, who often stood on a raised platform. Although worship services were held throughout the week, the major service was on Sunday. It was a lengthy and formal event with a two-hour sermon (minister's lecture) that opened and closed with long prayers. Worshipers stood during the prayers and throughout much of the service. Sometimes the congregation would take a lunch break after the morning service and return for another session in the afternoon. Singing or chanting psalms (song-poems from the Bible) was allowed, but with no musical accompaniment (an instrumental or vocal part designed to support a melody). A person called a "liner" would sing a line, and the congregation would repeat it in whatever tunes individuals chose to follow.

Community enforces covenants

Since the Puritans lived close together, they observed one another to make sure everyone obeyed the covenants. As a result, there was no privacy in Puritan communities. If trouble arose in a family, church elders (leaders who were not ordained ministers) would take action. They had the authority to remove children and servants from households that did not meet community standards. The husband was the head of the household and represented the family at public and church events. He was also responsible for raising his children in a strict manner to save them from the temptations of Satan (another name for the Devil). A woman obeyed her husband and supervised private household affairs. Puritans assumed that the Bible provided all necessary laws for a moral society, so they did not write an official set of laws until 1641. They also established schools to ensure that everyone could read the Bible. In 1636 Harvard College opened its doors in Cambridge, Massachusetts, to prepare Puritans for the ministry. (It was the first institution of higher learning in the colonies.)

Since Puritans frowned on any activities that did not glorify God, they had strict rules against dancing, card playing, drinking alcohol, and other "immoral" or "frivolous" pastimes. They did not observe the holy days traditionally celebrated in the Catholic Church and the Church of England—not even Christmas (the celebration of the birth of Jesus of Nazareth) and Easter (the commemoration of Jesus's resurrection, or rising from the dead). They thought the Catholic Church had simply made up religious holidays to fit the dates of pagan (non-Christian) rituals so it would be easier to convert nonbelievers to Christianity.

"the young brood doth much afflict me"

Puritan children were brought up in a strict religious environment. Parents were responsible for teaching their children to read and write so they could understand the Bible, and the community enforced rigid moral codes. Nevertheless church leaders worried about the "ungodliness" of young people. For instance, in 1657 Ezekiel Rogers, a Puritan preacher, expressed dismay over the behavior of the "rising generation" in a letter to a fellow minister in England. Rogers confided that he could not find any servants—most of whom were fourteen to eighteen or nineteen years old—who would set a good moral example. He wrote:

Do your children and family grow more godly? I find the greatest trouble and grief about the rising generation. Young people are little stirred [to godly behavior] here; but they strengthen one another in evil by example and by counsel [talking among themselves]. Much ado have I with my own family; hard to get a servant that is glad of catechizing [receiving religious instruction] or family duties. I had a rare blessing of servants in Yorkshire [England], and those that I brought over were a blessing, but the young brood doth much afflict me. Even the children of the godly here, and elsewhere make woful proof [of following Puritan teachings].

Reprinted in: Earle, Alice Morse. Child Life in Colonial Days. *New York: Macmillan, 1899; reprinted, Stockbridge, Mass.: Berkshire House Publishers, 1993, p. 235.*

Influence declines

The Puritans' strict rules often caused conflicts with those who did not share their beliefs. Challenges to Puritan control gained momentum with the arrival of new colonists. By 1660 non-Puritans were pouring into New England in greater numbers, seeking economic opportunity rather than joining the religious community. Church membership declined rapidly, and soon few could claim to be saved. In desperation, some Puritan churches adopted the Half-Way Covenant, whereby children of any baptized person could be admitted to the church regardless of whether their parents were church members. Others took the Presbyterian position that anyone who led a moral life could join the church. In 1692 Massachusetts Bay was placed under a royal charter (direct control of the English monarch) with Plymouth, forming the single colony of Massachusetts. The Puritans were now New Englanders, and their religion became known as Congregationalism.

Congregationalism

Traditional Puritanism had declined by the early 1700s and was replaced by Congregationalism. The

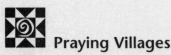

Praying Villages

New England colonists made a widespread effort to convert and "civilize" Native Americans during the seventeenth century. Most of the activity took place in the Massachusetts Bay Colony, where English Puritan missionary John Eliot established fourteen "praying villages" for Christian natives. He initiated his project in 1649, with funding from A Corporation for the Promoting and Propagating the Gospel among the Indians of New England, a missionary organization based in London, England. Eliot had an ambitious mission. He believed converted Native Americans should become independent and adopt the European way of life—live in houses, wear European-style clothes, and own land. He envisioned the settlements as self-governing Puritan villages, where Native Americans would be free to manage their own affairs under Massachusetts Bay laws. In 1651 the first town of "praying Indians" was established at Natick. The first Native American church was also founded at Natick in 1660 and was active until 1716. In 1663 Eliot published a Bible in the Algonquian language. Native American conversion thrived in Massachusetts until it was stifled by Metacom's War (1675–76; also known as King Philip's War). This devastating conflict between the colonists and the Wampanoag broke out when a Christian Native American was murdered, possibly on orders from the Wampanoag chief Metacom. Although many Christian natives fought for the English colonists, they were mistrusted by Puritans and other Native Americans. Eliot himself came under suspicion for his efforts at segregation. As a result, the number of Christian natives began to decline. In 1674, before the war, there had been about thirty-six hundred converts in the fourteen settlements. When the war ended two years later, the number of "praying villages" had dropped to four and the population of Christianized Native Americans had significantly decreased.

original ideal of the Puritan fathers was that separate congregations would all share the same beliefs and promote the same practices in following church covenants. Yet over time Puritans had broken into separate congregations with different views, and it was difficult for church leaders to maintain unity. Another problem was that congregations no longer placed the welfare of the community above self-interest. They also relaxed standards for admission into church membership—some did not even bother to observe the Half-Way Covenant. In New England coastal cities, merchants chose churches that emphasized leading a private moral life but required no commitment to the community. These churches accepted anyone who professed a Christian belief as members. Even the physical appearance of church buildings had changed, reflecting the growing wealth and sophistication of the congregations. Structures became larger and more luxurious and even featured steeples. Balconies had more seats for worshipers, and tall windows flooded the interior with light. Altars appeared in the front of the church, with an elaborate, winding staircase that led to a pulpit (an elevated platform used in church services) high above the worshipers' heads.

Faced with these dramatic changes, church leaders were worried that Christians had lost their way and salvation was no longer possible. They thought the solution was to impose basic requirements on Congregational churches. One such effort was the Saybrook Platform, which a Connecticut group called the clerical party enacted into law, with the support of the governor, in 1708. It created a Presbyterian-type church organization, with a central council that would oversee county districts. The main council would set standards for local churches, appoint supervisors to implement the standards, and ordain ministers. Yet the colony still had to abide by English law and tolerate other religions, so the Connecticut legislature grudgingly passed a Toleration Act, which few communities actually followed.

Revivalism sweeps congregations

Despite an appearance of order and formality in the churches, many

A portrait of minister Jonathan Edwards, who motivated his congregation to seek spiritual awakening through his powerful sermons.
Reproduced by permission of Archive Photos, Inc.

Congregationalists longed for conversion, or an intense personal commitment to the teachings of Jesus. This longing increased with news of the exciting revivals staged by Solomon Stoddard (1643–1729), a pastor in western Massachusetts. Stoddard had abandoned all Puritan church covenants and offered the Lord's Supper (holy communion) as an opportunity for conversion. He also advocated a Presbyterian-style organization. But he was most famous for his powerful sermons, which inspired a spiritual awakening in his listeners. The urge for a new kind of religious experience was heightened by Jonathan Edwards (1703–1758), Stoddard's grandson, who motivated other ministers to stir the souls of their congregations. By 1737, when Edwards published *Faithful Narrative of the Surprising Work of God,* which described his revivals, awakenings were regular occurrences throughout New England. However, it took the appearance of English evangelist (a minister who preaches conversion) George Whitefield (1714–1770) in 1740 to fan these scattered flames into a roaring fire called the Great Awakening.

Presbyterianism

Many Puritans in New England called themselves Presbyterians. Presbyterianism was a democratic system (demonstrating social equality) of church organization in which ministers and elders formed the governing body in a district. Like Puritanism, Presbyterian beliefs were based on the teachings of French reformer John Calvin. From the beginning Presbyterian leaders worked closely with other Protestant denominations in worship, ministerial education, and mutual support. Congregation members came from Ireland, Scotland, England, Wales, Sweden, Germany, and France. By the early eighteenth century Presbyterians were the fastest-growing religious group in the colonies, primarily because of a large number of Irish immigrants (people who move from one country to another). Waves of Irish

Presbyterians first flooded into the middle and southern colonies, which tolerated their religious beliefs, and then flowed into the unoccupied western regions.

Churches isolated

Most of these immigrants lived on isolated farms, so they had to travel some distance to attend services. They usually formed small congregations that often had trouble supporting a minister. Before a congregation could hire a minister, each family pledged a contribution to his salary in the form of food, firewood, or money. If this was not sufficient, two or three congregations shared a minister and conducted their own worship services when he was visiting another church. Larger congregations relied on pew rents (rental of church benches), with more desirable pews going for a higher fee. Worship services were similar to those of the early Puritans in New England, except that several congregations might join in the Lord's Supper. Sometimes this event lasted for two days. One minister would preach a sermon of preparation, after which local clergy would dispense communion tokens to worthy members. The tokens were used as tickets to sit at chosen tables, which were roped off to keep out the "undeserving."

Struggle to define beliefs

Forming an American denomination was a great challenge. Presbyterians found themselves divided on such

Makemie Organizes

The Irish Presbyterian minister Francis Makemie (c. 1658–c. 1707) is credited with joining scattered American congregations into an organized denomination. A tireless traveler, he first journeyed throughout the colonies and down to Barbados in 1683, preaching and organizing churches as he went. In 1706 he organized the first presbytery (a representative gathering of ministers and church elders) in Philadelphia, Pennsylvania, which was attended by seven local ministers and their elders. Within ten years there were four presbyteries and a synod (central council) operating in the colonies. A few months after the first presbytery meeting, Makemie became the center of attention when Edward Hyde, Viscount Cornbury—the governor of New York—had him arrested for preaching without a license. Makemie's defense was that he had been granted a license as a dissenting minister in Barbados, which was valid in all British domains. The court acquitted him, but a vengeful Cornbury

Francis Makemie. *Reproduced by permission of The Library of Congress.*

ordered him to pay the entire cost of the trial. New Yorkers were so incensed that the assembly passed a law prohibiting such assessments and Cornbury was recalled in disgrace. By this time Makemie had died, but many dissenters had moved into the Presbyterian fold.

issues as whether to adopt the Westminster Confession of Faith. The Westminster Confession of Faith (or creed) was established by the Presbyterian-controlled British Parliament (lawmaking body) at the Westminster Assembly (1643–49) as the basis of church doctrine (policy and teachings). The creed recognized the absolute authority of God and the Bible in government, morality, and religion. English Presbyterians accepted baptism and communion, but they opposed the intervention of the church in state affairs. Many American colonists accepted these views, while others objected to having a man-made creed, as opposed to one from God (i.e., the Bible). Debates raged from 1721 until 1729, when the American synod (central council) adopted the Westminster Confession as a guide to church government, but they did not require individual congregations to adopt it.

Presbyterians spark revivals

Presbyterians remained loosely organized into the 1720s, but they were united in their desire to convert others to their beliefs. Around 1726, a young minister in New Jersey named Gilbert Tennent (1703–1764) became acquainted with Theodorus Frelinghuysen, a neighboring Dutch Reformed clergyman. Frelinghuysen was holding religious meetings called revivals, where he preached emotional sermons and urged personal conversion. Tennent wanted to start his own revivals and was soon joined by his brothers and a few others who had been tutored by Gilbert's father, William Tennent (1673–1746), in what was later known as the "Log College." Along with Frelinghuysen they intruded on the congregations of neighboring churches, accusing clergymen of being unqualified to lead others to salvation. Several of Tennent's followers could not meet the educational requirements for ministers set by the Westminster Directory in England, so they fought to have the requirements abolished.

Many sympathized with their position, since lowering standards would make more ministers available for vacant Presbyterian churches. In 1738 the synod compromised by passing the Examination Act, which required ministerial candidates without a university degree to be approved by a synod committee. In 1746 the Presbyterians founded the interdenominational (open to all religious groups) College of New Jersey at Elizabethtown for the training of Presbyterian ministers. The school was moved to Princeton, New Jersey, in 1754 and was officially named Princeton College in the 1760s. (It is now Princeton University.)

Baptists

In 1639 Roger Williams (1603?–1683) and fellow refugees from the Puritan Massachusetts Bay Colony founded the first Baptist (a shortened form of Anabaptist) church in America. They rejected infant baptism, which was practiced in all Christian churches at that time. Williams and his followers believed that only adults were capable of understanding the true meaning of the commitment to lead a life according to the teachings of Christ. They therefore advocated adult baptism, which involved immersion in a river or stream as a way to be cleansed of past sins and start a new life.

Diverse groups formed

By the 1700s the Baptist Church was composed of several groups. Among them were the General Baptists (also known as Six Principle Baptists) from England, who believed in free will (the idea that all people can make voluntary choices or decisions independently of God). They settled mainly in Rhode Island and formed a yearly meeting in 1700 to serve as an advisory board for their numerous churches. Another group, called Particular Baptists, came from Wales and advocated a doctrine of predestination (belief that God has determined one's earthly fate by divine decree). They worked closely with the Presbyterians, who also believed in predestination. The Philadelphia Baptist Association soon attracted other newly organized churches in Virginia and North Carolina. These churches had a strong representation of General Baptists, who later changed their name to Regular Baptists.

Baptists support Great Awakening

Baptist congregations remained small and relatively weak until after the Great Awakening, a series of revivals (intensely emotional religious meetings) in the early 1740s. This movement had a profound impact on all Protestant denominations in the colonies. The message of the Great Awakening was that conversion (a personal commitment to the teachings of Jesus) was the only genuine Christian experience. A true religious conversion, revivalists argued, is the result of a new spiritual awareness that comes when an individual can understand the meaning and importance of a religious life. Revivalists also protested against requiring churches to hire educated and ordained ministers and sup-

 **Baptism**

In 1639 Roger Williams and fellow refugees from the Puritan Massachusetts Bay Colony formed what is called the first Baptist church in America. The name originated from the baptismal experience, which was the center of Baptist beliefs. After an individual had undergone a spiritual conversion, or awakening, the congregation would witness as he or she was submerged in a river or stream. Upon emerging from the water, the person would be cleansed of past sins and ready to start a new life and relationship with God. This practice had its roots in biblical accounts of John the Baptist, the Jewish prophet who preceded Jesus. He was baptizing people as they awaited the new Messiah, whom Christians believed was embodied by Jesus.

porting the ministers with taxes. These views struck a responsive chord in New England, Virginia, and other areas where established (officially organized) churches were the center of society. In New England groups calling themselves the "New Light" separated from established congregations and formed voluntary churches. The Baptists adopted this new style of church formation, creating an environment that encouraged the revivalists. The most influential "New Light" leader was New Connecticut clergyman Isaac

Isaac Backus, the most influential leader of the "New Light" groups.
Reproduced by permission of The Library of Congress.

Backus (1724–1806), who was converted in 1742 and launched a half-century of service. He was instrumental in educating Baptists about their history and the cause of religious freedom. His efforts bore fruit throughout the eighteenth and nineteenth centuries as traveling evangelicals took their message to the southern colonies.

Lutheranism

Lutheranism arose as a result of the Protestant Reformation initiated by German reformer Martin Luther (1483–1546) in the 1520s against the Roman Catholic Church. Charging that Catholicism was corrupt, he left the church when he realized that reform was not possible. According to Luther, salvation comes only to those who have faith in God's mercy (willingness to forgive sins), which leads to a new life based on the teachings of Christ. Luther argued that the Bible was the only source of knowledge about God, so Christians had to be able to read the Scriptures for themselves. Therefore salvation could not come from being moral, doing good works, or relying on the assistance of priests. All of these ideas were contrary to the teachings of the Catholic Church, which relied on priests, bishops, and rituals for interpretation of the Scriptures, forgiveness of sin, and rewards for doing good works.

Although Luther rejected Catholicism, his new religion retained some of the same beliefs. Like the Catholics, for instance, Luther considered all human institutions, including government, to be ordained by God. Luther also accepted the Catholic view that during the sacrament of the Eucharist (holy communion; the Lord's Supper), Christ was actually present in the bread and wine taken by church members. (In holy communion, bread represents the body of Christ and wine is his blood.) Luther's reform movement quickly spread throughout Europe, inspiring numerous sects (small religious groups) that became Protestant denominations in the seventeenth and eighteenth centuries. Luther's ideas strongly influenced the French reformer John Calvin, whose system of religious doctrines was adopted by the Puritans.

Lutherans among earliest settlers

The first Lutherans in America were Swedes who settled New Sweden, which was founded by the West India Company on the banks of the Delaware River in 1638. New Sweden was served by a continuous line of ministers, the most famous of whom was John Campanius (1601–1683), a missionary to Native Americans who translated Luther's catechism (religious instructions) into the Delaware language. The church went into decline after Dutch colonists in New Netherland drove the Swedes out of New Sweden in 1655. The English took over New Netherland and renamed it New York in 1664, and the Swedes then came under the control of the English. When the king of Sweden realized Lutheran churches in the colonies had no ministers, he sent a large supply of books and three ministers, who arrived in 1697. They established the Holy Trinity at Tranhook Church near Wilmington, Delaware, and Gloria Dei at Wicaco near Philadelphia. For seventy-five years all national branches of the Lutheran Church were supervised by a provost, or personal deputy of the archbishop of Sweden, who was allowed to ordain ministers.

By 1719 fourteen Lutheran churches had been established in America, but there was only one minister for all of them. Deacons and overseers (church leaders who are not ordained ministers) were running congregations when a great wave of German immigrants began arriving in the colonies. Most of them settled in Pennsylvania. The loosely organized congregations were prime targets for small religious sects that appeared in the colonies around the same time. American Lutherans appealed to Europe for more ministers, but their requests went unheeded. Finally, Count Nikolaus von Zinzendorf (1700–1760) arrived in 1741. Although he was an ordained Lutheran minister, he was more interested in promoting Moravian beliefs, and he placed Moravian ministers in Lutheran churches.

Mühlenberg unites Lutherans

In 1742 Henry Melchior Mühlenberg (1711–1787), a German Lutheran missionary, arrived in Pennsylvania to take over three congregations. He found them occupied by others, including von Zinzendorf. Within a month Mühlenberg had reclaimed all three, and within six years he had organized Swedish and German pastors and delegates in the Pennsylvania Ministerium. This central organization had the authority to ordain ministers, form churches, and prepare a book of common prayer (the text used in all Lutheran worship services). At the next meeting the group elected Mühlenberg as overseer of all Swedish and German Lutheran churches. He held this office for many years, expanding Lutheranism in America. The shortage of minis-

A portrait of Henry Melchior Mühlenberg, who united the Lutheran congregations in Pennsylvania. *Reproduced by permission of Corbis-Bettmann.*

ters continued, however, and congregations often held simple services in homes and barns.

Dutch Reformed Church

The Dutch Reformed Church was the state church of Holland (the Netherlands) and was governed by the Classis of Amsterdam (main church council). Like Puritanism, the church was based on the teachings of French religious reformer John Calvin. The first Dutch Reformed congregation arrived

in America when the Dutch West India Company established trading outposts in New Netherland in 1624. However, the first ordained minister did not reach the colony until five years later, so the congregation was led by laymen (unordained church leaders) called *Krankenbesoeckers* (comforters of the sick). For several years the church coexisted with other denominations in the interest of attracting settlers. When the English took over New Netherland and renamed it New York in 1664, there were twelve struggling Dutch Reformed congregations and six ministers, three of whom left immediately. Yet the church grew, spreading into New Jersey and Pennsylvania and welcoming Dutch Reformed or Presbyterian preachers. In the early 1740s the American church seriously considered joining with the Presbyterians. The union did not take place, however, because Dutch Reformed leaders insisted that services be conducted in the Dutch language. Yet in New York several Dutch ministers used the English language and even adopted the worship service of the Anglican Church.

Dutch Reformed churches in New Jersey went in a new direction after the arrival of Dutch preacher Theodorus Jacobus Frelinghuysen. In 1735 he and two other preachers spurred a series of spontaneous revivals with evangelical (being in agreement with the Christian gospel) sermons in Dutch and a minimum of ritual. They also criticized established clergymen as "lifeless formalists" (those who rely too much on set rituals and teachings). Dutch Reformed congregations began to split into two warring factions—those who supported the traditional church and others who were attracted to the revival movement. This development forced the Amsterdam Classis in 1748 to establish a coetus (governing council) in America with the power to ordain its own ministers. The church was granted more independence after 1750.

Judaism

Judaism (the religious beliefs, practices, and way of life of Jews) was introduced in America by Dutch Jews who arrived in New Amsterdam in 1654. (New Amsterdam was renamed New York city by the English when they took over New Netherland in 1664; see Chapter 4.) Jews share many traditions with Christians, but they do not view Jesus of Nazereth as the Messiah and son of God. Jewish laws and customs are based on the Torah (the five books of Moses). Thirty-four other books were later added from the Hebrew Bible (called the Old Testament by Christians). Jews had been active in the Dutch West India Company settlement in Brazil but were expelled when the Portuguese retook the post. The Netherlands had provided a place of refuge for Sephardic Jews (those of Iberian, or Spanish, descent) after they were expelled from Spain in 1492 and from Portugal in 1496. In the Netherlands they flourished as merchants and tradesmen. Initially there were no rabbis (Jews trained and ordained for professional religious leadership) among the Jews who emigrated to America. This fact did not present an obstacle, however, because only ten adult males were needed to form a synagogue (congregation).

As soon as Jews were granted the right to public worship in New York City in the late 1600s, they established a congregation. By 1729 they had built a house of worship. Other Jews arrived in small groups, especially after 1740, when the British Parliament allowed them to become naturalized citizens. They moved to other colonies, but were declined political rights because they were not Christians and could not take oaths on the Bible. They settled primarily in coastal cities and practiced their faith quietly. Cantors (chief singers during Jewish worship) took on the role of ministers, and well-educated congregation members preserved the teachings and traditions of Judaism. Many settled in Rhode Island, where they organized a synagogue, built a school, and started a social club. At the end of the colonial period the Jewish community in Rhode Island included about two hundred people. The first of the English colonies to provide religious toleration for Jews was Carolina (later South Carolina; see Chapter 4). Four shop-keepers were granted citizenship between 1697 and 1698. Sephardic Jews from London, England, and the West Indies arrived in Charleston, South Carolina, in the late 1730s. In 1740, they were joined by Jews fleeing Savannah, Georgia, who had heard rumors of a Spanish invasion (see "Georgia" in Chapter 4). In 1749, the Jewish community organized a Sephardic-rite synagogue, Beth Elohim. Around two hundred Jews lived in Charleston by the end of the colonial period.

German Reform Church

The German Reform Church was a Protestant religion similar to the Dutch Reformed Church, and their histories were intertwined. The German church was established in the Palatinate and Rhineland provinces and overseen by a council called the Heidelberg Reform Group. European wars in the early eighteenth century drove many Germans to the middle colonies, mainly Pennsylvania. Because few of the immigrants came to America as organized religious groups, they had no ministers. For instance, an early German Reform Church was started in 1719 in Germantown, Pennsylvania, but it operated without a minister. Other churches were built as community centers, with schoolmasters and laymen conducting services.

In 1727 the Amsterdam Classis took responsibility for the German Reform Church. In 1746 the Classis sent German minister Michael Schlatter to the colonies to organize the church. Within a year he had brought together four ministers and twenty-seven elders representing twelve churches to form a coetus that would meet annually. Although the German Reform Church could not ordain ministers and was still under the control of Dutch Reformed headquarters in the Netherlands, it was on a firmer foun-

dation. Schlatter went on to organize congregations from northern New Jersey to the backwoods of Virginia.

Society of Friends

The Society of Friends (also known as Quakerism) was founded during the mid-1600s by English religious leader George Fox (1624–1691). The name "Quaker" reportedly originated when Fox was ridiculed for telling a judge to "tremble [quake] at the words of the Lord." Quakers were persecuted in England, so they sought religious freedom in other countries. The first Quakers in America settled in the tolerant Rhode Island colony, and from there they sent missionaries to Puritan New England. They preached and paraded in the streets, mocked the clergy, and challenged the Puritan way of life. Quakers believed that all humans possessed the "Inner Light" of Christ, which was more important than the Scriptures. They ordained no ministers, held no formal worship services, and recognized no sacraments (holy rituals such as baptism and communion). Instead, men and women alike gathered and spoke at the prompting of the Inner Light. Believing in the equality of all people, the Friends recognized no hierarchy (social class system) and refused to engage in customary social rituals, such as tipping their hats in the presence of their betters. They dressed plainly without any ornamentation to signify that the material life was unimportant. They refused to bear arms (carry weapons in war) or to take the oaths required in courts of law.

Pennsylvania founded for Quakers

In 1681 William Penn (1644–1718), a prominent English Quaker, founded Pennsylvania as a model colony based on the Friends' beliefs (see Chapter 4). Penn traveled throughout Europe, inviting Quakers to settle in Pennsylvania and offering generous grants of land. He guaranteed freedom of thought with his Frame of Government and, later, the Charter of Liberties. The right to vote and hold office in the assembly (lawmaking body) was open to almost every free man, and oaths were not required. Penn also set the tone for relations with Native Americans, treating them with the same respect he accorded fellow colonists.

Quaker meetings

Friends gathered at least once a week, usually in simple meetinghouses but also in private homes and barns. The meetinghouses were plain, rectangular buildings with windows high in the walls, which were often whitewashed to heighten spiritual intensity. They were also sparsely furnished, with no pulpit, altar, or ornaments of any kind. Members arrived quietly, with men and women entering through separate doors and sitting apart. Seating was by order of arrival, not rank, except for the elders (church leaders). A time of silence allowed everyone to

A woman preaching during a Quaker meeting in Pennsylvania. William Penn founded the colony based on Quaker beliefs. *Reproduced by permission of Archive Photos, Inc.*

turn inward and listen to their Inner Light. As the spirit moved them, men, women, and children stood and spoke. When there seemed to be no more

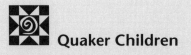

Quaker Children

Quaker families relied on spiritual love rather than strict discipline to maintain harmony in the home. Parents were openly affectionate toward their children, whom they regarded as innocent and incapable of sin until at least eleven years old. Then they used rewards and reason to encourage proper behavior. Quakers devoted little attention to giving children a formal education, other than teaching them to read and write so they could work in practical trades. Quakers felt that too much book learning might obscure the Inner Light. Adolescence was the most dangerous time, for Quakers viewed sexual desire as a sin. Young people were watched closely by the elders and forbidden to have physical contact. They could marry within the faith, but only with their parents' consent.

messages, the elders rose and shook hands, and the meeting ended. Those who had a gift for speaking of the spirit and leading others to contact the Inner Light were called Public Friends (ministers). These men and women traveled around the colonies, ministering to Quakers and non-Quakers alike.

A crisis among Friends

In 1689 the Society of Friends underwent a crisis when Scottish Quaker George Keith (c. 1638–1716) arrived in Philadelphia from New Jersey. He set out to purify the faith by imposing stricter discipline. He demanded that Quakers adopt a creed, test the religious faith of members who attended meetings, and rely more directly on the Scriptures. His followers even organized separate meetings, calling themselves Christian Quakers and causing a split among the Pennsylvania Quakers. In 1692 Penn denounced Keith, who went back to England, where he was forced out of the Society of Friends. After becoming an Anglican, he returned to Pennsylvania as a missionary with the Society for the Propagation of the Gospel (see box on page 297).

Keith's charges struck a nerve among the Friends, however, who responded by acting on many of his suggestions. Meeting groups appointed overseers who asked members standardized questions to test their faith. The Philadelphia Yearly Meeting prepared papers on discipline and practice, which all of the lower meetings (congregations) were directed to follow. Special quarterly meetings were instituted where children were to be drilled in their duties. "Weighty Friends" (wealthy and respected elders) took a greater role at meetings where Public Friends had once been dominant.

Prosperity changes way of life

By the 1740s prosperity was taking a toll on the Quaker way of life as wealthy merchants built bigger homes and purchased finely crafted household furnishings. They acquired wardrobes made with the best and most expensive fabrics—but still in dark colors and with no ornamentation. Young people began engaging in more games and social activities, often with non-Quakers, and some married outside the faith. Although Friends refused to bear arms, government officials were under increasing pressure to vote for military spending to defend the western frontier from Native American attacks. The resulting political conflict led the Quakers to withdraw and let non-Quakers govern the colony.

Moravians

Many American colonists belonged to pietist sects, or small groups that rejected formal religion. They emphasized individual study of the Bible and intense spiritual experience. Generally the pietist sects were offshoots of Lutheranism, and most started coming to the colonies from central European countries, such as Switzerland and Germany, in the late 1600s. These groups were welcomed by the Quakers of Pennsylvania, who were committed to religious toleration.

Among the more prominent pietist sects were the Moravians, or the Renewed Church of the United Brethren. It is difficult to categorize Moravians, but they seem to have functioned like a sect. They concentrated on awakening Christians to a spiritual awareness that transcended denominations. According to the Moravians, once people had had the ecstatic experience of union with God, they could be assured of salvation. The first Moravian immigrants arrived in Georgia in 1735 to minister to Native Americans and slaves. Because they were pacifists (those who oppose war), they were forced to leave and moved into Pennsylvania. Zinzendorf joined them in 1741 and founded several missionary towns. Over the next decade many Moravians went to North Carolina.

Embrace early Christian practices

Moravians revived such early Christian practices as the love feast and foot washing. They held land and property in common and worked in small groups organized by age and sex. Women had considerable control over their own lives, an unusual practice for the time. Moravians supported extensive missionary networks that ministered to Native Americans with great success. Initially they enjoyed good relations with other pietist sects and Reformed denominations because they were willing to follow local religious customs wherever they were preaching. Later, however, they were suspected of trying to steal members from established congregations. The Moravians joined early revivalists (those preaching a renewal of Christian commitment) in the 1730s prior to the Great Awakening but then split with them over philosophical issues. The Moravians increasingly turned their focus inward toward their own settlements, eventually separating themselves from neighboring communities.

Dunkers

The Church of the Brethren, a pietist sect, received the name "Dunkers" because they believed in complete immersion in a stream or river during baptism. They arrived in Pennsylvania from Germany in 1719. A prominent Dunker leader was Christopher Sower, who established Sunday schools and a printing press that issued a German-language newspaper and an edition of Martin Luther's Bible. It was the second Bible printed in America; the first was John Eliot's Bible in the Algonquian language. Perhaps the most colorful Dunker was Johann Conrad Beissel, who established the Ephrata Cloister in 1720. Beissel's group believed that Adam originally had the feminine quality of wisdom and the male attribute of divinity in equal proportions. This balance was disturbed, however, after Eve was created from one of Adam's ribs. The result was that men and women were doomed to having sexual desires. The Ephrata Dunkers believed that only by rising above sexuality could humans return to unity with God. Therefore, Ephrata brothers (men) and sisters (women) lived separately, performing their unique but equal tasks. The group ran a printing press, painted illuminated manuscripts, and composed and performed musical works. The Ephrata Cloister also served as a cultural center for Germans in Pennsylvania.

Great Awakening

The Great Awakening was the most significant religious event in the American colonies during the eighteenth century. It was sparked by George Whitefield (pronounced Whitfield), an English Anglican minister who had become famous for sermons in which he attacked the Anglican Church. In his electrifying speeches he hurled charges at the Anglican clergy, accusing them of relying on outdated doctrines and neglecting the spiritual welfare of their congregations. Soon after being ordained he was barred from preaching in Anglican churches. He therefore held outdoor revival meetings (religious events based on spontaneous spiritual awakening) in England, Scotland, and Ireland, where he attracted huge crowds.

Whitefield was a marvelous performer. He acted out his speeches and created imaginary dialogues with biblical characters in tones that carried to the farthest edges of the crowd. He shouted, stomped, sang, and always wept. People regarded his cross-eyed stare as a sign of a supernatural presence that enabled him to keep one eye on heaven and the other on hell. Whitefield's message was simple: "Repent and you will be saved." He did not understand theology (religious philosophy), which he considered unimportant to his mission of driving people to seek salvation.

Colonies eager for rebirth

In 1739 Whitefield embarked on a tour of the colonies, where revival efforts were already under way in New England and the middle colonies. One of the first to use publicity to his advantage, Whitefield had sent out press releases (notices printed in newspapers) that described his miraculous conversion of masses of people. (Conversion is a personal commitment to follow the teachings of Jesus of Nazareth, the founder of Christianity). By the time Whitefield arrived in Philadelphia, he was already a celebrity among eager revivalists who were clamoring to hear his message. Philadelphians rushed to meet this "boy preacher" (he was only twenty-five years old). He toured through Pennsylvania and New York, usually preaching outdoors and attacking the clergy of established denominations. Whitefield then set out for the southern colonies, traveling through Maryland, Virginia, the Carolinas, and Georgia, where he started an orphanage. He was greeted enthusiastically wherever he went—the Great Awakening had swept America.

Edwards fuels revival

On a return trip to New England, Whitefield went to Boston, Massachusetts. There he met Jonathan Edwards (1703–1758), the famous Congregationalist preacher, who soon moved to the forefront of the Great Awakening. Impressed by Whitefield's success in lifting Christians out of their "lethargy" (lack of religious fervor), Edwards invited the reformer to preach to his congregation at Northampton, Massachusetts. Edwards's own "fire and

 Famous Sermon

New England preacher Jonathan Edwards was one of the leaders of the Great Awakening. His "fire and brimstone" approach to salvation reached a peak in 1741, when he delivered his most famous sermon, "Sinners in the Hands of an Angry God." Edwards stunned his listeners with a graphic picture of the uncertain nature of life and the eternal punishment awaiting unrepentant sinners. Now considered a masterpiece of public speaking, "Sinners" bombarded the audience with frightening images of a hell filled with tormented souls who burned eternally like live coals. Edwards compared sinners to a spider dangling from a single silken thread held fast only by God, who had every reason to let them drop unless they asked him for forgiveness. During George Whitefield's tour throughout the colonies, Edwards was invited to preach, and each time he presented "Sinners." His audiences were convulsed in "great moaning," crying out, "What shall I do to be saved—oh I am going to Hell!" So intense was their anguish that Edwards had to stop several times whenever he delivered the sermon. He eventually published "Sinners" to great acclaim.

brimstone" approach to salvation reached its peak in 1741, when he delivered his most famous sermon, "Sinners in the Hands of an Angry God."

English evangelist George Whitefield helped to spread the message of the Great Awakening. *Reproduced by permission of Archive Photos, Inc.*

Whitefield causes splits

By the time Whitefield returned to England in 1740, evangelical magazines had sprung up throughout the colonies to praise his amazing success. He had had the most effect on Presbyterians in the middle colonies and the Congregationalists in New England. Eventually Whitefield became notorious for his abusiveness, however, and critics accused him of engaging in self-promotion. In fact, he had been instrumental in splitting congregations and producing wounds that would not be healed for years. On a later trip to the colonies Whitefield actually apologized for his excessive behavior.

Awakening changes America

By 1743 the emotionalism of the revivals had already begun to die down. Yet the Great Awakening had an impact on all of the colonial denominations and sects. It created a new awareness of individual religious experience, as people began defining their own beliefs rather than accepting the views of church authorities. Churches formed interdenominational networks that helped break down isolation. Baptists and Presbyterians spread into New England and the South, which had once been strongholds of Congregationalism and Anglicanism. There was an outburst of missionary activity among Native Americans and African slaves, as well as a growing movement against slavery. The Great Awakening also led to the founding of several colleges, such as Princeton, which were initially intended to educate ministers and then became liberal-arts institutions. Perhaps one of the most significant developments was increased opposition to the Anglican Church, which represented English control of the colonies. A democratic spirit was emerging in religion, and this spirit soon rippled into other aspects of colonial life. In fact, some historians regard the Great Awakening as the key to the society that later started the American Revolution.

Education  12

Native Americans were among the first pupils in European schools in North America. Religious education was a tool of conquest used by all European colonizers in the New World (the European term for North and South America). Driven by "God, Gold, and Glory," the Spanish, French, Dutch, and English were determined to spread Christianity to "heathen" peoples. Yet conversion was not their only goal: they also wanted to seize land so they could exploit the rich natural resources and expand their nations' empires in North America. The Spanish and French established mission (church) schools where they converted Native Americans to Roman Catholicism and enforced European customs and traditions. (Roman Catholicism is a branch of Christianity based in Rome, Italy, and headed by a pope who has supreme authority in all church affairs.) The Dutch and the English used a similar approach, attempting to convert Native Americans to various Protestant beliefs. (Protestantism is a branch of Christianity that formed in opposition to Catholicism; it consists of many denominations, or separate organized churches.)

Franciscans in Spanish borderlands

In the 1590s the Spanish occupied La Florida (present-day Florida, Alabama, and South Carolina) and the Southwest (present-day New Mexico, Arizona, and Texas), areas called the borderlands. By 1650 Franciscan friars (members of the Roman Catholic religious order of Saint Francis of Assisi) had established a chain of 38 missions serving 26,000 converts among numerous Native American tribes in La Florida. During this time Franciscans had also moved into New Mexico, founding 20 missions that served 750 Pueblo converts. In both regions the friars tightly regulated mission life, requiring the Native Americans to reject their own beliefs and accept Roman Catholicism. They also introduced native peoples to Spanish handicrafts and farming methods.

The Franciscans' efforts in La Florida ended in failure because tribes either resisted expansion of the missions or formed alliances with English settlers and raided them. At the end of the French and Indian War in 1763, the Spanish surrendered La Florida to the English. The Spanish government evacuated thirty-one hundred settlers, friars, and Native American converts to Cuba and New Spain (Mexico). The Franciscans in New Mexico initially had better luck with the Pueblo, who willingly integrated Catholicism into their own religious traditions. Nevertheless the Pueblo finally rebelled and drove the Spaniards back into Mexico in 1680 (see "Pueblo turn against Span-

ish" in Chapter 2). The Franciscans returned to New Mexico twelve years later, and this time they allowed the Pueblo to follow their own traditions. By 1750 the Franciscans were educating ten thousand Native American converts and the children of four thousand Spanish settlers.

Jesuits embrace Native American ways

In the meantime, the Spanish had sent Jesuit missionary (a member of the Society of Jesus) Eusebio Kino (1645–1711) and two other Jesuit priests to Primería Alta (northern Mexico and southern Arizona; see Chapter 2). Unlike the Franciscans, the Jesuits believed that Native American religion should be combined with Christianity. Beginning in 1687 Kino established about twenty missions where he introduced wheat and cattle, along with other European crops and livestock, to the Pimas and the Papago. Carefully teaching Catholic beliefs, he appointed Pima and Papago converts as teachers who assisted him in the schools. Between 1687 and Kino's death in 1711, the Jesuits baptized (admitted to the church through anointment with water) more than thirty thousand Native Americans. After Kino died, however, the missions were neglected and eventually abandoned.

Between 1717 and 1724 Franciscans started ten missions along the west coast of the Gulf of Mexico to keep the French out of the region. They taught Christianity to the Apache, Comanche, and clans known as the

Noteños. The missionaries also schooled the native peoples in various trades, with the goal of making the settlements self-sufficient. This work was extremely dangerous because other native groups allied with the French often attacked the missions. By 1742 there were only eighteen hundred Spaniards and thirteen hundred converted Native Americans in Texas.

Jesuits start missions in New France

In 1609 French explorer Samuel de Champlain (c. 1567–1635) founded New France (present-day Canada; see Chapter 3). Soon afterward he brought in the Recollects and the Capuchins, two branches of the Franciscan order. As was the case with Spanish Franciscans, these missionaries thought they had to "civilize" the Native Americans. They encouraged the Huron and Montagnais tribes to give up their nomadic (move from place to place) habits, settle near French villages, and send their children to Catholic schools. The project was a failure. Between 1615 and 1627 the priests baptized only fifty-four Native Americans, forty-one of whom later stopped going to church services.

The Jesuits were better equipped to teach Native Americans. In 1625 priests Charles Lalemand, Jean de Brebeuf, and Ennemond Masse began working among the Hurons, a mighty nation of thirty thousand who lived around the Great Lakes (a chain of five lakes along the present-day bor-

"One must be very careful . . ."

In 1647 Jesuit priest Paul Rogueneau was teaching the Hurons. He expressed more tolerance and patience than many other clergymen attempting to educate the "heathens":

One must be very careful before condemning a thousand things and customs, which greatly offend minds brought up and nourished in another world. It is easy to call irreligious what is merely stupidity, and to take for diabolical [evil] workings something that is nothing more than human; and then, one thinks he is obliged to forbid as impious [lacking in proper respect] certain things that are done in all innocence, or, at most, are silly but not criminal customs. . . . I have no hesitation in saying that we have been too severe in this point.

Source: Eccles, W. J. The Canadian Frontier, 1534–1760, rev. ed. Albuquerque, N. Mex.: University of New Mexico Press, 1983, p. 48.

der between Canada and the United States). Rather than dismissing Native American culture as paganism (having little or no religion), the Jesuits merged Christianity with native traditions. They traveled and lived among the Hurons, learning their languages. By blending into native society, the Jesuits were eventually teaching twelve thousand converts. Between 1648 and 1650, however, the Hurons were attacked by their enemies, the Iroquois, who killed thousands and drove out the survivors, including the Jesuits.

The Jesuits then traveled into the area that is now the United States, and many became explorers. The most prominent was Jacques Marquette (1637–1675), who explored the Mississippi River with Louis Jolliet (1645–1700) in 1673 (see Chapter 3). The Jesuits eventually moved into *le pays des Illinois* (Illinois country) and down the Mississippi River, starting missions along the way. They also taught the French language, occasionally sending Native American boys to Quebec or Montreal for further study. A few of these young men went to France to attend grammar school (high school) or college. The results were not encouraging: when the young men returned home, they found they were accepted by neither the French nor the Native Americans. Boys who had learned French and remained with their tribes, however, became translators and guides, serving as a valuable link between the two cultures.

Dutch fight "heathenish tricks and deviltries"

Dutch traders and Iroquois chiefs formed an early alliance in the area that is now New York State. The Iroquois served as middlemen in the fur trade between the Dutch and western Native American tribes. When the Dutch West India Company founded New Netherland in 1624, the charter directed the colonists to convert the Iroquois to Christianity. The first Dutch Reformed preacher, Jonas Michaelius, arrived in New Amsterdam (now New York City) in 1628. (The Dutch Reformed Church was the established religion in Holland; see Chapter 11.) Michaelius believed that Native American children should be separated from their parents so they could be taught the Dutch language and the Christian religion before they learned "heathenish tricks and deviltries." However he had no success because the parents would not let their children leave home. In 1642 Johannes Megapolensis became the minister at Rensselaerswyck, the patroonship (large estate) of the van Rensselaer family, in the area that is now Albany, New York. He worked among the Mohawk, even learning their language, but he had no luck in educating them. Megapolensis went back to Holland and returned with Samuel Drisius, another preacher, around 1655. Together they managed to convert one Native American. Two years later they reported that the man got drunk, sold his Bible (the Christian holy book), and "turned into a regular beast, doing more harm than good among the Indians." Within nine years the English took over New Netherland and renamed it New York.

English try various methods

English efforts to educate Native Americans did not gain momentum until the mid-1700s—and even then religious leaders had little success. At first prospects looked promising at Jamestown in Virginia, when Anglican (the official state religion; also known as Church of England) minister Alexander Whitaker converted the Powhatan "princess" Pocahontas (1595–1617) to Christianity around 1613 (see Chapter 10). Her later trip to England built public support for starting a college for Native Americans at Henrico, a community near Jamestown. The project collapsed, however, when the Powhatans massacred Jamestown colonists in 1622. Virginia Company officials (investors in England who sponsored the colonization of Virginia) then concluded that the Native Americans could not be educated. Nevertheless in 1693 a charter for the College of William and Mary called for a school with one professor who would teach reading, writing, arithmetic, and religion to Native American boys. Funds for the school were provided by scientist Robert Boyle (1627–1691), inventor of vacuum pump, who is called father of modern chemistry. In 1723 Brafferton Hall was built to house Native American students. (The building still stands on the William and Mary campus.) Few students enrolled at the school until the 1740s and 1750s, when Shawnee and Cherokee hostages were brought there during colonial wars. Many died of European diseases, and others simply ran away. Efforts at educating Native Americans elsewhere in the southern colonies were equally unsuccessful.

Eliot starts "praying villages"

Meanwhile, Puritan preachers Thomas Mayhew Jr. (1593–1682) and John Eliot (1604–1690) had been converting Native Americans in Massachusetts during the 1640s. From 1651 to 1665 Eliot established more than fourteen villages for "praying Indians" of the local Wampanoag tribe. With financial support from the Society for the Propagation of the Gospel in New England based in London, England, he built settlements where Christianized Native Americans would live in houses, wear European-style clothes, and own land. Most important, Eliot envisioned that the settlements would be self-governing under the laws of Massachusetts. He also compiled an Algonquian translation of the Bible and trained at least twenty-four Native American preachers. Eventually the Wampanoag's resentment toward the colonists for taking their land grew. During King Philip's War (1675–76; see "King Philip's War" in Chapter 5) the Wampanoag unsuccessfully tried to drive out the English, bringing a virtual end to Eliot's villages. In 1674 about thirty-six hundred converts were living in the fourteen settlements. Following the war there were only four settlements, and the number of Christianized Native Americans had significantly decreased.

Beginning in the 1720s New England leaders tried other education methods. One idea was placing native children as apprentices in "English and Godly Families," where they would learn to read and write English. (An apprentice is a child or teenager who learns a trade with a master craftsman in return for his labor.) This scheme failed when Native American parents refused to part with their children.

Eleazor Wheelock, who established one of the best-known schools for Native Americans in the colonies. *Reproduced by permission of The Library of Congress.*

Later, ministers started boarding schools in order to remove Native American youths from their "heathen" environment. Both boys and girls attended the schools, so that male graduates could find "civilized" mates. One of the best-known schools was founded by Presbyterian minister Eleazar Wheelock (1711–1779) in Lebanon, Connecticut, in 1753. Among his students was Samson Occom (1723–1792), the famous Native American preacher, who established Presbyterian congregations among the Montauk tribe on Long Island. Occom also made a fund-raising trip to England and collected money for expanding the school. Yet in the 1760s Wheelock grew tired of the project and turned his attention toward starting Dartmouth College in New Hampshire.

After taking over New Netherland and renaming the colony New York in 1664, the English worked with Dutch Reformed ministers in educating the Mohawk and Iroquois. One minister, Godfriedus Dellius, had moderate success, baptizing more than one hundred and admitting sixteen to communion (the ritual in which wine and bread represent the blood and body of Jesus of Nazareth, the founder of Christianity). In the early 1700s the Anglican Society for the Propagation of the Gospel in Foreign Parts made numerous conversion efforts intended to lead to education. Frustrated missionaries finally gave up. William Andrews expressed the general feeling: "Heathen they [Native Americans] are and Heathen they shall be." Nevertheless Anglican missionaries continued trying to convert and educate the Mohawk and the Iroquois until the end of the colonial period. Historians note that they succeeded mainly in ensuring that the Iroquois Confederacy (an alliance of Native American groups) was loyal to Britain after the American colonies declared their independence in 1776. The grand plan to turn Native Americans into educated Englishmen, however, had more or less failed.

Education of Europeans

Religion was also central to the education of young Europeans in North America. Although several colleges were founded during the colonial period, greater emphasis was placed on schooling below the college level. In the Spanish borderlands and New France, the Roman Catholic Church controlled formal schooling, making sure that academic standards and religious instruction were maintained. In New Netherland and the English colonies, schooling was closely allied with various Protestant denominations (organized religious groups).

By the turn of the eighteenth century, education had become more diverse and more widely available in the English colonies. Schools were still stressing religion, but many had added areas of secular (nonreligious) study that were popular in Europe. The attitudes of parents strongly influenced education throughout colonial North America, causing a shift from authoritarian (extremely strict) to more permissive child-rearing methods, particularly among the upper classes. Yet schools continued to reflect the class system, and, except in New France, boys were much more likely to be educated than girls.

Spanish borderlands

Despite the frontier circumstances of many settlers in the borderlands, their attitude toward child rearing reflected the strongly class-conscious, patriarchal (headed by the father) family structure of Spain. Honor was at the heart of family relations. For children to disobey their parents was to dishonor the patriarch in particular and the family in general. Women were responsible for the religious education of children, especially before puberty (the condition of being or the period of becoming first capable of reproducing sexually). Mothers trained daughters for their future roles as wives and mothers, with particular emphasis on chastity (sexual purity), modesty, and submissiveness. Children of the elite usually learned reading and writing in church schools, but the literacy rate among the general population of settlers was low.

Craftsmen were in high demand in the borderlands, and boys had to know how to read and write before beginning an apprenticeship. More often fathers taught sons the family trade and initiated them into the code of honor that governed males. While sons were taught to protect their sisters and other female relatives from predatory males, the *machismo* culture of the borderlands encouraged men to express their sexual prowess through seductions, both with Native American and European women.

Mission schools are dominant Franciscans supervised the schooling of settlers' children in present-day New Mexico, Texas, Arizona, and Florida. Schools were scarce outside Native American missions until near the end of the eighteenth century. Parents were required by law to provide religious training to their children and servants, and it was common among the upper classes to have live-in tutors. During the Spanish conquest of the Southwest, children of the Native American elite were educated in the missions, serving as a bridge between the Spanish rulers and Native Americans. This system, known as the Calmecac, was also followed in other borderland regions. Young Native Americans educated in the Calmecac were called *doctrineros,* and they were used in the missions as teachers. Around 1700 a school for reading and writing was established in Santa Fe, New Mexico.

Education above the primary level did not exist in the borderlands. However, children of the borderland elite might go to Durango, in northern Mexico, for Latin schooling and seminary training (preparation for the priesthood). Although educated laymen and clergy lived in Spanish territory, no colleges were established there during the colonial era. Children of the elite in Florida sometimes returned to Spain for a college education or attended college in Santo Domingo or Mexico City. Those from the provinces of New Mexico and Texas either went back to Spain or to Mexico City.

New France

French culture and the Catholic Church both supported a strongly patriarchal view of the family among French settlers in Canada, the Illinois country, and the Mississippi River valley. The shortage of labor in New France, however, gave children and wives more leverage in dealing with fathers and husbands. Children's labor was valuable, and for that reason the child's wishes regarding work assignments had to be heeded, at least to a degree. A young woman from the middle or upper class went to a school headed by a priest or nun (a woman who belongs to a religious order), while a boy of similar social status was more likely to work with his father or perhaps be apprenticed. Craft apprenticeship was the dominant form of nonreligious education in New France, and the boy's family made certain that the master treated his apprentice fairly and taught him well. Some apprenticeship agreements required masters to teach boys to read and write.

Primary schooling Most children in New France received little formal education beyond a year of religious instruction, which was required as preparation for their first communion around age ten. (The first communion marks a young person's admission into the Roman Catholic Church.) Some priests conducted primary schools for both girls and boys, in which they taught reading, writing, and arithmetic as well as catechism (religious instruction that involves questions and answers). In the families of farmers and fur traders, known as the *habitants,* young women were more apt to receive additional schooling than young men. The Sisters of the Congregation of Notre Dame were particularly active in establishing schools for girls; they founded ten schools by 1707, primar-

A Spanish mission in New Mexico. Several of these missions were established to educate Native Americans. *Reproduced by permission of The Granger Collection.*

ily in rural parishes (areas of church jurisdiction). More than half the parishes had at least one girls' school by 1763. Boys rarely attended school because there was such a demand for farmworkers, trades apprentices, and workers in the fur trade.

Boys of the French upper classes might attend the Sulpicians' Latin school at Montreal, where they were given a background in the Roman and Greek classics (languages, literature, and history). Bishop François Laval de Montigny began a seminary in 1659 mainly for the education of priests, but other young men were allowed to attend. Laval's seminary, however, was rigorous, and of the 843 who entered, only 188 stayed and went into the priesthood. The Jesuits at Quebec also established a school of hydrography (charting bodies of water) to prepare young men as pilots, navigators, and cartographers (mapmakers). Young ladies from the upper classes were likely to attend various schools founded by the Ursuline sisterhood (a Catholic order for women) in Quebec, Trois-Rivières, and Montreal. They were taught reading, writing, mathematics, chemistry, biology, and botany (the study of plants), and they were rigorously instructed in Latin before being taught French grammar and literature. Some of these young women later taught their own children and those of their neighbors, though they never established formal schools.

Educated young men from France were sometimes allowed to teach in schools in New France, but only under the supervision of the Catholic clergy. The only permanent school at Louisbourg in the French territory of Louisiana was for girls, founded by the Sisters of the Congregation of Notre Dame in 1727. Schooling was generally neglected in Louisiana, which did not even have a Catholic seminary. However, a Capuchin monk, Father Cecil, did operate a school in the territory from 1725 to 1731. Young men from wealthy families generally went to France for their classical education. In 1727 the Ursuline sisters established a hospital and boarding school for girls in New Orleans. It relocated in 1734 to a building on Chartres Street that still stands.

College of Quebec The Jesuits founded the College of Quebec in 1635, but a full curriculum (set of courses) was not established until the 1660s. By 1712 the college was judged to be equal to or better than Jesuit colleges in France. Course offerings included Latin, rhetoric (public speaking), humanities, grammar, history, geography, science, philosophy, mathematics, and physics. The course of study at the College of Quebec usually took five years or more, and the science curriculum took three years. Students also studied drama and presented plays. Like other Jesuit colleges, the College of Quebec did not award degrees, but students regularly engaged in public discussions. Louis Jolliet, who became famous for his exploration of the Mississippi River (see Chapter 3), studied at the college.

New Netherland

The Dutch in both the Netherlands and the New Netherland colony had progressive attitudes toward child rearing. In fact, foreign observers accused them of indulging and spoiling their offspring. In 1638 Dutch Reformed Church leaders and the Dutch West India Company started a school for girls and boys in New

Netherland, emphasizing religious instruction, reading, and writing. Within ten years, however, New Netherland was in trouble, and colonists were looking for solutions to such problems as low population and ineffective government. In 1648 Dutch Reformed minister Johannes Backerus wrote, "I think we must begin with the children, for many of the older people are so far depraved they are now ashamed to learn anything good." Director general Peter Stuyvesant (c. 1610–1672) had arrived the previous year to bring order to the colony. He told Everardus Bogardus, the Dutch Reformed pastor at New Amsterdam, to begin recruiting schoolmasters. By 1664, when the English took over New Netherland, ten teachers were attached to the Dutch Reformed Church. New Netherland did not have a college, but several young men from the Dutch colony attended Harvard College in Cambridge, Massachusetts, and others returned to the Netherlands for their education.

English colonies

A variety of schools emerged in the English colonies during the colonial period. This was the result of a growing population and the increasing importance of literacy (the ability to read and write). Although schools differed from region to region, the trend throughout the colonies was the same: formal education was becoming more accessible to everyone. Petty (elementary) schools were sponsored by various Protestant denominations for religious instruction and the teaching of reading, writing, and arithmetic. Latin grammar schools were the main institution for secondary education, but the "English school" soon became popular among the middle classes. Unlike grammar schools, which were affiliated with churches, English schools were privately run. They offered not only English grammar but also mathemat-

From *The New England Primer*

The Dutiful Child's Promises (c. 1690)

I will fear GOD, and honour the KING.

I will honour my Father & Mother.

I will obey my Superiours.

I will submit to my Elders.

I will love my Friends.

I will hate no Man.

I will forgive my Enemies, and pray to God for them.

I will as much as in me lies keep all God's Holy Commandments.

I will learn my Catechism.

I will keep the Lord's Day Holy.

I will reverence God's sanctuary.

For our GOD is a consuming fire.

Now I Lay Me Down to Sleep (1737)

Now I lay me down to take my sleep,

I pray the Lord my soul to keep.

If I should die before I wake

I pray the Lord my soul to take.

Reprinted in: Warfel, Harry H., and others, eds. The American Mind: Selections from the Literature of the United States, *Volume I. New York: American Book Co., 1963, pp. 65–66.*

Now the Child being entred in his Letters and Spelling, let him learn these and such like Sentences by Heart, whereby he will be both instructed in his Duty, and encouraged in his Learning.

The Dutiful Child's Promises,

I Will fear GOD, and honour the KING.
I will honour my Father & Mother.
I will Obey my Superiours.
I will Submit to my Elders.
I will Love my Friends.
I will hate no Man.
I will forgive my Enemies, and pray to God for them.
I will as much as in me lies keep all God's Holy Commandments.

A page from one of the earliest editions of *The New England Primer* giving children instructions of how they should behave.
Reproduced by permission of The Granger Collection.

ics, modern languages, and such practical courses as commerce (the buying and selling of goods), navigation, and surveying (measuring and describing an area of land). Located mainly in larger cities and towns, these schools reflected the trend away from classical and religious education to a more secular emphasis.

Petty schooling Most colonial parents who were literate themselves began teaching their children to read and write at home, usually as a way to provide religious instruction. Young apprentices sometimes received additional literacy training from their masters or went to evening school for two or three months in the winter. Poor children might attend a church school for free, whereas children of congregation members would pay a small fee. Wealthy parents hired tutors or Latin masters to teach their children English as preparation for studying the classical languages in Latin grammar school.

Elementary education was sometimes separated into reading and writing schools. Reading was the first to be taught, usually through recitation of the alphabet as the catechism was being learned. The child's first textbook, called a hornbook, usually contained the alphabet, simple syllables, the Lord's Prayer (the prayer that Jesus taught his disciples), and basic catechism. The hornbook was a piece of parchment paper attached to a thin piece of wood—measuring only four or five inches long and two inches wide—that had a small handle at the end. Covering the paper was a yellowish transparent sheet called a horn. The paper, wood, and horn were held together with a narrow strip of metal or brass tacked down with tiny nails. Students carried their parents' used hornbooks, as did female teachers who ran so-called dame schools. At dame schools girls were often given lessons in cooking and sewing as well as reading.

When students began learning how to write, the primer replaced the hornbook. The primer was about five inches long and three inches wide, consisting of eighty pages. A typical primer began with the alphabet followed by lists of syllables, such as "a-b" "ab" and "e-b" "eb" (sometimes called a syllabarium). Woodcut prints adorned *The New England Primer,* many of them illustrating the alphabet and accompanied by simple rhymed verse. For example, a woodcut of a figure picking an apple from a tree is followed by "In Adam's Fall, We sinned all." Next came moral lessons for children, the Lord's Prayer, the Apostles' creed, the Ten Commandments, the names of the books of the Bible, and finally the Westminster Catechism (the form approved by the church) and the famed catechism *Spiritual Milk for Babes,* written by Puritan minister John Cotton (1585–1652). Children were expected to read, reread, and recite from the primer. Much of the recitation was done in unison so that more advanced students could encourage the less skilled.

In nearly all petty schools, prayer and Bible readings marked both the beginning and end of the day. Both town schools and schools sponsored by religious groups required masters to bring their pupils to church on Sunday for catechizing (reciting the catechism) by the pastor. Few children attended petty school for more than three years, and seldom more than a couple of months each year after that. Poor parents had little money to spend on education and usually needed their children to help out on family farms.

 An Arithmetic Problem

Crocker's Arithmetick (1688), published in London, was a popular text in the American colonies. The following problem appeared under "The Backer Rule of Thumbs":

> *I did lend my friend 3/4 of a Porteguise [coin] 7 months upon promise that he should do as much for me again, and when I should borrow of him, he could lend me but 5/12 of a Portuguese [sic], now I demand how long time I must keep his money in just Recompence [repayment] of my loan, accounting 13 months in the year.*

Source: Earle, Alice Morse. Child Life in Colonial Days. New York: Macmillan, 1899; reprinted Stockbridge, Mass.: Berkshire House Publishers, 1993, p. 141.

Latin grammar schools As in England, boys destined for college or leadership in a profession had to study Latin and some Greek, the languages of scholarship and learning. The largest number of grammar schools were in New England, where Puritans required trained ministers and people were generally well educated. In the middle colonies and the South, knowing Latin and at least some Greek was a mark of upper-class status among gentleman (noblemen) planters and clergymen. The curriculum of the grammar school remained essentially the same throughout the colonial period, although individual masters and tutors may have varied their approaches somewhat. Reading, memorization, oral recitation, and writing were heavily relied upon, with an emphasis on rote memory (learning through repetition and memorization). Girls in the upper classes occasionally learned some Latin by studying along with their brothers under a tutor's guidance, but females were generally not taught the language.

Years of study Typically, young boys began grammar school at the age of seven or eight, and the course of study lasted seven years, usually six days a week. For the first three years boys memorized a Latin primer called an "accidence." In their fourth year they studied Latin grammar, often using the sixteenth-century text by William Lily. Ezekiel Cheever, the legendary master of the Boston Latin School, compiled a Latin text that was also used in the grammar schools. At this time students also began reading more advanced works by Erasmus, Aesop, and Ovid. The fifth year emphasized writing Latin prose and verse, continued reading of Erasmus and Ovid, and introduction to Cicero's letters. The sixth year was usually devoted to classics such as Cicero's *De Officiis,* Virgil's *Aeneid,* and Ovid's *Metamorphoses.* Students also began studying Greek and rhetoric.

In the seventh year other Roman authors such as Horace, Juvenal, and Homer were added to the reading list. A special challenge was reading the New Testament (the second part of the Christian Bible) in Greek and learning Hebrew. While studying Latin grammar, most students also continued learning English grammar. They might spend part of the early morning or late evening attending an English reading and writing school, or the Latin master might teach English grammar along with classical languages. At the end of seven years, at age fourteen, a young man was expected to be ready to pass the language requirement for college admission.

Private English school The Latin grammar school was the main form of secondary education throughout the colonial era. During the eighteenth century, however, merchants, tradesmen, and craftsmen created a demand for education in English that would prepare young people for commerce and trade. Various kinds of schools were started throughout the colonies, especially in seaport towns. In addition to teaching English grammar, schoolmasters offered instruction in surveying, accounting, navigation, and mathematics, which were necessary for road and bridge building. Instruction in the "practical arts and sciences" was always in English, so the schools became known as "English schools." Yet schoolmasters taught many different subjects, including college preparatory courses in Latin, Greek, Hebrew, and rhetoric. Although the schools were intended for young men, girls frequently took courses in sewing, reading, and writing.

Teachers Teachers usually came from the middle or lower classes and had acquired some formal education. In the

"The Flying Spider"

When Puritan minister Jonathan Edwards was twelve years old, he wrote "The Flying Spider," a composition for his schoolmaster, on the web-making genius of spiders. The excerpt below is the first part of his long essay.

May it please your Honour [Edwards's schoolmaster],

There are some things that I have happily seen of the wondrous way of the working of the spider. Although every thing belonging to this insect is admirable, there are some phenomena relating to them more particularly wonderful. Everybody that is used to the country, knows their marching in the air from one tree to another, sometimes at the distance of five or six rods [82 to 100 feet]. Nor can one go out in a dewy morning, at the latter end of August and the beginning of September, but he shall see multitudes of webs, made visible by the dew that hangs on them, reaching from one tree, branch and shrub, to another; which webs are commonly thought to be made in the night, because they appear only in the morning; whereas none of them are made in the night, for these spiders never come out in the night *when it is dark, as the dew is then falling. But these webs may be seen well enough in the day time by an observing eye, by their reflection in the sunbeams. Especially late in the afternoon, may these webs, that are between the eye and that part of the horizon that is under the sun, be seen very plainly, being advantageously posited to reflect the rays. And the spiders themselves may very often be seen travelling in the air, from one stage to another amongst the trees, in a very unaccountable manner. But I have often seen that, which is much more astonishing. In very calm and serene days in the fore-mentioned time of year, standing at some distance behind the end of an house or some other opake [opaque] body, so as just to hide the disk of the sun and keep off his dazzling rays, and looking along close by the side of it, I have seen a vast multitude of little shining webs, and glistening strings, brightly reflecting the sunbeams, and some of them of great length, and of such height, that one would think they were tacked to the vault of the heavens. . . .*

Reprinted in: Warfel, Harry H., and others, eds. The American Mind: Selections from the Literature of the United States, *Volume I.* New York: American Book Co., 1963, p. 82.

seventeenth century provincial governments tried to license teachers, mainly to make sure students were receiving proper religious instruction, but the laws were not enforced after 1700. Although women taught in petty schools, most teachers were men. They were rarely paid enough to support a family, so they were often town clerks, farmers, or shopkeepers as well as teachers. In New England, grammar schoolmasters were either young college graduates looking for a job as a minister or older preachers supplementing their pastor's salary. Schoolmasters earned about forty pounds (English currency) a year in addition to their board, while petty-school teachers made about

"inconvenient exchanges"

Historian Alice Morse Earle noted that colonists who could not afford the school fees paid teachers "in any of the inconvenient exchanges which had to pass as money at that time,—in wampum, beaver skins, Indian corn, wheat, peas, beans, or any country product known as 'truck.' It is told of a Salem [Massachusetts] school, that one scholar was always seated at the window to study also to hail passers-by, and endeavor to sell to them the accumulation of corn, vegetables, etc., which had been given in payment to the teacher."

Source: Earle, Alice Morse. Child Life in Colonial Days. *New York: Macmillan, 1899; reprinted Stockbridge, Mass.: Berkshire House Publishers, 1993, p. 69.*

twenty pounds a year. Most tutors on southern plantations were paid around thirty pounds annually.

New England requires schooling In 1642 the General Court (the Massachusetts government) passed a law requiring parents and masters to teach their children, apprentices, and servants to read and understand the Bible and the laws of the colony. This was followed by the famous "Old Deluder Satan" law of 1647, which called upon towns of fifty or more families to establish a petty school to teach reading and writing. (The idea was that education would eliminate ignorance, which was the work of the devil, and lead to understanding of the Bible, or the word of God.) Towns of one hundred or more families were also required to provide a Latin grammar school. Over the next decade all eight of the large Massachusetts towns complied with the grammar-school requirement, but perhaps fewer than one-third of towns with at least fifty families set up petty schools.

As the colony expanded, magistrates required teachers to hold classes in different sections of the towns over the period of a year. This "moving school" method made the teacher less accountable to the people of any given district and limited students' access to schooling. The next stage was development of the district system, which took authority away from towns. Connecticut, Plymouth, and New Hampshire followed the lead of Massachusetts in establishing schools. However in Rhode Island, where religious freedom was protected, the government did not require schooling for fear that one religious sect might be favored above another.

Schools are limited by diversity Religious and ethnic diversity limited government's involvement in education in the middle colonies. In New York, schools were affiliated with various religious groups. Towns and counties exercised authority over orphans, poor children, and apprentices, but there

An illustration of a class in session in an one-room colonial schoolhouse.
Reproduced by permission of Corbis-Bettmann.

were no public schools because people did not want public funds to help one religious sect over another. A Latin school was legislated for New York City in 1702 and again in 1732, but neither lasted because of religious conflicts. In both New York and Pennsylvania, non-English settlers wanted to preserve their own religions, languages, and educational traditions. The Quakers in Pennsylvania did not approve of extended education at all. They thought that reading, writing, and arithmetic were sufficient and any learning beyond these basic skills would encourage idleness. Similarly,

Germans thought education would make farm boys lazy. For this reason there were no strict requirements for teachers in the middle colonies. In fact, former indentured servants (laborers contracted to work for a specific length of time) or even exported convicts frequently worked as teachers. Drunkenness was a continuing problem among male teachers.

Schoolhouses in New York and Pennsylvania were made of logs. Some had rough wood flooring, while others had dirt floors that turned to dust, which rowdy students would then kick up to disrupt classes. Desks were made by hammering wood pegs into the log walls about 4 feet from the floor and then laying boards atop the pegs. Older pupils sat at these desks with their backs to the room, and younger students sat on log benches. The teacher sat at a desk in the middle of the room. A fireplace was usually at one end of the room or in the middle. Firewood was provided by parents as part of their school fees. (If a child's parents forgot to send wood, the schoolmaster would make the child stand in the coldest corner of the schoolroom.) There was no glass in the windows and no blackboards. During the eighteenth century students in most colonies used slates, hung by strings around their necks, on which they wrote with slate pens. Paper was in short supply, so birch bark was used for making textbooks and writing tablets.

In the Chesapeake region where the Anglican Church was established, the government was involved only in the education of poor children and orphans. As early as 1642 Virginia passed laws on the apprenticeship of poor children, requiring masters to teach apprentices to read and write. Few church parishes built schools or paid a teacher to instruct the poor. Some preachers taught reading and writing as part of religious instruction, but they were the exceptions rather than the rule. During the colonial era nine schools were established specifically to educate poor children with funds left in the wills of generous Virginians. The other southern colonies followed Virginia's apprenticeship legislation for poor and orphaned youth. In 1696 Maryland set up a government-sponsored corporation to raise funds for establishing a Latin school in every county. But only one school, King William's School (later called St. John's), in Annapolis, was started in Maryland. Another Maryland law in 1723 was designed to start schools in several counties, but religious disputes among settlers prevented the law from taking effect. Similarly, South Carolina made several unsuccessful efforts to establish free Latin schools.

Colleges in English colonies

Higher education was also emphasized during the colonial period. Five colleges built in this era were established in order to train ministers. They were: Harvard, William and Mary, Yale, Princeton, and King' College. A sixth college, The Academy of Pennsylvania, which was founded in 1751, became the first institution of higher education to offer colonial students a chance to study areas other than religion.

Harvard College In 1636 Harvard College opened its doors in Cambridge, Massachusetts, as the first institution of higher learning in the colonies. Harvard was named for John Harvard, a Puritan minister who donated a large sum of money and his private library toward starting a college for training ministers. Courses in the classics and philosophy were offered in addition to religion, but men who wished to study law or medicine had to go to Europe.

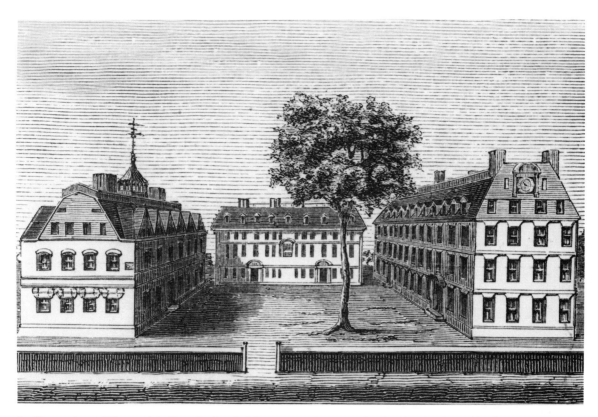

An illustration of Harvard College in Cambridge, Massachusetts, the first institution of higher learning established in the colonies. *Reproduced by permission of Corbis-Bettmann.*

For half a century Harvard was the only college in America, and it served mainly to educate the sons of Puritans.

For several decades Harvard struggled to survive because there were often no more than ten or twenty students at a time, only one or two teachers, and hardly any discipline. The situation had changed by the 1750s, however, and life at the college was quite strict. At least ninety students were enrolled and they were required to follow a rigid routine. They got up each morning at five o'clock, attended chapel at six, and had breakfast at seven. Classes started at eight, and then the afternoon was set aside for study until supper at six. Students had some free time until curfew, when they snuffed their candles, put out fires in fireplaces, and went to bed. In addition to following this rigid schedule, they were forbidden to tell a lie, drink alcohol, or play cards. They could not go skating without permission, and they were required to observe the Sabbath (Sunday), a day set aside for church services and religious contemplation. All violators were fined ten shillings (a sum of British money equal to about $1.20) for each offense. No one was

" . . . I said, this is certainly a tavern."

In 1680 New York colonists Jasper Danckaerts and Peter Sluyter paid a visit to Harvard, where Puritans studied for the ministry. The New Yorkers expected to see an impressive institution, but instead they found that only ten students were enrolled and the college barely had enough funds to stay open. Danckaerts and Sluyter were also surprised that the students were heavy smokers and could not even speak Latin (which was one of the basic requirements for admission to Harvard).

We started out to go to Cambridge, lying to the northeast of Boston, in order to see their college, and printing office. We reached Cambridge, about eight o'clock. It is not a large village, and the houses stand very much apart. The college building is the most conspicuous [noticeable] among them. We went to it, expecting to see something curious, as it is the only college, or would-be academy of the Protestants in all America, but we found ourselves mistaken. In approaching the house, we neither heard nor saw anything mentionable; but, going to the other side of the building, we heard noise enough in an upper room, to lead my comrade to suppose they were engaged in disputation [argument].

We entered, and went up stairs, when a person met us, and requested us to walk in, which we did. We found there, eight or ten young fellows, sitting around, smoking tobacco, with the smoke of which the rooms was so full, that you could hardly see; and the whole house smelled so strong of it, that when I was going up stairs, I said, this is certainly a tavern. We excused ourselves, that we could speak English only a little, but understood Dutch or French, which they did not. However, we spoke as well as we could. We inquired how many professors there were, and they replied not one, that there was no money to support one. We asked how many students there were. They said at first, thirty, and then came down to twenty; I afterwards understood there are probably not ten. They could hardly speak a word of Latin, so that my comrade could not converse with them. They took us to the library where there was nothing particular. We looked over it a little. They presented us with a glass of wine. This is all we ascertained [found out] there. The minister of the place goes there morning and evening to make prayer, and has charge over them. The students have tutors or masters.

Source: Colbert, David, ed. Eyewitness to America. New York: Pantheon Books, 1997, pp. 37–38.

allowed to leave the college grounds without a good reason and permission from his tutor (teacher).

College of William and Mary In 1693 the College of William and Mary (named for English monarchs William III and Mary II) was established in Williamsburg, Virginia, to train Anglican ministers and to provide a college for the sons of Virginia plantation owners. Within fifteen years William and Mary had added courses in law and medicine. In the meantime Harvard had been influenced by educational trends in Europe. The college expanded its curriculum (program of study) to include the liberal arts (grammar, rhetoric, logic, arithmetic, geometry, astronomy, and music) as well as science, philosophy, politics, and other subjects being studied in Europe. Harvard also added another year of study at the freshman level, dropping the average age at entry to between fifteen and sixteen. The basic requirement for admission was a solid background in the Latin language.

Yale College   Harvard alumni (graduates) eventually became concerned that the college had strayed from Puritan teachings because fewer graduates were going into the ministry. In 1701 they started a college to educate ministers in a traditional Puritan curriculum. For several years the school was moved among various locations in Connecticut. Finally in 1720 a permanent building was constructed in New Haven, Connecticut, and the college was named Yale College for Elihu Yale, who had contributed a large sum of money to the enterprise. Yet by 1760 Yale had also adopted European trends and become essentially the same as Harvard.

Princeton College and King's College
Colleges were established much later in the middle colonies. Unlike New England and the southern colonies, New York was populated by numerous religious groups, so no church had enough dominance to open an institution of higher learning. The Quakers

still controlled Pennsylvania, but they had no interest in starting a school because they did not have ordained ministers. Yet Presbyterians (a branch of Puritanism) were arriving in Pennsylvania in increasing numbers. At first their ministers attended Harvard, but they soon saw a need for their own college. In 1746 the Presbyterians founded the interdenominational (open to all religious groups) College of New Jersey at Elizabethtown. The school moved to Princeton, New Jersey, in 1754 and was officially named Princeton College in the 1760s. In 1754 King's College (now Columbia University) opened in New York City as a nondenominational institution.

Academy of Philadelphia   The first institution to abandon religious requirements was the Academy of Philadelphia, founded in 1751 with the support of statesman Benjamin Franklin (1706–1790). His goal was to provide a "useful" education, with courses in astronomy, arithmetic, accounting, and geometry, as well as English, history, botany, agriculture, mechanics, Greek, and Latin. In 1755 the academy was renamed the Academy and College of Philadelphia (now the University of Pennsylvania), and is now regarded as the basis for the public education system that was later adopted in the United States.

By the end of the colonial period six colleges had been established in America, all of them admitting only male students. With fewer men entering the ministry, the colleges were increasingly fulfilling nonreligious educational goals. Yet there were still no professional schools, and young men who wanted to become doctors or lawyers continued to earn their degrees in Europe. Those who could not afford a European education attended colonial colleges and then practiced for two or three years with a qualified professional. Women were not permitted to attend any of these schools, a situation that remained long after the colonies had become the United States.

Education of Africans in Spanish and French colonies

The Catholic Church influenced the nature of slavery and slave education in both the Spanish and French colonies. In the Spanish borderlands, the church gave religious instruction to both African and Native American slaves. In addition to religious training slaves were generally educated in a particular skill, such as household servant, cook, carpenter, or other type of artisan (craftsman). Training began in early childhood. It is assumed that few slaves learned to read and write. A similar situation existed in New France. In 1685 Jean-Baptiste Colbert (1619–1683), chief minister under King Louis XIV, issued a Code Noir (Black Code) for the French West Indies (islands in the Caribbean Sea), which also applied to New France and the Louisiana territory (the Mississippi River valley and the Gulf of Mexico region). All slaves were to receive religious instruction and be converted to Catholicism. Yet frontier conditions, especially in Louisiana, kept the Code Noir from being enforced. If African women had children by white men, the women and children could win their freedom. Interracial children were therefore eligible to be educated, but freed slaves seldom got any schooling. They were more likely to learn their life's work through formal or informal apprenticeship.

Education of Africans in New Netherland

The status of a slave was more flexible in New Netherland than in most other colonies. The Dutch West India Company, which founded New Netherland, made huge profits from importing slaves into Brazil and Spanish America. There were both slaves and free blacks in New Netherland, but a slave code was never passed. The Dutch West India Company regularly granted freedom to slaves, allowing them to own property and live with their families. Whether slave or free, most African parents taught their children the trades they knew, including housekeeping, farming, and crafts. Many blacks joined the Dutch Reformed Church, where they received religious instruction. New Netherland director general Peter Stuyvesant hired a schoolmaster for the slave children on his farm, and local free blacks' children may also have been taught to read and write.

Education of Africans in English colonies

In Virginia and Maryland, slaves were taught at a very early age the tasks involved in the tobacco trade—stripping tobacco leaves from the stalk, curing the tobacco, and preparing it for shipment to England. Young slaves were also introduced by their elders to household work as well as the crafts necessary to maintain the plantation. Teaching slaves to read and write was considered inappropriate because of their low status. Even the question of religious instruction was controversial because Christians could not own fellow Christians. If a slave became a member of the church, he or she would therefore become a free Christian man or woman. To bypass this touchy problem, between 1664 and 1706 all the southern colonies and New York passed laws declaring that Christian baptism did not determine whether a person was slave or free. Nevertheless, in 1740 South Carolina prohibited teaching slaves to read and write, and most slaves in that colony did not receive religious instruction. Despite this law, Africans were taught to read and write at schools in Charleston. One of the schools was founded by the Anglican Society for the Propagation of the Gospel in Foreign Parts (S.P.G.) in 1743 and operated for the next twenty years. As many as sixty students were enrolled at a time. Other S.P.G. missionaries spread out through the Carolinas and Georgia, teaching slaves and giving religious instruction. Quakers also went into the Carolinas and Virginia, preaching the Christian message and often teaching literacy skills. Historians conclude, however, that relatively few slaves were affected by these efforts.

The S.P.G. and the Quakers were also active in the middle colonies. In New York City, several S.P.G. clergymen maintained an evening school for adult slaves, which opened in 1704, for many years. In Pennsylvania prominent Quakers opened a school for black children in 1700. Growing Quaker opposition to slavery produced more opportunities for slaves to obtain schooling in Pennsylvania by the 1740s. A school for black children opened at the Anglican Christ Church in Philadelphia in 1758. Education of slaves was minimal in New England, however, because the African population was relatively low (only 3 percent prior to the American Revolution in 1774). Puritan leaders such as John Eliot and Cotton Mather advocated teaching slaves to read and write, and there is evidence that some children of freed slaves attended schools with white children. Yet literacy training for blacks was limited and took place mainly in households rather than classrooms.

Arts and Culture

13

The earliest known European artists in North America were Dutch portrait painters in New Netherland (which became New York in 1664, when the English took over the colony). The Dutch brought a rich artistic tradition with them from the Netherlands. They decorated their homes with oil paintings and prints, including landscapes, still lifes, and religious subjects. Although historical records show that Dutch painters in New Netherland were quite productive during the seventeenth century, only three works survived: portraits of New Netherland governor Peter Stuyvesant, Nicholas William Stuyvesant, and Jacobus Strycker, which were probably painted sometime between 1661 and 1666 by Huguenot (French Protestant) artist Henri Couturier.

Most Dutch painters were "limners" (that is, delineators, or artists who depicted their subjects by drawing). They usually earned their living at other trades such as house-painters or glaziers (people who place glass in windows), and they were sometimes self-taught. Many traveled from place to place in search of commissions (contracts). One of the earliest limners was Evert Duyckinck (1621–c. 1703), who headed a family of artists. None of his paintings has survived, but coats of arms (family emblems or crests) enameled on the windows of the Dutch Reformed Church (a Protestant religious group based in Holland) at Albany, New York, in 1656 are known to be his work. At least ten portraits are attributed to his youngest son, Gerrit Duyckinck. Gerrit's son, Gerardus Duyckinck, painted *The Birth of the Virgin* (1713), the earliest dated and signed New York painting. He also specialized in portraits and biblical works. Evert Duyckinck III painted portraits in a style similar to that of his cousin Gerardus.

Dutch painters continued to arrive in New York and the neighboring New Jersey colony during the early 1700s. Among them was Pieter Vanderlyn, who painted portraits of leading New York families. Another artist was John Heaten, who married a Dutch woman and was active as a portraitist in the upper Hudson Valley during that period. He is also known for landscapes and genre paintings (those depicting scenes from everyday life). After the English took control of New Netherland, however, wealthy Dutch colonists began to favor English styles of painting.

Painting in New England

New England Puritans rejected religious paintings and other forms of decoration as being too closely associated with Roman Catholicism. (Puritans were a Protestant Christian group that observed strict moral and religious codes. Protestantism was formed partly in opposition to the elaborate decorations and rituals used in the Catholic Church.) Yet they approved of portrait painting, not as an art form but as a practical way for people to have a picture of an important leader or a beloved family member. As in New Netherland, the first New England portrait painters often made a living as housepainters or glaziers, while others were sign painters. Like limners, they traveled from town to town looking for work. One of the most talented was Augustine Clement, a glassmaker from Reading, England, who arrived in Boston, Massachusetts, in 1635. Unsigned portraits of Puritan leaders Richard Mather, John Clark, and John Endecott were probably painted by Clement. The portrait of Clark and an unsigned portrait of Elizabeth Eggington were both inscribed (dated) in 1664, making them the earliest New England portraits that can be dated with certainty.

Portrait style

Seven unsigned paintings of parents and their children, dated between 1670 and 1674, are examples of early New England portrait style. Scholars believe they were done by Boston artist Samuel Clement. All of the portraits—*Mr. John Freake, Mrs. Elizabeth Freake and Baby Mary, The Mason Children, Alice Mason,* and three individual pictures of children in the Gibbs family—feature rich colors and close attention to facial details. The portraits were painted in a style that had gone out of fashion in London but was still practiced in rural England. For example, the trend in London at the time was to create the illusion of three dimensions with perspective and shading. This artist, however, used bright colors, flattened patterns, and symbolism such as a bird to represent the soul.

Colonies attract portrait painters

In the early eighteenth century, rising prosperity in the colonies began to draw trained artists to growing port cities. Henrietta Johnston, a painter of miniatures (tiny pictures), arrived in Charleston, South Carolina, in 1705 and remained active there until her death in about 1728 or 1729. She was followed by Swiss artist Jeremiah Theüs, who operated a studio that lasted until 1774. German painter Justus Engelhardt Kühn was active in Annapolis, Maryland, from 1708 until his death in 1717. Scots painter John Watson settled in Perth Amboy, New Jersey, in 1714. English painter Charles Bridges arrived in Virginia in 1735 and spent the next few years traveling from plantation to plantation, painting portraits of the Virginia aristocracy (nobility class). He did not stay in the colonies long enough, however, to have much of an influence on other artists.

Hesselius and Smibert have great influence

Two artists who were largely responsible for the development of American painting for the rest of the eighteenth century were Gustavus Hesselius (1682–1755) and John Smibert (1688–1751). Hesselius was born in Sweden and received part of his artistic training in England. In the early 1700s he moved to Philadelphia, Pennsylvania. Except for spending a few years in Annapolis in the 1720s, he lived and worked in Philadelphia until his death. In 1735 Hesselius painted portraits of Delaware chiefs Tishcohan and Lopowinsa, thus becoming the first European artist to depict Native Americans in a sensitive manner. The *Last Supper,* which he did for Saint Barnabas's Church in Queen Anne's Parish, Maryland, was the first painting commissioned for a public building in America. The work has since been lost.

When Smibert arrived in Boston from England in 1729, he was already an established portrait painter. Two years later he completed his best-known work, *The Bermuda Group.* The large portrait features Anglican (Church of England) bishop George Berkeley, members of Berkeley's family, and others—including Smibert—who participated in Berkeley's failed plan to start a college in Bermuda (an island in the Caribbean Sea). The painting became a model for later American group portraits. Although Smibert had done his best work by 1730, he brought a new sophistication to painting in New England. He did portraits of the leading Boston citizens, and he is credited with organizing the first art show in the colonies.

Smibert also influenced a number of younger American artists.

John Smibert's painting of Benjamin Coleman. *Reproduced by permission of The New Britain Museum of American Art.*

Among them was Robert Feke (c. 1705–c. 1750), who was born in Oyster Bay, Long Island. *Family of Isaac Royall,* which Feke painted in Boston in 1741, has been compared to Smibert's *The Bermuda Group.* Considered by some art historians to be a more imaginative painter than Smibert, Feke influenced other young painters in the 1740s and 1750s. Though the two men may never have met, Feke also influenced John Singleton Copley, whose earliest works were modeled on portraits by Feke and Smibert. By 1754 American portrait painting was on the verge of a great leap forward with the emergence of Benjamin West, as well as Copley and Charles Willson Peale.

Printmaking

The most popular art form in the British colonies was the print. A print is made by carving or etching an image into wood, stone, or metal. The printmaker then applies ink to the surface of the image and presses it onto paper to produce a picture. The prints that colonists used to decorate their homes were usually small engravings, most often portraits of prominent people. The first known portrait print made in the colonies was a woodcut portrait of Puritan minister Richard Mather made by Boston printer-engraver John Foster in 1670. By 1710 colonial artists were making mezzotints, which are engraved images on copper or steel that appear to be more three-dimensional than simpler engravings. The earliest mezzotint may

 Influential Mezzotint Artist

The best-known colonial mezzotint artist was Peter Pelham, who had been a printmaker in London before he set up shop in Boston in 1727. His most famous mezzotint is a portrait of Puritan minister Cotton Mather, from which he also made an oil painting. After portrait painter John Smibert arrived in Boston in 1729, Pelham based many of his mezzotints on Smibert's portraits of notable New Englanders. Pelham passed on his knowledge of printmaking to his stepson John Singleton Copley, one of the best artists of the Revolutionary period.

have been a portrait of four Iroquois chieftains, made by engraver John Simon in 1710. Another prominent engraver was William Burgess, who worked in Boston from 1716 to 1731 and made mezzotints of scenes and landmarks around the city.

The first historical print published in the colonies was a line engraving of a battle plan by Thomas Johnson. Colonists also began producing portrait prints for use in books and almanacs. A copperplate engraving of Puritan minister Increase Mather, made by Thomas Emmes in 1728, became a model for prints in books published by clergymen. Boston printer James Franklin studied print-

A colonial tombstone with elaborate carving found in a New England cemetery.
Reproduced by permission of Corbis-Bettmann.

making in London, England, and is believed to have made most or all of the illustrations for the books and almanacs he published.

Early sculpture

The majority of seventeenth-century colonists were struggling to survive in North America, so they paid little attention to artistic trends in England or elsewhere in Europe. They did not have their portraits painted or decorate their homes with landscape paintings and prints by well-known artists. When most colonists created designs, they decorated objects that served a practical purpose. They were producing the earliest form of American sculpture, and they based their work on the traditions of their native countries. The first American sculptors were stonecutters and carpenters who carved designs onto gravestones and wooden objects such as trunks and Bible boxes.

Grave markers

Grave markers are some of the best examples of colonial stone carving, although only a few markers made before 1660 still exist. The first decorations on gravestones were simple geometric designs such as rosettes, pinwheels, and radiating suns. Such ornaments could be carved with simple tools by craftsmen with no artistic training. By the end of the 1600s, the winged skull—a depiction of a human skull with wings on the sides—had become the most widely used design on gravestones. It continued to dominate graveyard art throughout the eighteenth century.

Portrait sculptures By the early eighteenth century the first American portrait sculptures began to appear on gravestones. (A portrait sculpture is a picture of the deceased that has been carved into the stone.) The earliest of these works may be the portrait signed "N.L." on the stone of the Reverend Jonathan Pierpont in Wakefield, Massachusetts. By the 1740s such carvings could be found in graveyards throughout the colonies. There are two types of stones: two-dimensional and three-dimensional. Examples of both types can be found in the Congregational churchyard in Charleston. The stone of Mrs. Richard Owen, like many of the early colonial portrait paintings, is simple and two-dimensional. It depicts a smiling Mrs. Owen, but the image is flat, with no sense of depth. The Congregational burial ground contains two of the more realistic three-dimensional gravestones—for Elizabeth Simmons and Solomon Milner—which were carved by Henry Eames of Boston.

Other popular eighteenth-century gravestone designs show the increased skills of colonial stone carvers. They include coats of arms, ships, and cherubs' (angel's) heads.

Wood carvings

Early seventeenth-century colonial wood-carvers were also untrained craftsmen. Their carvings were usually geometrical designs (basic shapes such as circles, squares, and rectangles) that could be made with simple carpenters' tools such as the chisel, gouge, and mallet. In the 1650s, however, American carvers were influenced by more intricate European styles. Wood-carvers were frequently called on to produce figureheads for the bows (front end) of ships, so they set up shop in the wharf (ship docks) sections of port cities. They also made shop signs and ornaments for furniture. As early as 1717 professional wood-carvers were working throughout the colonies, from New England to the Carolinas. For instance, Henry Burnett was a noted craftsman in Charleston in the 1750s. Yet Boston was the center of activity for talented carvers during most of the eighteenth century. Among them was Samuel More, who began making figureheads as early as 1736. Another prominent carver was John Welch, who made a decorative figure called the "Sacred Cod" that now hangs in the Old State House in Boston. Moses Deshon carved the coat of arms (official emblem or crest) for Faneuil Hall (a public meetinghouse and marketplace) in 1742.

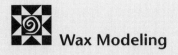

Wax Modeling

Wax modeling was another popular form of sculpture in the colonies during the eighteenth century. Since wax melts easily, few examples of wax sculpture have survived. Working with wax was also a hobby because wax was plentiful and easy to mold. As early as 1731 upper-class women in New York City were offered classes in sculpting fruit and flowers. The August 28, 1749, issue of the *New York Gazette* newspaper advertised an exhibit of wax figures of members of European royalty. Around that time artists were making small portraits in wax, an art that became more widespread and further refined during the second half of the century.

First American statue A well-known carved figure from the colonial period is *The Little Admiral,* which can be seen today in the Old State House in Boston. It is widely considered the earliest free-standing statue created in the American colonies. Some twentieth-century art historians believe *The Little Admiral* was made by Samuel Skillin, who was a notable craftsman in his day. In a short story titled "Drowne's Wooden Image," however, New England author Nathaniel Hawthorne suggested that the figure was made by Shem Drowne, a Boston tinsmith (one who makes objects from tin). Although someone later painted the date "1770" on the base of this wooden figure, art historians believe it was actually carved in the 1740s or 1750s. Because *The Little Admiral* once held an object such as a beer stein (a large mug) or nautical instrument (a device used to chart sea routes), it is thought to have been made as a trade sign. In fact, some scholars believe the figure was the image of British admiral Edward Vernon and stood outside the Admiral Vernon Tavern in Boston in 1750. Another expert, however, says *The Little Admiral* is the portrait of a Captain Hunnewell that stood outside a nautical-instruments shop in the city.

Music

Music was one of the first forms of culture in North America. When European settlers arrived in the Southwest and along the Atlantic coast, they encountered Native American musical traditions that had existed for thousands of years. Native American music was primarily vocal (made with the voice) and sung mostly in groups as a way to communicate with supernatural powers (holy spirits). Chants and songs were accompanied by drums, rattles, flutes, and whistles. Native Americans performed music to ensure success in battle, appeal to the gods for rain, or cure the sick. There were various kinds of songs. Traditional songs were passed down from generation to generation, while ceremonial and medicine songs appeared to individual tribal members in their dreams. Native Americans also performed songs that celebrated tribal heroes, inserting a hero's name to fit the particular occasion.

Native American music had little influence on Europeans, except in the Southwest, where the Franciscans (members of a Catholic religious order) used Native American music for religious education. They adapted Christian music and drama to the traditional feasts and ceremonies of Native Americans. They also encouraged Native Americans to compose music in the European tradition. For instance, Native American choirs learned chants for Catholic masses (church services) as well as carols (popular songs expressing religious joy) and other traditional religious songs of the Spanish settlers. Though much of this early music has since been lost, some evolved to become part of the folk tradition of the Southwest.

Colonial religious music

Colonial churches used different hymnbooks, but most followed the directive of the Puritan leader John Calvin (1509–1564) that worship services include the singing of verses from the book of Psalms in the Old Testament (a part of the Christian Bible that contains song poems). The Puritans of seventeenth-century New England did not approve of professional singers, singing in harmony, or any sort of accompaniment such as organ music. These were features of the Roman Catholic service, which Puritans rejected as unnecessarily elaborate.

(The Roman Catholic Church is a Christian faith based in Rome, Italy, and headed by a pope who has supreme authority in all religious affairs.) Yet even Anglican (Church of England) churches, which did not oppose these practices, did not have organs or use music other than simple hymns in their services. Musical instruments were too expensive for early colonial churches, and few parishioners were trained singers.

When the typical congregation (a separate group of church members) sang a hymn, a deacon (church official), called a "liner," announced which tune would be sung, usually from a choice of only four or five melodies. The liner then read out each line before it was sung. As memories of church music in England grew dimmer and fewer churchgoers could read the music printed in increasingly scarce music books, American music became dramatically different from—and worse than—English music. Especially among the rugged individualists of New England, everyone seemed to sing a different tune and sometimes slipped from one melody to another while paying no attention to tempo (the beat of a piece of music).

Singing schools By the turn of the eighteenth century ministers throughout the colonies were calling for singing schools to instruct people in reading music and singing psalms. Anglican singing instruction began in Maryland as early as 1699, and there were singing classes in Virginia in

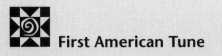

First American Tune

Until the second half of the eighteenth century little original music was composed in the colonies. The first piece of new music written in America may have been "Southwell New Tune," a brief hymn published in the Reverend Thomas Walter's *The Grounds and Rules of Musick Explained,* a popular songbook. The 1723 edition of John Tufts's *A Very Plain and Easy Introduction to the Art of Singing Psalm Tunes* (first published in 1721) includes another song, "100 Psalm Tune New," that was probably written in America.

1710. Four years later the first school for psalmody (hymn singing) was advertised in Boston. Such schools were most popular in New England from 1720 to about 1750, after prominent clergymen such as Benjamin Colman, Thomas Symmes, Cotton Mather, and Thomas Walter spoke out in favor of singing reform. Once Congregationalists (Puritans) accepted singing reform, they began appointing "choristers" (singing leaders) to sound the first note by voice or pitch pipe (a device for giving the first note of a tune) and then lead the singing. The use of the pitch pipe aroused controversy because some traditionalists considered it a violation of the ban on musical instruments. Many of the same people were also alarmed when young singing-school graduates asked permission to sit together and perform some of the religious songs they had learned. The first New England congregation to agree to such a request was the West Church in Boston, which designated "singers' seats" in 1754. By the end of the 1760s twenty-three churches in New England had made similar arrangements.

Organ music Elsewhere in the colonies, churches were increasingly incorporating organ music into their services. The Anglican King's Chapel in Boston installed an organ in 1714, and the other two Anglican churches in the city had them by 1744. The first known organ in New York City was installed at the Dutch Reformed Church in 1724. During the first half of the eighteenth century Anglican churches in South Carolina, Pennsylvania, Rhode Island, and New York City installed organs. Between 1737 and 1767 five Virginia churches obtained organs.

Secular music emerges

As new settlers continued to bring their own musical traditions to North America, a distinctly American form of secular (nonreligious) music began to take shape. In the Spanish Southwest ancient songs about European wars were turned into ballads (narrative songs) that reflected the everyday experiences of the settlers. British colonists fitted new lyrics on contemporary topics to old ballad or hymn tunes. In the eighteenth century English colonists adapted new music from England, such as marches or stage and opera music. While poorer people continued to enjoy folk music and dancing, prosperous colonists wanted to copy the latest trends in music and dancing among aristocratic circles in England. They bought instruments and music books and hired professional music tutors and dancing masters. They also enjoyed listening to performances by British and European musicians.

Music flourishes in cities Boston led the way in supporting musical culture in the colonies. Thomas Brattle, a wealthy merchant, installed an organ in his home in 1711 and four years later donated another to the Anglican King's Chapel. Edward Enstone, who arrived from England in 1715 to work as an organist, started a music and dancing school and began holding public balls. By 1717 he had also opened a store where he sold and repaired musical instruments, as well as offering sheet music and instruction books. In 1729 he sponsored the first documented public concert in the colonies. The following year the Men's Musical Society of Boston sponsored a concert in honor of Saint Cecilia, patron saint of music. An early documented private concert was held in 1710 in New York City, where in 1714 musicians were hired for a parade and ball celebrating the coronation (the celebration of the crowning) of King

 African American Music

During the colonial period African Americans preserved their musical traditions in the slave quarters of the great southern plantations. They sang songs and played homemade African-style drums and reed instruments. They also introduced a string instrument called the *banjer* or *banjar*, which they brought from West Africa in the seventeenth century. A gourd with an attached handle and four catgut strings, it was the basis for the banjo, which American instrument manufacturers began making in the nineteenth century. The first European instruments played by African Americans were violins, or fiddles, which were often homemade but other times were given to them by white masters. Some slave owners also taught their slaves to play European-style music for white audiences. Over time black musicians began incorporating their own musical ideas into European music.

George I. The Philadelphia Assembly, a dancing club founded in 1748, also encouraged musical performances.

Musical diversity in rural areas Diverse ethnic groups introduced their own musical traditions throughout the colonies. English and Scots-Irish settlers in remote regions of the Appalachian Mountains brought ballads and tunes, many of which are still being played and sung today. Isolated French settlers in northern New England also maintained their musical traditions, as did German musicians in Pennsylvania. Eighteenth-century Moravian communities in Pennsylvania and North Carolina were well-known for their ability to perform a wide range of European sacred and secular music. By the eighteenth century secular music was exceptionally popular in the South, where people from outlying plantations often came together during sessions of the courts or legislatures. During that time they attended concerts, plays, and balls and took home the music they heard at those events. By 1735 musicians in Charleston were giving public concerts honoring Saint Cecilia. The Tuesday Club of Annapolis met from May 1745 until February 1756 and fostered its members' musical interests. By 1752 the club included five string players, two flute players, a keyboardist, and perhaps a bassoonist. Songs written by several members for performance at club meetings may be the earliest secular music written in America.

Literature

When Europeans arrived in North America, they discovered that Native Americans had created rich oral traditions over thousands of years. Stories, poems, and myths were passed on by storytellers from generation to generation. The language of Native American oral performances, which some-

what resembled European poetry, was highly musical. The narrator conveyed meaning through the way he delivered the words. Jesuit missionaries (Catholic priests who belonged to the Society of Jesus and traveled to foreign lands to do religious work) in New France (present-day Canada) were among the first to make written records of Native American oral presentations. In yearly reports to their superiors in France, they described how the Hurons, Iroquois, and other tribes gave speeches and told stories. The Jesuits also attempted to translate some of the speeches and stories, but they could not fully convey the meaning, which depended on the performance of the Native American speakers.

Among the Jesuits who wrote these accounts were Paul Le Jeune, Paul Rageneau, Jacques Marquette, and Louis Hennepin. In his report for 1645 and 1646, Rageneau described a story-telling session at a meeting of elders who had gathered to elect a "very celebrated Captain." They used the occasion to pass on tribal history by telling stories about their ancestors. Hennepin mentioned Native American creation mythology (stories about how the world was made) in a report on his explorations of North America in 1697. He was one of many Europeans who attempted to prove that the lost tribes of Israel were the ancestors of Native Americans. (According to the Bible, the Christian holy book, ten Israelite tribes were taken to Assyria after the Assyrians conquered Israel in 722 B.C. No one knows what happened to the tribes. Early Christian leaders claimed Native

North Americans were the descendants of these lost tribes.)

Literature written by Europeans during the colonial period consisted mainly of histories based on their experiences in North America. Many colonists also wrote poetry, which was the primary literary form in Europe at the time.

Spanish

The earliest literature written by Europeans in North America came from sixteenth-century Spanish explorers who published reports on their journeys after they returned to Spain. The first was Alvar Nuñez Cabeza de Vaca, whose account of an eight-year overland journey from Florida to the west coast of Mexico in the 1520s and 1530s was published in 1542 (see Chapter 2). In 1605 Spanish military leader Garcilaso de la Vega published *La Florida del Ynca* (Florida of the Inca), a colorful description of the expedition led by Spanish explorer Hernando de Soto in the Spanish territory of La Florida, which is now the southeastern United States (see Chapter 2). It was based on firsthand accounts from expedition members. In the 1560s Pedro de Casteñeda wrote about his experiences as a member of Francisco Vásquez de Coronado's expedition in the American West (see Chapter 2).

Spanish poetry Much of the early literature of Spanish colonies in the Southwest (present-day New Mexico, Arizona, and Texas) was passed on

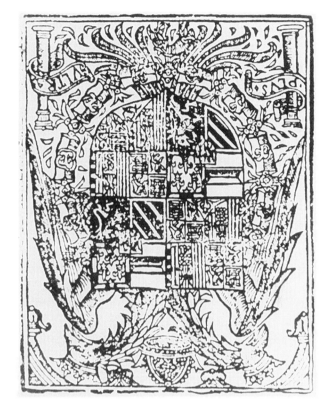

The title page from Alvar Nuñez Cabeza de Vaca's account of his journey from Florida to Mexico. *Reproduced by permission of Arte Público Press.*

orally. Hoping to convert Native Americans and to educate colonists, Franciscan missionaries often staged religious dramas that were either versions of Spanish plays or plays written in Mexico. Some of the songs and poems from these plays inspired traveling troubadours (poets and musicians of knightly rank whose theme was love) to compose their own verses. Spanish settlers also passed on long romance poems, narratives that had moral or religious messages. Another popular tradition was the telling of *cuentos,* or prose tales

A New Mexico Epic

The earliest literature by Europeans in North America came from sixteenth-century Spanish explorers who published reports on their journeys after they returned to Spain. Among these accounts was an epic poem, *Historia de la Nuevo-Mexico* (History of New Mexico), by Gaspar Pérez de Villagrá. He was one of the six hundred colonists who established the first Spanish settlement in New Mexico in 1598. Beginning with a brief description of earlier expeditions, Villagrá wrote a thirty-four-part poem that included a detailed eyewitness account of the colonists' adventures. *Historia de la Nuevo-Mexico* is still consulted by modern historians seeking information about the Spanish colonial period.

(stories in nonpoetic form), which originated in Spain but were modified over time in North America.

French

The earliest French colonial writings were also historical accounts. They included *Histoire de la Nouvelle-France* (History of New France; 1609–1618) by Marc Lescarbot and *Voyages de la Nouvelle France* (Voyages of New France; 1632) by Samuel de Champlain, founder of New France (see Chapter 3). The Jesuits' annual reports, *Jesuit Relations,* were begun by Paul Le Jeune in 1632 and continued through 1673. The most notable French colonial history to mention Louisiana was published by Jesuit priest and travel writer Pierre-François-Xavier de Charlevoix (1682–1761). His *Histoire et description de la Nouvelle France* (History and Description of New France; 1744) was a report on his travels down the Mississippi River to New Orleans.

French poetry Mock-heroic poems (comic or satirical depictions of heroic events) were another popular form of literature in New France. René-Louis Chartier de la Lotbiniére wrote a verse epic about a military expedition against the Mohawk led by Rémy de Courcelle in 1666. Probably not intended for publication, this comic picture of military life seems to have been circulated widely in New France and France. French officer and traveler Louis-Armand de Lom d'Arce de La Hontan (1666–1715) also gave satirical descriptions of politics and society in "Nouveaux Voyages" (New Voyages) and "Dialogues," both published in 1703. The first surviving poem written in Louisiana was Dumont de Montigny's "Poème en vers" (Poem in Verse), a history of the province from 1716 to 1746. Written in the 1740s, it remained unpublished until 1931. As in the Spanish colonies, there was an active oral tradition in New France. When folklorists (scholars who study the traditional customs of a country) began col-

Books and Reading in the Colonies

The first European settlers in North America brought books with them or imported books from their home countries. Even in New England, where a printing press was established at Cambridge, Massachusetts, in 1638, most books of any length came from England. Printers set up shop in New Amsterdam in the 1650s, Boston in 1675, Philadelphia in 1683, and New York in 1693. By 1750 there were also printing presses in Connecticut, Rhode Island, Virginia, and South Carolina, and Pennsylvania. Yet printing a long work required more type and equipment than colonial printers could afford, so most books sold in America were imported from Britain and Europe until after the American Revolution. Colonial printers concentrated mainly on government documents, almanacs, sermons, and other pamphlet-length works such as primers, political tracts, and essays on contemporary issues. Although many colonists could not read, in New England an estimated 90 percent of white males and 40 percent of white females were literate by 1750. In the other English colonies literacy rates for white males ranged from about 30 percent to more than 50 percent. (Different figures are often given for literacy rates.) In most literate households, however, the only books might be a Bible, an almanac, and possibly a hymnbook. There were impressive private libraries in all the colonies, but the general public used subscription libraries that began springing up during the eighteenth century. The earliest was the Library Company of Philadelphia, which Benjamin Franklin founded in 1731.

lecting Canadian stories and songs in the nineteenth century, some were discovered to have originated in France.

New England colonies

Early New England historians tended to focus less on events than on showing that God had chosen the Puritans as instruments of his will and fully supported their ventures in North America. The Puritan mission was the focus of seventeenth-century histories of the Massachusetts Bay Colony, such as Edward Johnson's *Wonder-working Providence of Sions [Zion's] Saviour in New-England* (1654) and Nathaniel Morton's *New Englands Memoriall* (1669). Many gave accounts of King Philip's War, the bloody conflict between the Puritans and the Narraganset tribe (1675–76; see Chapter 4). Among them were Increase Mather's *A Brief History of the Warr with the Indians of New England* (1676), William Hubbard's *A Narrative of the Troubles with*

A Puritan Defends Native Americans

Most Puritan historians took a negative view of Native Americans, whom they regarded as agents of the devil. An exception was Daniel Gookin, who spent more than twenty years as Indian superintendent in the Massachusetts Bay Colony. He attempted to give a more positive account of Native Americans in his *Historical Collections of the Indians in New England,* which remained unpublished until 1792, more than one hundred years after his death. Gookin also took the side of Native Americans in *An Historical Account of the Doings and Suffering of the Christian Indians in New England in the Years 1657, 1676, 1677* (1836). He wrote this book in response to Increase Mather's and William Hubbard's accounts of King Philip's War, which depicted Native Americans as evil devil worshippers.

Increase Mather and grandson of two first-generation New England men of God (John Cotton and Richard Mather), Cotton Mather published 444 works (mostly pamphlets) during his lifetime. He is considered one of the most published American authors of all time.

Thomas Prince, another clergyman who believed in the Puritans' mission, wrote *A Chronological History of New-England.* Two of the most useful documents for modern historians were not published during their authors' lifetimes. Plymouth Colony governor William Bradford (see Chapter 4) wrote *Of Plimoth Plantation* in 1630 and 1646 to 1650, and it was first published in 1856. Massachusetts Bay Colony governor John Winthrop (see Chapter 4) kept journals from 1630 to 1649; they were first published in part in 1790.

the Indians in New-England (1677), and *Duodecennium Luctuosum* (Two Decades Full of Sorrow; 1699) by Cotton Mather (1663–1728).

Cotton Mather was the most productive Puritan author. In his major work, *Magnalia Christi Americana* (The Great Works of Christ in America; 1702), he wrote the biographies of more than sixty Puritan "saints" (a term the Puritans used to describe those who were "saved"). The son of

New England poetry The first colonial printing press opened in Cambridge in 1638. For this reason the published works of New England poets far outnumbered those by residents of the other English colonies. Many of the earliest poems were elegies (expressions of sorrow) written by Puritan clergymen or brief verses about months and seasons in almanacs. Puritans were also fond of creating anagrams (words or phrases formed with the letters of other words or phrases) from people's names and then using them as the starting points for poems. For example, Puritan minister John Wilson turned "Claudius Gilbert" into "Tis Braul I Cudgel" and then wrote a

Two pages of poems from Anne Bradstreet, whose *The Tenth Muse Lately Sprung Up in America* was the first book published by a woman in the colonies.
Reproduced by permission of The Granger Collection.

poem about the "brawling" of the Quakers and other dissenters (those who protest against the established church) and how God "cudgeled" (beat) them with his holy word.

The first book published in Cambridge was *The Whole Booke of Psalmes* (better known as *The Bay Psalm Book*; 1640), a hymnbook that contains some of the earliest Puritan poetry. Clergymen Thomas Welde, John Eliot, Richard Mather, and others rephrased or summarized verses from the Book of Psalms in the Bible so that they could be sung to traditional hymn tunes. Welde and his colleagues did not like existing translations of the psalms, so they went back to the original Hebrew to make a "plaine translation" that aimed for "fidelity rather than poetry." For example, the current translation of the opening lines of the twenty-third psalm was "The Lord is my Shepherd. I shall not want." Welde and the others gave their "plaine translation" as: "The Lord to mee a shepherd is, want therefore shall not I." *The Bay Psalm Book*, which could be found in many New England homes, went through twenty-five editions. By the mid-eighteenth century, however, it had been replaced by the hymns of English religious leaders Isaac Watts, John Wesley, and Charles Wesley.

Nathaniel Ward Another Puritan pastor, Nathaniel Ward (1578?–1652), wrote an entirely different kind of poetry in *The Simple Cobbler of Aggawam in America* (1647). The speaker in the poem is a shoemaker who reflects on the religious and political issues of the day. Ward used word-play to express his distrust of such practices as religious debate. At one point the Cobbler of Aggawam says that the devil "cannot sting the vitals [internal organs] of the Elect [Puritan leaders] morally," but he can "fly-blow [make impure] their Intellectuals miserably."

Anne Bradstreet Ward also wrote a poem of dedication for the first book by an American woman, *The Tenth Muse Lately Sprung Up in America* by Anne Bradstreet (1612–1672), which was published anonymously in 1650. Modern readers admire Bradstreet's love poems, including "To my Dear and Loving Husband," which begins with the memorable lines:

> If ever two were one, then surely we
> If ever span were lovd by wife, then thee;
> If ever wife was happy in a man
> Compare with me ye women if you can.

New England colonial readers admired Bradstreet's philosophical and religious poems, marveling at the extent of her knowledge and the quality of her verse. In his dedication Ward wrote, "It half revives my chil frost-bitten blood,/To see a Woman once, do ought that's good."

Michael Wigglesworth Bradstreet's poetry was widely read by New Englanders, especially after her husband had an enlarged edition of *The Tenth Muse* published in Boston, again anonymously, in 1678. Yet the most popular poet at the time was Michael Wigglesworth (1631–1705), whose book-length poem *The Day of Doom* (1662) is considered the first American best-seller. *The Day of Doom* had gone through seven editions by 1751, and the sixth edition of his popular second book, *Meat Out of the Eater* (1670), was published in 1721. These books were so often read and reread that no copies of the first edition of either have survived. Wigglesworth's sermons in verse did not appeal to later generations, but his contemporaries admired and heeded his warnings about the hellfires that awaited sinners bound for eternal damnation.

Edward Taylor Another important New England poet was Edward Taylor (c. 1645–1729). Yet the only verses by him that appeared in print during his lifetime were two stanzas from "Upon Wedlock and Death of Children" (written in 1682 or 1683), which Cotton Mather included in his *Right Thoughts in Sad Hours* (1689). While Taylor is believed to have read a few of his poems to his congregation in Westfield, Massachusetts, he was virtually unknown until scholars discovered manuscripts of his poems and published them in the twentieth century.

Today Taylor is considered a major American poet, and more than two hundred of his *Poetical Meditations* (written between 1682 and 1725) have been called the most important poetic achievements of colonial America. Taylor accepted the stern religious beliefs of his fellow Puritans, but he often focused on God's grace and the experience of religious joy:

> God is Gone up with a triumphant
> Shout
> The Lord with sounding Trumpets
> melodies.
> Sing Praise, sing Praise, sing Praise,
> sing Praises out, Unto our King
> sing praise seraphickwise.
> Lift up your Heads ye lasting Doore
> they sing
> And let the King of Glory Enter in.

By the eighteenth century literary tastes were becoming more secular throughout the colonies. Prosperity gave colonists the opportunity to learn about the latest cultural trends in England through imported books, magazines, and engravings. The change became apparent even in New England, where Boston clergyman Mather Byles (1707–1788), nephew of Cotton Mather, wrote sermons in which he concentrated more on style than on religious insights. In later years he became known for his wit. Another eighteenth-century Boston poet, Joseph Green, wrote humorous verses that poked fun at prominent people and public events, including "A Parody on a Hymn by Mather Byles" (1733). Green's most popular work was "Entertainment for a Winter's Evening" (1750), a satire (humorous treatment) on the Freemasons (Free and Accepted Masons, a fraternal organization with secret rituals), in which he named actual people.

Middle colonies

The earliest history of New Netherland (renamed New York in 1664) was written by lawyer Adriaen van der Donck and published in the Netherlands in 1649. His later work, *A Description of the New Netherland* (1655), was the first book published in New Netherland. Daniel Denton's *A Briefe Description of New-York* (1670) attracted English settlers to the colony after Britain took it over. Similarly, William Penn lured settlers to his colony with *Some Account of the Province of Pennsilvania* (1681) and other pamphlets.

One early history, *Good Order Established in Pennsilvania & New-Jersey* (1685), was written by Thomas Budd, who successfully recommended public education. An important later history was *The History of the Five Indian Nations Depending on the Province of New York* (1727) by Cadwallader Colden. Colden admired Native Americans and believed that the Iroquois (a powerful tribal alliance in the New York region) could play a role in protecting New York against the French and their Huron allies in New France.

Middle colonies poetry Dutch colonists in New Netherland included some notable poets. Jacob Steendam's "Spurring-Verses" were published in

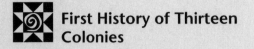

First History of Thirteen Colonies

New Yorker William Douglass is sometimes called the first American historian to examine the thirteen colonies as a single unit. He wrote *A Summary, Historical and Political of the First Planting, Progressive Improvements, and Present State of the British Settlements in North America* (1747–1752) in response to what he called the "intolerably erroneous" work of Cotton Mather and other New England historians. Later historians charged, however, that Douglass's own work was sloppy and unreliable.

Peter C. Plockhoy's *Kort en Klaer Ontwerp* (Short and Clear: Antwerp; 1662) to encourage settlement in New Netherland. According to Steendam, the colony was a paradise where "birds obscure the sky," the land was filled with wild animals, the waters were teeming with fish, and oysters were "piled up, heap on heap, till islands they attain [until they become islands]." Henricus Selyns, a Dutch Reformed minister, wrote marriage poems, epitaphs for prominent colonists, satires, and verses in Latin. Nicasius de Sille, who held important administrative posts in the colony, also wrote poems. The best known was "The Earth Speaks to Its Cultivator," in which the main character is a "New Adam" (Adam was the first man on Earth, according to the Christian Bible), an image of the European settler in North America that was used throughout American literature well into the nineteenth century.

Although New Netherland became New York in 1664, the transition to English cultural traditions did not gain momentum until the second half of the eighteenth century. Consequently, there were only a few English New York poets writing verse during the colonial period. Among them were William Livingston and Richard Steere, but only Steere achieved any recognition for his work. He was an English Puritan who fled to Boston in 1682 or 1683 after his verses angered British authorities. He then offended Puritan leaders in Boston by voicing unorthodox religious views. Steere finally settled on Long Island in 1710. The poems contained in his collection *The Daniel Catcher* (1713) include some of the earliest examples of American nature poetry. Steere is also credited with writing the first American poem in blank (unrhymed) verse. Pennsylvania also produced few notable poets during the colonial period. However, James Logan, who came to America as secretary to Pennsylvania founder William Penn, is said to have written original poems in the 1730s and 1740s.

Southern colonies

The best-known work about Virginia is *A True Relation of Such Occurences and Accidents of Noate as Hath Hapned in Virginia* (1608) by John

Smith, one of the founders of Jamestown, the first permanent English settlement (see Chapter 4). Smith wrote several books about his experiences in Virginia and New England, concluding with *The True Travels, Adventures, and Observations of Captaine John Smith* (1630). One of the earliest descriptions of Native North American customs was *A Briefe and True Report of the New Found Land of Virginia* (1588) by Thomas Harriot, a surveyor (a person who measures and describes an area of land) with Richard Grenville's 1585 expedition to Virginia (see Chapter 4). The book had been reprinted seventeen times by 1610 and attracted thousands of English settlers. Other influential pamphlets promoting the southern colonies were John Hammond's *Leah and Rachel, or The two fruitfull sisters Virginia and Maryland* (1655), George Alsop's *A Character of the Province of Mary-land* (1666), and John Lawson's *A New Voyage to Carolina* (1709).

In *The History and Present State of Virginia* (1705), Robert Beverley (1673–1722) openly criticized several royal governors (colonial officials appointed by the English monarch) for infringing on Virginians' personal liberties. At the same time he praised the simple traditions of Native Americans. Beverley's fellow Virginian William Byrd II made a valuable and humorous contribution to knowledge about life in rural Virginia. In *The History of the Dividing Line Betwixt Virginia and North Carolina* (published in 1841) and *The Secret History of the Line* (published in 1929), he wrote accounts of establishing the boundary between Virginia and

 African American Oral Tradition

The first Africans arrived in Virginia as slaves in 1619. They brought a rich heritage of orally transmitted stories and folktales, some of which eventually became part of mainstream American literature. Since most slaves were not taught to read and write English, they passed on Anglicized (adapted to English) versions of African stories orally. The first African Americans to write in the English literary tradition and have their work published were poets Jupiter Hammon and Phillis Wheatley. Hammon's first published poem appeared in 1760, and Wheatley's first poem was published in 1767, when she was only thirteen or fourteen. By about 1760 African Americans were also writing autobiographical narratives to describe their experiences as slaves.

North Carolina in 1728. Byrd also kept diaries that are quite famous today. Since many of the experiences he wrote about were considered immoral, he used a shorthand code that he invented. Twentieth-century scholars managed to figure out the code and published the diaries, which provide modern readers with fascinating glimpses into the life of a colonial Virginia gentleman. In *A True and Historical Narrative of the Colony of Georgia* (1741) several Georgia colonists— Patrick Tailfer, Hugh Anderson, David

Douglas, and others—used satire and "tall tales" to attack the administration of James Oglethorpe, the founder of the colony (see Chapter 4). In particular they criticized his opposition to slavery and the rum trade.

Southern colonies poetry Ebenezer Cook, a lawyer who wrote satiric verse on life in colonial Maryland, has been called the father of traditional Southern humor writing. Cook's best-known poem, *The Sot-Weed Factor* (1708), tells the story of an English tobacco (sotweed) merchant (factor) who was cheated out of all his possessions in a series of scams by Maryland colonists. Cook depicted a land "where no Man's Faithful, nor a Woman Chast [chaste; a virgin]," making fun of Englishmen who expected to get rich fast in North America. Another Marylander, Richard Lewis, is known as the best early American nature poet. He based his poems on close observations of nature, such as this vivid description of a hummingbird in "A Journey from Patapsco to Annapolis" (1731):

> He takes with rapid Whirl his noisy Flight,
>
> His gemmy Plummage [gem-like feathers] strikes the Gazer's Sight
>
> And as he moves his ever-flutering Wings,
>
> Ten thousand Colours he around him flings.

Theater

According to Gaspar Pérez de Villagrá's *Historia de la Nuevo-Mexico*, the first European play produced within the boundaries of the modern-day United States was a *comedia* (a drama that ends happily) by Captain Marcos Farfán de los Godos. It was staged on the banks of the Rio Grande in New Mexico on April 30, 1598. Villagrá described this play, which is now lost, as a drama about the willingness of Native Americans to convert to Christianity. He also mentioned a production of a Spanish drama called *Moros y Cristianos* (The Moors and the Christians) and a *comedia*, perhaps by Farfán, at San Juan de los Caballeros, near present-day El Paso, Texas, in 1598. Throughout the Southwest Spanish priests made extensive use of religious plays in their attempts to convert Native Americans to Christianity. The French also brought their theater traditions to the New World (European term for North and South America). Marc Lescarbot's *Le Théâtre de Neptune en Nouvelle-France* (The Theater of Neptune in New France) was performed at Port Royal, Acadia (later Annapolis Royal, Nova Scotia), on November 14, 1606. It was the first play written and staged in French Canada, and from 1640 until 1699 plays were frequently performed in Quebec.

English colonies

Distinctly American drama was the last cultural form to develop in the colonies, mainly because hardworking settlers in the New World had little time for entertainment. Puritans in New England and Quakers in Pennsylvania also placed religious and moral restrictions on theatrical performances. Even in the southern colonies, where there were few Puritans or Quakers, plays were suspected of encouraging undesirable behavior in the lower classes (servants and laborers).

Amateur productions The first known performance of a play in the thirteen original colonies was an amateur production of *Ye Bare and Ye Cubb* by William Darby in Accomac County, Virginia. (There are no surviving copies of this play, which is known only through court records.) After Darby and some of his friends gave their performance on August 27, 1665, they were arrested for playacting. They were eventually found not guilty. In 1690 Harvard College students in Cambridge also earned the disapproval of local authorities by staging a play called *Gustavas Vasa*. According to Virginia records, in 1702 students at William and Mary College in Williamsburg gave a recitation of a "pastoral colloquy."

Professional theater During the first half of the eighteenth century, professional theater began to take hold in the southern and mid-Atlantic colonies. In 1716 or 1717 authorities in Williamsburg allowed a theater to be built, and amateur actors staged plays there for the next several years. In 1723, despite the antitheater sentiment of Quakers, strolling players performed outside the city limits of Philadelphia. During the 1730s amateur acting groups built theaters in Charleston and New York City.

 First Published American Play

In 1705 Robert Hunter, the governor of New York and New Jersey, wrote a play titled *Androboros* (Maneater), which was not intended for performance. It appeared in print in 1714, thus becoming the first published American play. *Androboros* was Hunter's attempt to sway public opinion in his favor during a political dispute. He was involved in a conflict with the assembly, the Anglican Church, and the royal commissioner of accounts, Francis Nicholson. The play was set in a mental institution and featured several thinly disguised characters. The keeper of the institution was based on Hunter himself, and the character of Androboros was meant to represent Nicholson.

Although theatrical performances remained controversial throughout the eighteenth century, the Quakers had slightly eased their opposition by 1749. That year a British company headed by Walter Murray and Thomas Kean staged English playwright Joseph Addison's tragedy *Cato* and other plays in a Philadelphia warehouse. In 1750 they took the play to New York City and performed regularly in a large room of a New York building. They met with such success that they presented fifteen more plays in a second season. After closing the production in New York in 1751, the company moved on to Williamsburg, where they opened in October in a recently constructed theater building.

First professional company The Company of Comedians is considered the first professional theater company to perform in English-speaking North America. They arrived in Williamsburg in 1752, hoping to recover financial losses from a poor season in London. The proprietor of the Company of Comedians was William Hallam, whose brother Lewis Hallam was the actor-manager. Lewis's wife was one of the actors. The company remained in Williamsburg for eleven months, performing about twice a week. They then proceeded to New York, where they built the first theater in the city and spent several months trying to get permission to perform. They finally opened with the comedy *The Conscious Lovers* by English playwright Richard Steele in September 1753. Meeting with great success, the company performed two or three times a week until March 1754. The final stop on their North American tour was Philadelphia, where, despite strenuous opposition from local Quakers, they played for two months before sailing to Jamaica. Though the Hallams' tour was successful, it did not spur an upsurge of theatrical activity in the colonies. The Company of Comedians was later renamed the American Company. On April 24, 1767, in Philadelphia they staged *The Prince of Parthia* by American poet and playwright Thomas Godfrey. It is considered the first professional production of a play by an American.

Architecture

The most lasting contribution of Spanish colonists to American culture was architecture. Buildings dating from the earliest period in La Florida differ from those found in the Southwest. Nevertheless both architectural styles were derived from the tastes of seventeenth-century Spanish aristocrats (upper social class) and adapted to New World conditions by Franciscan missionaries. In the Southwest in particular, the Spanish also drew upon Native American traditions.

The Spanish Southwest

In the Southwest, where the Spanish adapted the building practices of the Pueblo Indians, Native American builders created the only examples of American architecture in which the traditions of the native culture significantly altered European styles. An important example is the Governor's Palace in Santa Fe, New Mexico (1609–1614); it was rebuilt in 1680 and at several later dates. Constructed from adobe (brick or building material of sun-dried earth and straw) and featuring a long covered porch, it is believed to be the oldest surviving structure built for Europeans in the United States. San Estiban in Acoma, New Mexico, which was completed before 1644, is the earliest of many Spanish mission churches still in existence in the United States. Three eighteenth-century mission churches can be seen in Texas. Nuestra Señora de la Purisima Concepción de Acuna was dedicated in 1755, and the chapel at the Presidio la

The Governor's Palace in Santa Fe, New Mexico, shows the Native American influence on European architecture. *Reproduced by permission of The Library of Congress.*

Bahia in Goliad was established in 1749. The church at the mission of San Antonio de Valero was started in 1744 and completed after 1777. (San Antonio de Valero is now known as the Alamo, the site of a battle during the Texas Revolution in 1836.)

Florida

The earliest surviving buildings in present-day Florida date from around the middle of the seventeenth century. Of these the most notable is the Castillo de San Marcos in Saint Augustine, which was begun in 1672 and is often called the finest structure of its kind in the United States. Built around a 100-square-foot central courtyard, this castle has spear-shaped bastions (a projecting part of a fortification) at its four corners, massive walls made of coquina (a form of limestone made by cementing shells and coral together), and a 40-foot moat (a protective trench surrounding a fort). Comparing favorably to fortresses constructed in Europe at the same time, the Castillo provided a successful defense of Saint Augustine during attacks from English forces in 1702 to 1703 and in 1740.

Mississippi River valley

After René-Robert Cavelier, sieur de La Salle, explored the Mississippi River valley in 1682, the French began establishing trading posts at strategic locations in the region, from Canada all the way south to the Gulf of Mexico. The original seventeenth-century structures built at these settlements, however, were destroyed by fire or flood. The oldest surviving French house is the so-called courthouse in Cahokia, Illinois. It was built as a private residence around 1737 and converted to a courthouse and jail in 1793. This and other early French buildings were constructed of upright logs set in the ground or on stone foundations. The logs were hewn flat on the sides that faced the interior and exterior of the structure. The spaces between the logs were filled with stones, bricks, or clay mixed with binding materials such as moss, grass, or even hair. Often the outside was covered with lime plaster to slow erosion by wind and rain. Like later French houses in the New World, the Cahokia Courthouse has a high, double-pitched roof to accommodate a covered *galerie,* or veranda, around all four sides of the house. Especially adapted to hot climates, this style was also used in larger, often two-story plantation houses in Louisiana later in the eighteenth century.

New Orleans

The French settled New Orleans, Louisiana, in 1718. The earliest buildings were constructed according to a technique called *briqueté entre poteaux,* which involved setting massive wooden vertical posts in the ground and putting bricks between them to create walls. In France, these walls were often covered with boards or plaster, but in the New Orleans region they were sometimes left exposed and consequently suffered deterioration from the weather. Many early eighteenth-century buildings in New Orleans were destroyed by fires that devastated the city in 1788 and 1794. In 1727 François Broutin designed a *briqueté entre poteaux* building to serve as the first Ursuline convent (a Catholic religious community). The first major brick building in the city was the prison (1730), which was designed by Pierre Baron. The only public building in New Orleans that dates from before the city was ceded (handed over) to Spain in 1764 is the second Ursuline convent. It is a brick structure designed by Broutin in 1745 to replace the other convent, whose wooden timbers had not held up well in the humid climate of the city. The earliest plantation house, which is called Parlange, was built around 1750 in Pointe Coupée Parish.

British colonies

Colonists of several nationalities contributed to American architecture, but housing styles in the English colonies were predominantly based on British models. Nevertheless architectural trends were slow to reach the New World and were often modified to meet the demands of colonial life. Colonial builders were confronted with extreme temperatures that were uncommon in England, and they did not have enough skilled craftsmen to fashion ornate (elaborately decorated) architectural details. Colonists also modified plans to suit available construction materials. For example, wood was far more plentiful in North America than in England and Europe, where brick buildings were most prevalent. Conversely, a shortage of lime used for mortar made brick buildings expensive in New England.

New England The first full-scale houses in New England were built for ministers and important officials of the Massachusetts Bay Colony soon after the colonists' arrival. The most common house consisted of a heavy oak frame filled with clay and straw, wattle, or sun-dried brick and then covered with a layer of clay. The roof was usually thatched (made of straw mats that are fastened together). But the colonists soon encountered a problem: this kind of house could not withstand the cold winters and harsh storms of New England. Therefore colonists began covering the exterior of their houses with weather boards, eventually adapting this method to build a wood-frame house. Wood shingles also replaced the thatched roof.

Colonists probably lived in one-story or one-and-a-half-story wooden houses. Most surviving New England houses, however, are a two-story style called the "saltbox." It is two rooms wide and one room deep, with the second story extending over

The First Settlers' Houses

The earliest settlers of Jamestown in 1607 and New England in the 1620s and 1630s built simple shelters in the tradition of the English peasant class. They bent tree branches to make a frame for a small, one-room cabin or a "wigwam." They often made the walls of woven wattle, or willow rods and other slender tree branches, then covered them with daub, or a mud mixture. Typically the thatched roof had a hole in the middle to let out the smoke from a stone hearth in the center of the earth floor. Occasionally such a structure had a mud-and-stick chimney. In Connecticut, Pennsylvania, and eastern Long Island the earliest English colonists' shelters were dugouts in banks with roofs and walls formed of brush and sod. Some buildings, such as the church at Plymouth and houses in the English settlements of eastern New Jersey, were of palisade construction—that is, planks driven into the ground. The English most often used this construction technique for forts and churches.

the first story in the front to create an overhang. This style became more common in the late seventeenth century. Sometimes lean-to rooms on the back or extra gables (the vertical triangular end of a building) on the roof were added to provide more space. For windows, small, diamond-shaped

The New England Meetinghouse

The first public building in a New England village was the meetinghouse, which served as both church and town hall. The only surviving seventeenth-century structure of this type is the Old Ship Meeting House, which was built in 1681 in Hingham, Massachusetts. The roof looks like a ship's hull turned upside down, and the interior has been compared to the great halls of medieval Europe. In keeping with Puritan beliefs, however, the plain furnishings and simple exterior seem to have been modeled on churches in Protestant Holland. Similar meetinghouses are known to have been built in other New England towns during the seventeenth century.

panes of glass were held together with strips of lead. Because glass was imported from Europe and heavily taxed, windows were quite small and most did not open.

The earliest surviving New England house is the residence of Jonathan Fairbanks, which was begun in 1636 in Dedham, Massachusetts. It has been altered by later renovations and additions, so houses from a slightly later period are better examples of seventeenth-century New England architecture. In Massachusetts these houses include the Whipple House (1640) at

Ipswich, the "Scotch"-Boardman House (c. 1650) at Saugus, the Parson Capen House (1683) at Topsfield, and the John Ward House (1684) at Salem. Perhaps most famous is the Turner House at Salem, which was built in 1668 and was the inspiration for *The House of the Seven Gables,* a story by nineteenth-century author Nathaniel Hawthorne. Among notable seventeenth-century Connecticut houses is the faithfully restored Stanley Whitman House (c. 1660) in Farmington. It is one of the best-preserved examples of the typical New England saltbox style.

Middle colonies   Dutch settlers brought to New Netherland a rich tradition of brickwork that is still evident in Holland and Belgium. Though some bricks may at first have been imported from Europe as ballast (a heavy substance used to improve stability) on ships, kilns (ovens used for processing a substance by burning, firing, or drying) capable of producing good-quality bricks were established soon after the first settlers arrived in New Amsterdam in 1626. Before long the first settlement of thirty bark-covered houses and a palisaded blockhouse (fort) was replaced by a city that looked much like those found in Holland. Most of the buildings were brick with steep tile roofs and gables facing the street. On the gables were steplike features that were useful to chimney sweeps (workmen who clean chimneys), who would otherwise have had to climb on the dangerously slippery roof tiles. Similar houses were built in Albany and other larger settlements. Unfortunately, none of these early Dutch city houses has survived.

The earliest Dutch farmhouses were built in the same style, but they tended to have straight gables at the sides. Dutch farmers in the lower Hudson River valley, northern New Jersey, and western Long Island usually built houses of stone or wood or combined the two. The still-popular Dutch colonial house, with a double-hipped roof (called a gambrel roof), originated in colonial farm settlements. Buildings of this type were not found in the Netherlands. They may have been adapted to suit the weather and available materials of the region.

Southern colonies While early Virginians built wooden houses similar to those in New England, most seventeenth-century houses in the southern colonies were made of brick. One notable exception is Bond Castle, a wooden house built in Calvert County, Maryland, in the late 1600s. In most areas throughout the South, settlers had adequate supplies of lime for mortar, so brick construction was more common there than in New England. Like New England houses of the same period, the earliest Southern houses were only one room deep. While New Englanders usually put the chimney at the center of the house for maximum warmth, Southerners tended to put the chimney at either end, with a central passageway for ventilation during hot weather. In general Southern architecture of the

 The Log Cabin

The log cabin was the major architectural contribution of Swedish settlers in New Sweden, which was established in the Delaware River valley in 1636. (New Sweden was later taken over by the Dutch; under the English it became the colony of Delaware.) This type of house—made of round logs with notched corners and projecting ends—was unknown in England, Holland, and France. Some historians believe the German settlers of Pennsylvania brought similar construction traditions with them, but others suggest the Germans may have learned cabin building from their Swedish neighbors. In either case, the Swedes and Germans were responsible for teaching settlers of other nationalities how to build the log cabins that dominated the western frontier throughout the eighteenth century and into the nineteenth century.

seventeenth century was more varied than that of New England.

Georgian architecture

During the early eighteenth century a new architectural movement began throughout the American colonies. By this time many colonists had become quite wealthy and wanted to build houses that displayed their affluence and refined tastes. They had to look to England for house designs

Bacon's Castle

One of the most unusual and interesting Southern houses is Bacon's Castle in Surry County, Virginia. Built of brick around 1655 by Arthur Allen, the house was called Bacon's Castle because it was used as a fortress by protesting colonists during Bacon's Rebellion of 1676. With three diamond-shaped chimney stacks at each end, the building resembles houses that were built in England during the first forty years of the seventeenth century. The cross-shaped layout was similar to other Southern buildings of the period. The most notable of these was the fourth Virginia statehouse, which was constructed at Jamestown in 1685 and destroyed by fire in 1698. Newport Parish Church (Saint Luke's), begun at Smithfield, Virginia, in 1632, also has architectural features similar to those of Bacon's Castle.

and furnishings, however, because the Navigation Acts (passed by the British Parliament between 1650 and 1775) required them to import nearly all products—including books and furniture—only from Great Britain. English architectural design books became popular, and colonial gentlemen often had several volumes in their libraries. For instance, Virginia aristocrat William Byrd II owned ten design books published before 1730. During that period a style called neo-Palladian (also called Anglo-Palladian) was in

vogue in England. In 1715 Scottish architect Colin Campbell (d. 1729) revived interest in the work of sixteenth-century Italian architect Andrea Palladio (1508–1580). Palladio copied features—called the classical style—that he found in ancient Greek and Roman architecture. The classical style used columns and arches on the front of a two-story structure made of basic materials such as stone or brick. The floor plan consisted of a central hall surrounded by rooms arranged in a symmetrical pattern.

During the early eighteenth century the neo-Palladian style was adapted by English architects and came to be known as Georgian architecture (named for English kings George I and George II). The Georgian style was also influenced by the Dutch, who used red brick and white stone with white-painted wood trim. These features—sometimes with modifications—were typically used in houses, public buildings, and churches throughout the colonies. Many are still standing today. One well-known example is Stratford Hall, a house built between 1725 and 1730 by the Lee family in Westmoreland County, Virginia. Stratford features a symmetrical floor in the classical style. Westover, the plantation house of the Byrd family in Charles City County, Virginia, has an unbalanced floor plan and classical door frames. Westover also has two features that appeared for the first time anywhere in the colonies: dormers (a window projecting through a sloping roof) and sash (frame) windows. The first truly Palladian feature in America can be found on the Ionic-style door frame at Whitehall in Newport, Rhode Island. The first completely Georgian building in America is Drayton Hall, near Charleston. Built by John Drayton between 1738 and 1742, this house seemed to signal the arrival of the Georgian style, which dominated American architecture for the rest of the century.

Church architecture

The greatest influence on eighteenth-century colonial church architecture was English architect Christopher Wren, who designed fifty-one churches to replace those destroyed in 1666 during the Great Fire of London. Wren's spires (steeples) were widely copied in the colonies and sometimes added to existing churches. The spires were tall and tapered, sometimes featuring classical columns at the base. The distinctive feature was a steep pyramid-shaped roof. A Wren spire can be found on the Anglican Christ Church, or Old North Church, in Boston. Designed by William Price, the church was begun in 1723 and the spire was added in 1741. The Anglican Trinity Church in Newport is also topped with a Wren spire. The church was designed and built by Richard Munday in 1725 and 1726, and its spire was also added in 1741. Wren influences can be seen in the Congregationalist Old South Church of Boston, which was designed by Robert Twelves and built in 1729 to 1730. The building has a nearly square New England-meetinghouse shape, but many architectural features are similar to those of the Old North Church. The spire resembles the one Wren designed for Saint Mary-le-Bow in London.

Science and Medicine

In the late sixteenth century, Europeans began journeying to the region in North America that became the original thirteen colonies. Many explorers reported on the features of the land and the customs of native peoples. But their primary goal was to find a more direct sea route to Asia or acquire instant wealth from discovering precious metals. Then the English founded permanent settlements along the Atlantic coast. From that time on, North America was like a scientific laboratory, helping scientists test ancient theories about the size and shape of the Earth or the location of oceans. Mountains, rivers, lakes, and bays invited closer investigation. Soon ordinary colonizers and settlers became geographers, naturalists, and mapmakers as they ventured into the wilderness. Spanish naturalists (those who study plant and animal life) explored the American Southwest from their base of New Spain (now Mexico). In 1590 the Spaniard Jose de Acosta speculated on the origins of Native Americans in *The Naturall and Morall Historie of the East and West Indies*. From New France (now Canada) French naturalists set out on the Saint Lawrence River and explored the Great Lakes, eventually reaching the Mississippi

Early Scientific Experiments

English surveyor Thomas Harriot may have performed some of the earliest scientific experiments in North America. In 1585 he was a member of an expedition, headed by English adventurer Walter Raleigh, to Roanoke Island, where the English hoped to start a permanent settlement. Harriot had the task of surveying the island and the surrounding area. In addition to conducting one of the earliest known statistical land surveys, he helped another member of the 1585 expedition, German scientist Joachim Ganz, search for copper and other precious metals. Twentieth-century archaeologists excavated the Roanoke site and found equipment that Harriot and Ganz probably used to test metals and ores.

River. Because the British colonies were more established than French and Spanish settlements, however, English achievements in science were more noteworthy.

Earliest American sciences

The first European focus of scientific study in America was geography, and the map was one of the most important tools. Some of the earliest geographic descriptions of the area that is now the United States were written by Englishmen who explored the Atlantic coast along present-day North Carolina and around the Chesapeake Bay (Virginia and Maryland). They made three trips to the area, which was then called the territory of Virginia, during the 1580s to try to start a permanent settlement on Roanoke Island (see Chapter 4). During an expedition in 1585 English mathematician and astronomer Thomas Harriot (1560–1621) conducted a detailed survey of the geographic features of Roanoke, nearby islands, and portions of the mainland. He also kept a journal of his observations of Native American customs. In 1588 Harriot published *A Brief and True Report of the New Found Land of Virginia*, primarily to encourage English colonization in North America. It is considered one of the earliest known large-scale statistical land surveys and possibly the first description of Native Americans to be written in English.

After the colony at Roanoke failed, the English did not return to North America for nearly twenty years. Then in April 1607 a party of 105 men arrived at the James River in present-day Virginia. They selected a site for a settlement and a fort so they could begin trading with local Native Americans. Some of the Englishmen immediately went hunting for gold. They soon discovered they were surrounded by the Powhatans, a powerful Native American confederation. Over nine difficult months 67 settlers died, and the survivors became entirely dependent on the Native Americans for food.

Faced with an increasingly desperate situation, one of the colonists, an adventurer named John Smith (c. 1580–1631), decided to go exploring.

Smith emphasizes natural resources

As Smith sailed up the James River in search of food, he recognized the richness and abundance of the wilderness. He was one of the first Europeans to realize that success in America would not come from discovering gold or finding a waterway through the continent to China. Smith concluded that colonies should be established to cultivate and harvest the vast resources of the continent: crops yielded from the land, fish caught from the sea, and timber cut from the forests. Determined to discover the true riches of America, he journeyed north by boat to the Chesapeake Bay, where he visited and traded with Native Americans. He also recorded his observations of plant and animal life and made notes on the features of the land. Smith took a scientific approach to the New World: knowledge—not ships, guns, or gold—was the key to success in America.

When Smith returned to England in 1608, he began compiling the records he had kept in America. That year he published *A Map of Virginia*, a narrative description of the region accompanied by an accurate map of the Chesapeake Bay. Six years later, in 1614, Smith returned to America, this time voyaging along the northeast Atlantic coast and naming the area New England. Once again he took compass readings to produce an accurate map. His *Description of New England*, published in 1616, provided a wealth of information on harbors, islands, bays, and rivers. Smith described animal life, such as the "Moos, a beast bigger than a Stagge," and various types of fish found in the sea and rivers. He discussed the eagle, "diverse sorts of Hawkes," and other birds. He wrote about soil, vegetation, and the "most pure" waters "proceeding from the intrals [entrails; inside] of rockie mountaines." His description of Native American customs showed he had a gift for ethnography (the study of human cultures).

"Accidental" scientists expand knowledge

Smith was neither the first nor the last English explorer who found himself becoming an "accidental scientist," performing the tasks of geographer, cartographer (one who makes maps), naturalist, geologist, and ethnographer. Others who explored Virginia in the early 1600s and wrote about their travels were John Brereton, James Rosier, and William Strachey. A later generation of explorers yielded more information about North America when they ventured inland to the Appalachian Mountains. In 1651 John Farrer drew a map of Virginia that showed the Pacific Ocean to the west, on the other side of the mountains. Therefore, North America seemed to be

French explorer Samuel de Champlain became the first European to give a detailed description of the coast of New England.
Reproduced by permission of AP/Wide World Photos.

other side. During the next century British colonists became aware of French exploration of the Mississippi River valley and lands even farther west. In 1750 Thomas Walker discovered the Cumberland Gap, one of the many passes through the mountains to Kentucky and other fertile lands. By the late 1700s there were few Appalachian locales not known to colonists or featured on maps.

French are important naturalists

The founder of New France, explorer Samuel de Champlain (1567–1635), was equal to John Smith in describing the natural history of North America (see Chapter 3). In addition to exploring the Saint Lawrence River valley down to the Great Lakes (a chain of five lakes on the border between Canada and the present-day United States) in 1603, from 1604 to 1607 Champlain traveled around the northeastern part of the continent. He sailed along the coast of present-day Maine and journeyed 150 miles inland. On another trip, he went down the coast of New England to the island that is now Martha's Vineyard, off Cape Cod. Although the English were exploring in the same area and eventually established the Plymouth Colony in 1620, Champlain was the first European to give a detailed account of the region. He is credited with describing Mount Desert Island as well as most of the major rivers in Maine.

a long, narrow strip of land separating the Atlantic and Pacific Oceans. Twenty years later Thomas Batts and Robert Fallam reached the top of the Appalachians, where they saw a vast territory, not a sea, extending to the west.

A more accurate description of the continent came with John Lederer's account of his journey to the Appalachians. Upon reaching the eastern edge of the mountains (the Blue Ridge), Lederer confirmed that the Pacific Ocean was not located on the

In the late 1670s the French also led the way into the Mississippi River valley, which they called Louisiana in honor of King Louis XIV. Explorers who became naturalists were Louis Jolliet, Jacques Marquette, and Louis Hennepin. All three went down the Mississippi River, exploring the river's tributaries (streams or lakes), describing land features, and writing about native peoples (see Chapter 3). In 1718 French geographer Guillaume Delisle published a map of Louisiana that would guide explorers for the next half-century. Meanwhile, French and Spanish explorers were competing for control of the American coastline along the Gulf of Mexico. In the process they created maps that aided later ventures. From 1738 to 1743 the Frenchman Sieur de La Vérendrye and his two sons, Louis Joseph and François, traveled northwest to the Missouri River, describing the area that is now North Dakota and South Dakota. From accounts of their expedition Philippe Buache drew a detailed map of Louisiana and the Great Lakes in 1754.

Rocky Mountains sighted

During a journey from the Missouri River to Santa Fe, New Mexico, in 1739 and 1740, the brothers Pierre and Paul Mallet spotted unnamed mountains to the west—now known to be the Rocky Mountains. Spanish explorers penetrated the wilderness west and south of the Rockies. Eusebio Kino, an Austrian Jesuit missionary (a member

 "the most terrifying waterfall"

In 1678 Louis Hennepin, a Franciscan priest, led an exploring party from Fort Frontenac (Kingston, Ontario) down the Niagara River. Upon reaching Niagara Falls, he noted that they were "the most beautiful and altogether the most terrifying waterfall in the universe." Hennepin was the first person to write a description of the falls.

of the Roman Catholic Society of Jesus who travels to foreign countries performing religious work; see Chapters 2 and 12), explored and described the Southwest and California. His 1705 map showed California to be not an island, as cartographer Henry Briggs had speculated in 1625, but part of the mainland.

Settlers: Second wave of "scientists"

Settlers became the next American "scientists." They quickly realized that life in Europe had not prepared them for the wilderness. The basic necessities of life and society had to be constructed out of available resources. Adapting previously acquired knowledge to the requirements of the rugged environment, they developed their own tools and technologies. The most used resource in early America was

Women Naturalists

A few colonial women had the abilities and courage to challenge the male scientific establishment. Hannah Pemberton of Philadelphia questioned the accepted explanation of earthquakes as signs of God's wrath. She was familiar with publications of the Royal Society of London and used them as a source for her rational, scientific explanation of earthquakes. Hannah Williams of South Carolina was a great collector of reptiles and insects, especially butterflies. Eliza Lucas Pinckney was a planter who conducted agricultural experiments on her South Carolina plantation, keeping notes on how various plants grew at different seasons. In 1744 she successfully produced a strain of indigo, a plant used to make a rich blue dye, which later became the staple crop of South Carolina. Perhaps the greatest female naturalist of the colonial period was Jane Colden of New York. Trained by her scientist father Cadwallader Colden, Jane became proficient in the Linnaean system of plant classification. By 1757 she had compiled a catalog of almost four hundred local plants. She was a published author and corresponded with leading European and American scientists. Jane Colden's example showed that with proper education and training, American women could make significant contributions to science.

wood. Forests of elm, oak, pine, maple, cherry, birch, walnut, and ash provided the basic materials needed for shelter, warmth, transportation, and trade. For instance, colonists used oak to produce staves (narrow strips of wood) for barrels to store and ship dry and wet goods. Black oak made excellent keels (long narrow structure attached to the bottom of ships). Some oaks produced an ingredient used to make writing ink. Carpenters fashioned elm into chairs and wagon wheels, walnut into gun stocks, and hemlock (a tree in the pine family) into flooring. Ship carpenters used locust for tunnels (wooden pegs) and yellow pine for ship decks. White pines, the tallest trees in the eastern forest, were cut, dragged to rivers, and then floated to shipyards, where craftsmen used them to make masts for ships. Ash was the favorite wood for kitchen utensils and fence rails. Some families made beer from the black spruce. Colonists joined Native Americans in preferring birch bark to the bark of other trees in the crafting of durable canoes.

The ax was the most important tool for the first settlers as well as those who later moved onto the advancing frontier. (An ax is a wedge of iron sharpened on one end and fitted into a hickory or ash handle.) With axes the settlers cleared forests for planting, cut rails for fencing, and split logs for firewood. They also built roads, which were at first merely rough paths through the forest. Eventually they used surveying instruments to measure a roadway, teams of oxen to drag away fallen trees, gunpowder to split boulders, and crushed rock to lay a roadbed. In low-lying areas logs lashed together with hemp (a plant that has tough fibers often used for ropes) formed causeways over bogs and bridges over streams. Road builders often followed paths used for centuries by Native Americans.

Native American contributions

Settlers learned a great deal from Native Americans, who taught them basic skills for surviving in the wilderness. Hunters rarely got lost in northern forests once they learned that moss grows on the north side of trees, away from direct sunlight. Cooks learned how to make hominy (kernels of corn that have been soaked in a solution and then washed to remove the hulls), succotash, and upaquontop (a stew made from hominy and fish heads). Farmers learned to plant maize (corn). The easiest way to travel in early America was by water. Native Americans showed explorers of New England and New France how to build light but sturdy bark canoes, made by burning and scraping out logs to form floatable shells. During winter, when rivers were frozen and the snow was deep, natives demonstrated that snowshoes were excellent devices for traveling.

Colonists are "unscientific" farmers

All of the early colonists depended on farming to produce food. Again, they adapted to their environment by inventing their own agricultural techniques or learning efficient

 The Log Trap

Settlers learned a great deal from Native Americans. For instance, trappers without proper iron traps learned to catch beavers, martens, and minks by using the culheag (or log trap). The trapper made the culheag out of two logs joined at one end but open at the other, with one log resting on top of the other, much like a pair of scissors. The top log was supported with a stick that stood on another rounded stick, which lay on the ground. The trapper attached a bait of raw meat to the rounded stick. When the animal tugged at the bait, the raised log collapsed, crushing the animal's head. Colonists also learned from Native Americans that the softest leather came from soaking deerskin in a mixture of animal brains and fat.

methods from Native Americans. European observers often regretted that few settlers used advanced agricultural techniques. Native Americans never developed "professional" farm practices because they were confronted by an untamed wilderness. Before a farmer could start growing crops, for instance, he had to remove hundreds of trees from his land. Some farmers chose to cut down trees in June after the planting was done and then burn the dead branches in the summer. The main problem, however, was stump and root removal, which required both human and animal labor.

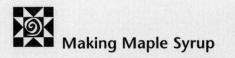

Making Maple Syrup

Early each year New England farmers placed wooden troughs (long, narrow containers) around the maple trees of the forest. They made the troughs by hand, using an ax, sometimes producing three dozen in a day. In March, when the winter nights were cold but the days were sometimes mild, the farmer cut a circular incision an inch or two in diameter in the maple tree to allow the sap to drip into the trough. Some maples gave two to three gallons of sap per day. After the farmer collected the sap in barrels, he brought it to a large outdoor fire over which hung large kettles. Women tended the kettles and boiled the liquid to a heavy maple syrup; repeated boiling produced sugar for candies and cakes.

The easiest method of clearing trees was girdling, which colonists learned from the Native Americans. Girdling worked best on land that did not need plowing. A farmer could often girdle dozens of trees in one day. The only tool he needed was a sharp knife or an ax. First he cut a deep incision around the trunk near the base of the tree that penetrated the bark into the wood. In time the leaves died and the branches became brittle. Eventually the tree would fall during a windstorm. The farmer then walked in and about the dead trees, digging small holes into which he dropped corn seeds. What had been a forest became a cornfield.

Native Americans also taught the New England Pilgrims how to fertilize the soil with small fish. Land was so plentiful, however, that many farmers did not bother to fertilize. Instead, when the soil gave out they simply cleared more land—a practice that later led to serious problems with Native Americans. The first colonists used hoes, spades, and sturdy sticks rather than plows to cultivate the soil. After 1650 more farmers used wooden plows with an iron plowshare (a blade that cuts deep into the soil). Plowed soil required a harrow (a large tree branch dragged by a team of horses or oxen) to break up clods of dirt. Through trial and error farmers learned that trees were the key to whether soil needed to be plowed. For instance, white oak meant that the soil was stony and hard, and therefore required plowing. Land dominated by beech, maple, and birch, however, indicated the soil was rich and would grow corn without plowing. Pine grew in a sandy soil that, although it often did not need the plow, lost its fertility within a few years.

Women master practical skills

Colonial women were as apt as men to use a commonsense, practical approach to survival in the American wilderness. A farmwife was simultaneously a cook, baker, butcher, candlestick maker, seamstress, and gardener.

For example, variety at mealtime depended on a woman's ability to grow different fruits and vegetables in the family garden. Baking bread was something of a science, requiring the perfect temperature in the fireplace and the right quantities of yeast, water, and grain. Acquiring yeast itself was a chore. The housewife used yeast from old dough or, in the words of one historian, "from the foamy 'barm' found on top of fermenting ale or beer." Cheese making was also a long and exhausting process. The housewife combined milk with rennet (the stomach lining of a farm animal), heated the mixture, scraped off the thickening curds, dried and pressed them, wrapped the curds in cloth, and let them dry and age in the basement. When the husband was ill or away, the wife managed all affairs of the farm.

New science sweeps Europe

During the early colonial period, colonists did not stay informed about European developments in physics and astronomy—they were too busy building towns and farms to keep up with the latest scientific discoveries. Colonial leaders, who were educated and therefore more likely to stay in touch with scientific trends, were primarily concerned with the practical challenges of starting and sustaining colonies. The gap between Europe and the colonies became even greater in the mid-seventeenth century. While settlers had been carving societies out of the wilderness, Europeans were adopting a "new science" and rejecting theories that had been accepted since ancient times.

For almost two thousand years the greatest European thinkers accepted the Greek scientist Aristotle's conception of the universe. Aristotle (384–322 B.C.) believed that the Earth was at the center of the universe, surrounded by the Moon, the Sun, the planets, and the stars. Each heavenly body orbited the Earth in a perfect circular motion. There was only one Moon in the universe. The Sun orbited around Earth between the spheres of Venus and Mars. Fixed stars were located at the outer edge of a small, limited universe. European scientists such as Nicholas Copernicus, Johannes Kepler, Galileo, and Isaac Newton, however, had different views. They believed that the Sun, not the Earth, was the center—not of the universe but of one solar system in one galaxy in a possibly unlimited universe. The Earth was one of several planets orbiting the Sun in an elliptical (oval) path. Other planets besides the Earth had moons. The universe operated according to precise forces, such as gravity, which made it logical and predictable. Therefore, according to the new science, the observations of astronomers helped humans understand the fundamental laws of the universe.

Can humans understand the universe?

The rise of modern science in the late 1600s sparked a debate over

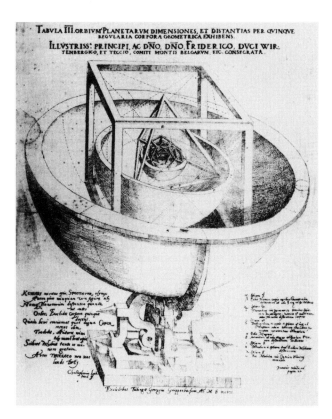

TABVLA III.ORBIVM PLANETARVM DIMENSIONES, ET DISTANTIAS PER QVINQVE REGVLARIA CORPORA GEOMETRICA EXHIBENS.

ILLVSTRISS: PRINCIPI, AC DÑO, DÑO. FRIDERICO, DVCI WIRTENBERGICO, ET TECCIO, COMITI MONTIS BELGARVM, ETC. CONSECRATA.

Johannes Kepler's model of the orbits of the planets. *Reproduced by permission of the New York Public Library Picture Collection.*

whether God had created a universe that could be understood by human beings. According to the new theories, science was a rational activity that enabled the scientist to analyze and control the forces of nature. They rejected the traditional view that the universe was created by God and would forever remain a mystery to humans. At that time religion was the center of life in the American colonies. Yet the most religious and devout Christians, the New England Puritans, ironically welcomed these views. They believed that the new science would lead to even greater reverence for God. For instance, knowing that the Earth was not the center of a possibly infinite universe was for Puritans proof of God's power and goodwill. According to Puritan thinkers, the scientific study of nature led to knowledge of God, resulting in a stronger faith.

During the next century, however, scientists and philosophers called deists came to different conclusions. To the deists, the new science proved that God had created the universe to run like a machine according to unchanging laws. In effect, God had set the universe in motion and then sat back to watch, never becoming involved or performing miracles. Deists were not atheists (those who deny the existence of a god), but they were not Christians either. The deists believed that faith, prayer, and worship were meaningless. Instead, it was the job of the scientist to use experimentation, reason, and mathematics to discover the predictable laws of the universe. In the colonies Puritans and deists continued their debate throughout the eighteenth century.

New science in America

Even though most American scientists were naturalists, botanists, and geographers, there were a few devoted to physics, astronomy, and mathematics. James Logan (1674–1751) of Philadelphia, Pennsylvania, for example, was one of the few Americans who could fully understand Newton's theories. Logan was interested in physics and taught himself mathematics. He studied astronomy and natural science and patronized (gave financial support to) such scientists as the botanist John Bartram (1699–1777). Many Americans developed extensive knowledge of the heavens. The first colonial astronomer of note was John Winthrop (1714–1779), descendent of John Winthrop, the founder of the Massachusetts Bay Colony (see Chapter 4). Winthrop owned two telescopes, which he used to observe comets and planets. In 1672 he donated a telescope to Harvard College. In 1680 Thomas Brattle used the telescope to make precise observations of Newton's Comet. By this time Harvard had established itself as the leader of scientific observation in the colonies. Over the next several decades Isaac Greenwood, Charles Morton, and other professors taught the theories of Copernicus and Newton. Harvard graduates such as Increase Mather, Samuel Sewall, and Thomas Robie observed the aurora borealis (northern lights), comets, eclipses (the total or partial covering of one celestial body by another), and planetary motions. Robie, a Harvard teacher and physician, calculated the distances of the planets to the Sun, observed the solar eclipse of November 1722 and the transit of Mercury in 1723, and tried to explain the aurora borealis. Logan and Cadwallader Colden of New York also made significant astronomic observations. Although few in number, these colonial Americans turned their attention from the practical affairs of everyday life to observe the motions of the heavens.

 ## Clergymen Are Scientists

The leaders of American science and medicine were often those with the most complete educations—the clergymen. The curricula of colonial colleges before 1750 focused on training young men for the ministry. While studying Christian writers, Greek and Roman classics, and languages, students at Harvard and Yale also took courses in science. One of the best courses was John Winthrop IV's class on experimental philosophy at Harvard. One of the greatest American scientists, the Bostonian Cotton Mather, was a minister. His counterpart in Virginia, the Reverend John Clayton, was one of the finest naturalists in the south. Isaac Greenwood was a minister who became the first Hollis Professor at Harvard, teaching math and physics.

Almanacs promote new science In the mid-1600s almanacs became a popular way for colonists to learn about science. Prior to this time Americans received their knowledge of the world from many sources: the neighbor next door, the clergyman on Sunday mornings, the stranger on the road. The annual almanac, a varied collection of news and facts, eventually became the most consistent source of information. In addition to predicting the weather and the date of the harvest moon, almanacs listed recipes, court dates and locations, and the routes and mileages

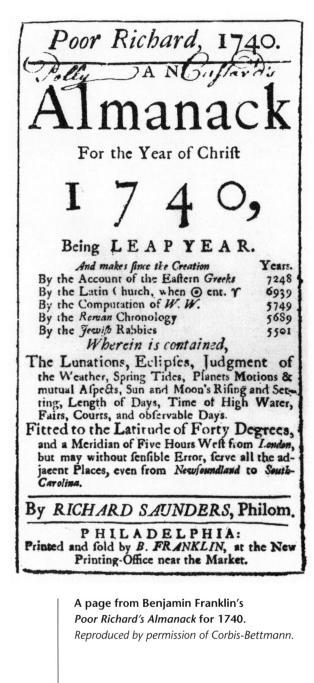

Poor Richard, 1740.

Polly AN *Guffard's*

Almanack

For the Year of Chrift

1 7 4 0,

Being LEAP YEAR.

And makes fince the Creation	**Years.**
By the Account of the Eaftern *Greeks*	7248
By the Latin Church, when ☉ ent. ♈	6939
By the Computation of *W. W.*	5749
By the *Roman* Chronology	5689
By the *Jewifh* Rabbies	5501

Wherein is contained,

The Lunations, Eclipfes, Judgment of the Weather, Spring Tides, Planets Motions & mutual Afpects, Sun and Moon's Rifing and Setting, Length of Days, Time of High Water, Fairs, Courts, and obfervable Days.

Fitted to the Latitude of Forty Degrees, and a Meridian of Five Hours Weft from *London,* but may without fenfible Error, ferve all the adjaecnt Places, even from *Newfoundland* to *South Carolina.*

By *RICHARD SAUNDERS,* Philom.

PHILADELPHIA:

Printed and fold by *B. FRANKLIN,* at the New Printing-Office near the Market.

A page from Benjamin Franklin's
Poor Richard's Almanack for 1740.
Reproduced by permission of Corbis-Bettmann.

of local roads. They provided chronologies of events and became the most important vehicle for spreading scientific knowledge in early America.

Few almanac publishers were original thinkers. They borrowed ideas from Europeans and then communicated them to the American reading public. The almanac became an effective textbook for promoting the new science. In the early 1600s most colonists thought the Sun literally rose and set in its orbit around the Earth, but by the mid-1700s more Americans realized this idea was wrong. Almanacs played a major role in bringing about this change in thinking. In 1659 the first almanac produced in America, Zechariah Brigden's *A Brief Explication and Proof of the Philolaick Systeme,* presented a formal attack on the Earth-centered universe. A 1674 almanac discussed Kepler's theory of the elliptical orbits of planets. A few years later the almanac of John Foster discarded the ancient idea of the "fixed stars" in favor of Galileo's idea of an infinite universe. During the eighteenth century almanacs carried information on Newton's laws of motion.

Alongside the most recent European discoveries, the reader of an almanac also found information on astrology (the study of the supposed influences of the stars and planets on human affairs). At that time there was still a widespread belief in astrology. Philadelphia printer Benjamin Franklin (1706–1790), who later became America's foremost scientist, included astrology and prophecies in his first edition of *Poor Richard's Almanack* (1732). Yet the first *Poor Richard's Almanack* also provided astronomers with the dates of two lunar and two solar eclipses. Three years later the almanac had a full

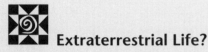

Extraterrestrial Life?

Since ancient times humans have debated the existence of life on other planets. The new scientists fueled these speculations by showing that the Earth was similar to other planets in that it orbited the Sun. If the Earth orbited a star (the Sun), they asked, why should there not be other stars with other planets capable of supporting life? Franklin took up the issue in *Poor Richard's Almanack,* where he contemplated the tremendous heat of the planet Mercury. He concluded that "it does not follow, that *Mercury* is therefore uninhabitable; since it can be no Difficulty for the Divine Power and Wisdom to acommodate the Inhabitants to the place they are to inhabit; as the Cold we see Frogs and Fishes bear very well, would soon deprive any of our Species of Life."

Finally, Franklin put himself in the place of possible inhabitants of Mars and wondered what they would see. "The Earth and Moon will appear to them, thro' Telescopes if they have any such Instruments, like two Moons, a larger and a smaller, sometimes horned, sometimes Half or three Quarters illuminated, but never full." Franklin was not willing to deny the possibility of life on the Moon, Jupiter, Saturn, and even comets. "If there are any Inhabitants in the Comets, they must live a Life wholly inconceivable to us." Franklin closed his discourse by speculating on the vast numbers of stars, the planets orbiting them, and the variety of life that must exist on those planets.

"description of the planets," in which Franklin provided a detailed guide for the amateur astronomer. As the years passed and Franklin's own knowledge increased, he included tables on planetary motions, descriptions and diagrams of eclipses, and information on such astronomical events as the transit of Mercury across the disk of the Sun. *Poor Richard's Almanack* for 1753 and 1754 included extensive analyses on the distance, appearance, and orbits of planets; an inquiry into the nature of comets; and a discussion of Newton's ideas on planetary astronomy.

Franklin a leading scientist

Franklin's most significant contribution to science was his experiments in electricity. For centuries Europeans had known about the static charge that results when two objects rub together. Scientists invented a primitive generator in the 1600s and a battery, the Leyden jar, in the next century. But the nature and uses of electricity were unanswered questions. During the eighteenth century in Europe electricity became the most popular scientific study, the source of entertainment at royal palaces, and the means by which seemingly magical tricks could be performed. Franklin's interest in electricity originated when he saw a traveling scientific lecturer, Archibald Spencer, perform an "electricity show" in Boston, Massachusetts. Soon Franklin acquired enough glass tubes, iron rods, silk, cork, and chains to perform his own experiments. By the late 1740s he was spending most of his time performing experiments in electricity and recording his results in various letters to American and European correspondents.

Conducts famous kite experiment
Franklin made several important discoveries about electricity. Contemporary European theories suggested that electricity consisted of two fluids, but Franklin found it was a single force. He realized that this force was present in nature in varying amounts, that its "particles" subtly penetrated matter, and that a net increase of electric charge in one body corresponded with a net decrease of electric charge in another. His most famous discovery confirmed what Europeans had long suspected—that lightning was an electrical phenomenon. In June 1752 Franklin constructed a silk kite with a metal wire protruding from its top. He flew the kite in a thunderstorm while standing in a shed for protection. In his hand he held twine tied to the kite. He tied a silk ribbon to the twine near his hand and attached a key as well. Lightning never struck the kite. Rather, the kite conducted (directed the course of) the electric charge of the clouds along the twine to the key. When Franklin moved his hand to the key, he felt a sharp electric spark. Franklin concluded in a letter to English botanist Peter Collinson, "from Electric Fire thus obtained, all the Other Electrical Experiments [may] be performed, which are usually done by the help of a rubbed Glass Globe or Tube, & thereby the Sameness of the Electric Matter with that of Lightning compleatly demonstrated."

Invents lightning rod Having shown that an object in a storm attracted an electric charge from clouds, Franklin advocated the use of iron rods to protect buildings and ships from lightning strikes. Indeed, in September 1752 Franklin installed a lightning rod on his own house in Philadelphia. The thin metal rod rose nine feet above the chimney and extended through the staircase to his study, where it split into two rods, each with a bell at the end. Between the two bells hung a metal ball attached to a silk thread. When the lightning rod conducted an electric charge from a storm, the charge forced the ball to ring the bells. "One night," Franklin wrote to a friend, "I was . . . awaked by loud cracks on the staircase." He found an intense electric charge of white light going from bell to bell, illuminating the entire staircase. Franklin was the first person in history to use a grounded lightning rod to protect a public or private building. He went on to gain international acclaim as a prolific inventor and practical scientist.

An illustration of Benjamin Franklin's famous kite experiment that proved that lightning was an electrical phenomenon. *Reproduced by permission of Corbis-Bettmann.*

American medicine

Medicine in early America was unspecialized and university-trained medical doctors were rare. The few qualified doctors had earned their degrees in London, England, or Edinburgh, Scotland. Most doctors were apothecaries (pharmacists) or barbers who had been educated under the apprenticeship system. In 1757 historian William Smith commented that in America "Quacks [untrained doctors] abound like locusts in Egypt." Indeed, for a young society colonial America had a high percentage of people who called themselves doctors. In one Virginia town in 1730 there was one physician for every 135 people. Even farmers living in rural areas could find treatment for illnesses. John Mitchell of Virginia was one of many physicians who earned a living by traveling throughout the colonies. They could prescribe herbal remedies, pull teeth, lance (to open) a boil (sore), and bleed or purge a patient. But they were helpless when faced with serious illnesses such as typhoid fever, smallpox, or dysentery (a disease characterized by severe diarrhea). Often both doctor and patient relied on home remedies

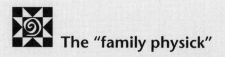

The "family physick"

An important part of the colonial wife's job was "family physick," or doctor. Women who owned *The Compleat Housewife; or Accomplished Gentlewoman's Companion* (1742) could find information on a host of homemade remedies for illnesses, pains, and injuries. Perhaps because of their experience in caring for family illnesses, many women became practicing physicians and apothecaries. Cotton Mather trained his daughter Katherine in "knowledge in Physic, and the Preparation, and the Dispensation of noble Medicines." The most common practitioner of medicine in early America was the midwife (a women who aids during childbirth). Obstetrics (the medicine of childbirth) was the domain of women, not men. Midwives rarely had formal medical training. Their knowledge came from experience and a great deal of folklore. They used garden herbs to relieve pain and fresh-churned butter as a lubricant. Often the midwife helped the mother stand, kneel, or squat to give birth. Midwives were assistants and helpers rather than crucial participants. In the case of an emergency they were helpless to save the mother or the child. Even so, midwives had remarkable success in delivering healthy babies.

learned from Native Americans. The feverish patient seeking relief sometimes followed the Native American practice of steam baths. Colonial

Americans and Europeans still believed in the ancient notion that disease was caused when the four "humours" of the body—blood, phlegm, black bile, and yellow bile—were out of balance. Many remedies involved trying to restore balance to the body, and patients were bled, given purgatives (a purging medicine), or subjected to the torture of "blistering" the skin. If at a loss for what else to do, early doctors turned to an almanac or the Bible for assistance. Frequently colonists treated themselves with home remedies published in manuals such as *Every Man his own Doctor* (1736).

Clergymen often doubled as physicians because of their education. There were so many deadly diseases in the colonies that it was convenient that the man who treated the sick could also pray for them and perform last rites. Death rates were particularly high in the southern colonies due to yellow fever (viral disease), malaria (disease characterized by cycles of chills, fever, and sweating), and hookworm (bloodsucking parasites), all of African origin. Diseases of European origin such as mumps, measles, and smallpox thrived in America as well, especially in the cities. The abundance of untrained physicians and the lack of a licensing system led to the widespread view that most doctors were quacks and the sick might as well treat themselves. There was no truly organized medical profession in America until the end of the colonial period. Communities did, however, develop techniques to prevent and combat disease. Cities such as Boston set aside

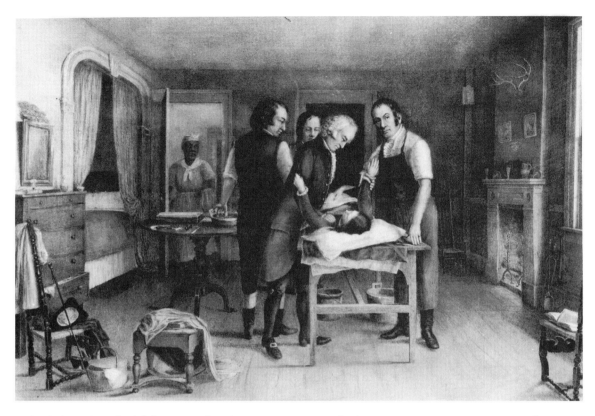

A depiction of a colonial doctor performing surgery on a patient.
Reproduced by permission of The Granger Collection.

places to quarantine (a state of enforced isolation) those who had communicable (contagious) diseases. (Boston used an island in the harbor.) These were the infamous pesthouses. The temporary residents of the pesthouses were frequently inoculated (injections to prevent a disease) for smallpox. In some cases towns tried to improve community sanitation and clean-water standards.

Medical community develops

During the early eighteenth century homespun medicine and trav-eling doctors were slowly replaced by physicians trained in European medical schools. Philadelphia physician Thomas Cadwalader, for example, studied in London and then taught medical techniques in Philadelphia. He performed the first autopsy (an examination of the body after death) in America. His contemporary, John Lining of Charleston, South Carolina, graduated from the University of Edinburgh. Concerned with the high death rate of the South (see Chapter 4), Lining kept statistics on the relation of disease to changes in the weather. He even observed and kept precise records on his own health. Another physician of the early eighteenth century was Bostonian William Douglass, a leader in the formation of the short-lived Boston Medical Society. There were other medical organizations in Charleston and in Massachusetts. Although these societies did not last long, they illustrated early efforts to establish the medical profession in America.

The smallpox inoculation controversy
In 1721 the Boston medical community was confronted with a smallpox epidemic (widespread outbreak of disease), which resulted in one of the first advances in American medicine. Smallpox was one of the most feared diseases of the eighteenth century. Highly contagious, it was marked by fever, vomiting, and the formation of pustules that scarred the body. For centuries Europe had been plagued with smallpox epidemics, but the disease was unknown in North America. After the arrival of Europeans, however, smallpox and other infectious diseases raged through Native American populations and thousands died. Americans were hesitant about sailing to Europe simply because of their fear of the disease. Yet the smallpox ultimately came to them.

In April 1721 a ship entered Boston Harbor whose crew had been infected with smallpox. Boston authorities immediately quarantined the sick men, but this failed to prevent the disease from spreading. Soon Boston was confronting an epidemic. Clergyman Cotton Mather (1663–1728) proposed a solution—smallpox inoculation (vaccination), which he had heard about from his slave Onesimus. Described by Mather as "pretty intelligent," Onesimus had reported that in Africa he had been inoculated for smallpox and had never caught the disease. In fact, Asians and Africans had been using the procedure for centuries: they drew pus from a pustule on an infected person who had a mild case of smallpox and inserted it into a healthy person. Nine times out of ten the healthy person developed a mild case of the disease, but it was not life-threatening. Once the disease ran its course, the person was immune to smallpox.

Mather publicly called upon doctors to inoculate uninfected Boston citizens. The only physician in Boston with a European medical degree, William Douglass opposed inoculation from the outset and organized most Boston physicians to protest the practice. Douglass argued that widespread inoculation without careful planning and application could actually spread the disease. He and his supporters also argued that Mather was interfering in divine matters. If God chose certain people to become sick, what human should dare oppose his will?

Surprisingly, Boston clergymen came out on Mather's side. One physician, Zabdiel Boylston (1679–1766), also agreed with Mather and inoculated his own six-year-old son and 2 slaves. Over the next few months Boylston inoculated 150 more patients. Other doctors eventually joined in the project, so that by the time the epidemic was over the following year, almost 300 people had been inoculated. Only 6, or 2 percent, of those who had received inoculation died from smallpox. Of the 5,000 Bostonians who caught the disease but who had not been inoculated, about 18 percent died. Clearly inoculation worked. Eventually Douglass accepted the practice and became a lifelong advocate of inoculation.

Sports and Recreation

15

By the time Europeans began arriving in North America during the late sixteenth century, Native Americans already had a long tradition of individual contests and team sports. Both men and women engaged in competitive recreation, especially various kinds of ball games. Southwestern native peoples played a form of basketball, and northern tribes competed in a version of modern-day lacrosse. (In lacrosse, players use a long-handled stick with a triangular mesh pouch attached at one end for catching, carrying, and throwing a ball into a goal.) A type of football, which involved kicking a leather ball against a post or posts, seems to have been popular among Eastern Woodlands tribes (native inhabitants of the region stretching from New England to Virginia). In Virginia it was played by women and young boys. European observers were all impressed with how civil the game was, how fairly the Native Americans played, and how little violence was indulged in by the players. Another favorite sport among native peoples was throwing spears at a rolling object. Frequently neighboring groups or towns challenged one another to spear-throwing contests. Native Americans also enjoyed swimming for recreation as well as for cleanliness.

A Native American Football Game

In the 1680s English traveler John Dutton gave an account of a Native American football game he observed near Boston, Massachusetts. Like many Europeans at the time, he remarked on how little violence the Native Americans indulged in—a sharp contrast to the cheating and foul behavior that marred some European games.

There was that day a great game of Foot-ball to be played [by local Native Americans]. There was another Town played against 'em as is sometimes common in England; but they played with their bare feet, which I thought very odd; but it was upon a broad sandy Shoar [shore] free from Stones which made it more easie. Neither were they so apt to trip one another's heels and quarrel as I have seen 'em in England.

Source: Earle, Alice Morse. Child Life in Colonial Days. *New York: Macmillan, 1899; reprinted Stockbridge, Mass.: Berkshire House Publishers, 1993, p. 358.*

European sports and recreation

Organized sports were virtually unknown in colonial America. Men and young boys frequently played spontaneous ball games or held contests of individual skill, but otherwise European settlers did not set aside time for leisure activities. They worked hard every day to earn a living or maintain their farms, so they were generally not interested in exhausting themselves during their spare time. New England Puritans also placed restrictions on entertainment, which mainly consisted of religious activities. The Sabbath (Sunday, observed by Christians as a day of rest and worship) was the only day they did not work, but church fathers required their congregations to attend morning and afternoon worship services on Sundays. By the mid-1700s, however, Puritan rules were less strict, allowing for a more relaxed Sabbath. In all of the colonies, summer markets, fairs, court meetings, and militia muster days (exercise and inspection of the citizen army) provided opportunities for socializing and recreation. The entertainment was usually formal and subdued in the North, although the monthly muster days were livelier events where women and children could visit with their neighbors as they watched men perform drills (military movements). The South was noted for more colorful activities such as traveling shows, music, and dancing. The gentry (upper or ruling class) also frequented taverns, where they could find various forms of entertainment, and organized horse races.

Few team sports in colonies

In their original homelands European colonists might have engaged in team sports, such as football games that pitted one town against another. Yet they seem to have left these practices behind. Except in New England, settlers came from various countries and had different traditions. American colonists also did not rely on the European calendar, which specified holidays when people would hold celebrations. Unlike Native Americans, settlers confined participation in most sports to males. According to European tradition, women rarely competed in games of skill, instead serving as spectators at contests between men. Major sports figures did not emerge from the colonial period because there were no professional athletes. Individuals probably excelled at certain feats, but their exploits were known only locally. The day of the sportsman (a gentleman who engages in or attends sporting events) was also yet to come. Wealthy colonial businessmen and planters (plantation owners) were too busy to devote themselves entirely to recreational pursuits.

Popular ball games

Team sports arrived in America relatively late in the colonial era. There are a few seventeenth-century descriptions of colonists playing football, but it appears to have been primarily a Native American game. Although cricket was popular in England, the sport was not widely adopted in the colonies. (Cricket is a game that is played with a ball and bat by two teams of eleven members each on a large field centering upon two wickets, or goals, that are defended by a batsman.) In 1708 Virginia planter William Byrd II (1674–1744) played a game he called cricket in Williamsburg, Virginia, but each team had only two men. At other times he played with

four men on a side. As a rule, however, colonists seemed more at home with contests that pitted individuals against one another.

Kolven

A favorite game among Dutch colonists was kolven, a combination of modern-day golf and hockey, which originated in Holland and is played either on the ground or on ice. Participants carry a stick that looks like a golf club, and they try to move a ball across a court and strike a post. Kolven must have remained a Dutch recreation, as English accounts from the period do not mention the game. It was probably the game translated as "golf" that was played at the van Rensselaer family estate, Rensselaerswyck, near Albany, New York, in 1650. Modern-day golf originated in Scotland and did not appear in America until after the Revolutionary War (1775–83).

Bowling Another individual sport was bowling, which the English and the Dutch brought to America. The most popular version was ninepins, played outdoors on a track or green (grassy area) about 20 or 30 feet long, where bowlers tried to knock down three sets of three pins with a wooden or stone ball. References to bowling appear in the earliest accounts of Jamestown, Virginia. For instance, John Smith, one of the founders of the settlement in 1607, noted in his journal that he had assigned work to men, but instead of completing their tasks they went into the countryside searching for gold or spent their time bowling in the streets. In 1636 a Virginia herdsman was punished for leaving his cows and playing ninepins. By 1654 there were bowling greens in Fort Orange (later Albany) and New Amsterdam (later New York City) in New Netherland. The greens were often owned by tavern keepers. In 1732 the Common Council of New York leased property in front of the fort to wealthy colonists so they could "make a Bowling-Green with Walks therein, for the Beauty and ornament of said street, as well as for Recreation." Charging only a token rent, the council obviously intended this facility to be open to the public. Two years later it was finished, fenced, and "Very Pretty, . . . with a handsome Walk of trees Raild and Painted." During the eighteenth century southern planters and northern merchants laid out private bowling greens on their estates.

Tests of physical skill

American colonists enjoyed tests of physical skill, such as footraces, boxing, and cudgel (a short, heavy club) matches. Footracing was popular throughout the colonial period. On muster days militiamen in Virginia and Maryland frequently held footraces and wrestling matches. Byrd mentioned several impromptu footraces in his diary. In New York, Governor Francis Nicholson celebrated Saint George's Day by sponsoring prizes for various sports, including footraces. (Saint George was a third-century Christian who died in Asia Minor.) Boxing was

also a popular pastime, both for fighters and spectators. Unlike the modern-day sport, which involves two men punching each other with heavily padded gloves, colonial boxers used their bare fists. Usually the fighters were lower-class men, and they could be badly hurt. This was a special attraction for gentlemen, who would bet on their favorite boxers. Another type of man-to-man combat was cudgels, a contest of physical skill in which each participant held a long, heavy stick with both hands. Using the cudgel to attack and parry (to ward off a weapon or blow), the fighters tried to wear down each other. The man left standing was declared the winner. Cudgel matches were held on muster days or during special celebrations. They were sponsored by taverns.

Outdoor recreation

Early European settlers were afraid to venture into the wilderness. Eventually colonists, especially in more established areas, came to enjoy walking in the open air during the summer. Some simply liked being outside, while others considered walking a healthful exercise. For instance, residents of the middle colonies visited sights such as Cohoes Falls near Albany or Passaic Falls in New Jersey. During the eighteenth century a popular pastime was strolling along streams and into wooded areas or climbing hills to view the scenery. Abigail Franks of New York City wrote to her son in London, England, that "you'll be Surprised that I have taken a ramble for a day twice this

Outdoor tea parties like the one illustrated here were common recreational activities for colonists. *Reproduced by permission of The Granger Collection.*

Summer." The Lutheran minister Henry Melchior Mühlenberg (1711–1787; see Chapter 11) "wanted a little exercise and some fresh air, so with our friends we climbed three miles up to the highest peak of the great mountain from which we were able to see about thirty miles in all directions." Almost daily Byrd rambled the grounds of Westover, his plantation on the James

Laws Against Sledding

Coasting downhill on sleds was a favorite winter sport for children in New York and New England. However the seemingly simple pleasure turned into an unlawful activity when "coasters" became a nuisance. According to historian Alice Morse Earle: "Many attempts were made to control and stop the coasters. At one time the Albany constables were ordered to take the 'small or great slees [sleds]' in which 'boys and girls ryde down the hills,' and break them into pieces. At another time the boy had to forfeit his hat if he were caught coasting on Sunday. The sleds were low, with a rope in front, and were started and guided by a sharp stick."

Earle noted that coasters were also a problem in Massachusetts: "There is a Massachusetts law of the year 1633 against 'common coasters, unprofitable fowlers and tobacco-takers,'—three classes of detrimentals. . . . coasting meant loafing along the shore, then idling in general, then sliding down the hill for fun."

Source: Earle, Alice Morse. Child Life in Colonial Days. *New York: Macmillan, 1899; reprinted Stockbridge, Mass.: Berkshire House Publishers, 1993, p. 350.*

River, frequently with his wife, Lucy Parke Byrd, and other companions. During the eighteenth century wealthy colonists in both the North and the South laid out gardens where they walked for pleasure and invited visitors, or sometimes even perfect strangers, to take a stroll.

Winter activities were especially popular among Dutch and Swedish settlers in the middle colonies. Frozen lakes and rivers provided raceways for sleighs pulled by horses. In 1663 Jeremias van Rensselaer, who lived near Albany, wrote to his brother in the Netherlands that the Hudson River froze for fourteen straight days, "so hard as within the memory of Christians it has ever done, so that with the sleigh one could use the river everywhere, without danger for the races, in which [the sport of racing] we now indulge [a good deal]." When a river was not available, people used ice-glazed roads or fields for sleigh competitions.

Another popular winter recreation was ice skating. People wore skates made of horn, wood, or metal, which they tied onto shoes and boots. Long, cold winters in New England and the middle colonies gave ample opportunity for skating, yet colonists as far south as Virginia could enjoy the sport when ice formed on lakes and ponds. In the Dutch colony of New Netherland (renamed New York when the English took over the colony) everyone skated—men and women, old and young. Charles Wolley, an English military chaplain who lived in New York at the end of the seventeenth century, was captivated by this sport. He was especially surprised to see women skating with men, since Englishwomen did not skate. As English customs replaced Dutch practices in the colony, women left the ice, but men of all classes continued to pursue the sport. A few colonists were "High Dutch" figure skaters, and others became speed skaters. According to some accounts, Africans in Philadelphia were among the more accomplished speed skaters.

Fishing

Fishing opportunities in America were a major attraction for European immigrants. Promotional literature sent out by the organizers of colonies announced that America offered an abundance of lakes, rivers, and streams overflowing with fish and shellfish. This pastime was popular among people of all classes, but it was especially appealing to servants, laborers, and slaves, who fished for food as well as for pleasure. Fishing was also one of the few recreations that men and women engaged in together. Since early settlements and all cities were built near water, most colonists had a fishing spot. Fishing was relatively easy and convenient, since all one needed was a line, a pole, and some bait. Most colonists used small boats or canoes to go out on the water. In the early 1730s William Moraley, an indentured servant, gave an account of fishing with a friend on the Delaware River near Philadelphia. Within twenty minutes, he wrote, "[we] caught between us 140 Perch and Roach." They sold about sixty of the fish for "Rum and Sugar" and served the rest at a dinner, complete with drink, for four friends.

 Elite Fishing Clubs

Philadelphia's location between two rivers made it an ideal site for recreational fishermen. During the eighteenth century wealthy Philadelphian gentlemen organized fishing clubs such as the Colony in Schuylkill, the Fishing Company of Fort St. David's, and the Mount Regale Fishing Company, all housed along the waterfront. Perhaps the oldest social organization in America, the Colony in Schuylkill was founded in 1732 to serve as a social club where members took turns serving dinner on the first Thursday of the month. Fort St. David's was a summer pavilion decorated with Native American artifacts. Members either went fishing themselves or feasted on fish they hired others to catch for them. The Mount Regale Fishing Company, composed of Philadelphia's gentlemen elite, met at Robinson's Tavern every other week in the summer.

Hunting

Promotional literature for the American colonies advertised the immense herds and flocks of animals available for hunting in the abundant new land. Yet during the seventeenth century most European immigrants were not hunters. On the surface, hunting might seem to have been a natural European sport, but this was not the case. For instance, English city dwellers had few opportunities to hunt in woods that were increasingly

An illustration of colonial gentlemen hunting and fishing. *Reproduced by permission of The Granger Collection.*

reserved for the upper classes. Ordinary people were prohibited from taking birds, deer, and rabbits from these reserves. While some poached the animals (took game or fish illegally), others never even tried their hand at hunting. Guns were also inaccurate, difficult, and time-consuming to operate. European colonists therefore did not bring hunting traditions with them to America. For Africans and Native Americans, however, hunting was a major part of male culture, so they were trained to use spears or bows and arrows from an early age.

Initially colonists bought wild game from Native Americans rather than kill it themselves. By the eighteenth century there was more leisure time for hunting but, except perhaps on the frontier, most settlers never relied on their hunting skills to put meat on their tables. In time, however, some became good marksmen (people skilled in shooting at a mark or target). Various colonies offered bounties on "vermin"—crows, foxes, squirrels, and wolves—animals that destroyed crops or killed domesticated animals. New England farmers hunted in pairs or groups of three. In the South larger hunting parties were assisted by Native Americans. Men hunted on foot and on horseback, and with or without dogs. South Carolina colonists hunted alligators from boats.

Marksmanship

Although most colonists were not interested in hunting, many men were proud of their abilities as marksmen. They often shot with guns or bows and arrows just for the joy of the sport or the chance to perfect their skills. For instance, Dutch settlers brought a game called "shooting the parrot" from the Netherlands. It originated when soldiers set either a live bird or a wooden replica on top of a pole and shot at it. The game was so popular in New Netherland that in 1655 Fort Orange magistrates granted a tavern keeper permission to have the burgher guard (member of a security patrol) shoot the parrot on the third day of Pentecost (a Christian feast on the seventh Sunday after Easter). The only rule was that "he keeps good order and takes care that no accidents occur or result therefrom."

By the eighteenth century English colonists were holding contests in which men shot at targets for prizes. For instance, Caesar Rodeney of Delaware helped organize several competitions. (He was the father of Caesar Rodeney Jr., who signed the Declaration of Independence, the document that formed the United States of America in 1776.) Rodeney was better off financially than the average colonist, so he had time to practice target shooting and could afford to buy ammuni-

An Unenthusiastic Hunter

John Winthrop, the first governor of Massachusetts, loved bird hunting as a young man, but he eventually gave it up for reasons that may explain why most English colonists were not hunters. Winthrop noted, "I have ever binne crossed in usinge it [hunting], for when I have gone about it not without some woundes of conscience, and have taken much paynes and hazarded my healthe, I have gotten sometimes a verye little but most commonly nothinge at all towards my cost and laboure."

tion for his guns. He was apparently a fair shot and competed for cloth, money, a hat, and a fiddle, which he also played. Anthony Klincken, who lived in Germantown, Pennsylvania, always took his gun when he went to nearby Philadelphia. According to an observer, Klincken "used to speak with wonder of seeing hundreds of rats in the flats among the spatterdocks [water lilies] at Pool's bridge, and that he was in the habit of killing them for amusement as fast as he could load [his gun]." Byrd shot targets with a bow and arrow, sometimes just for fun, but often in a contest with others.

Horse racing

The American enthusiasm for horse racing can be traced back to England, where it was first organized during the reign of King Henry VIII (1491–1547). Cities sponsored races during festivals as part of the entertainment. By 1600 a dozen or more English towns were sponsoring races. In time, silver trophies for first, second, and third places became commonplace. Towns marked off courses (also called tracks) and built grandstands, where spectators could watch for free and place bets. Races were as long as 4 miles and were run in several heats (a single round of a contest), which rewarded stamina as well as speed. The first specialized racecourse was developed by King James I at Newmarket, England, by 1622. While some members of the royal court rode in the races, others watched from permanent stands. Newmarket was so strongly identified with immoral court life that when the Puritans came to power during the English Civil War (1642–48), they demolished the stands and plowed up the track. The Restoration (return of the monarchy) in 1660 brought to power Charles II, an accomplished competitive rider who established an annual race, the Plate, which he himself later won. During Charles's reign Newmarket became the fashion center of the nation. Other courses developed later. Queen Anne (1665–1714) founded the famous races at Ascot and also established breeding lines known as "thoroughbred," which meant that a horse was descended from especially fine Arabian horses. Soon a breeding history known as the pedigree was developed, and some of the thoroughbred horses were taken to the colonies.

New York pioneers horse racing Informal races between riders on horseback undoubtedly occurred throughout the colonies. Formal horse racing was introduced by New York governor Richard Nicolls in 1668 when he sponsored an annual race at Hempstead Plain on Long Island. This oval, two-mile course was named Newmarket after the track in England. Races were run in the spring and fall, with the winners taking home an engraved silver porringer (a metal bowl with a single, flat, pierced handle). Horse racing became so popular that a second racetrack, Church Farm on Manhattan Island, opened by the 1730s. In 1744 wealthy New Yorkers Peter De Lancey and William Montague raced their horses (Ragged Kate and Monk, respectively) at Church Farm for a prize of 200 pounds (English currency). This was more than five times the amount a typical laborer earned in a year. Other tracks also opened in New York before the American Revolution (1775–83).

Puritan and Quaker disapproval of time-wasting entertainment such as horse racing meant that formal racecourses were slower to develop in New England and Pennsylvania. During the eighteenth century races were held in Boston and Philadelphia. By 1720 horses ran for money prizes at Cambridge and Rumney Marsh outside Boston. In Philadelphia, Race Street led to a racecourse, and before 1726 Sassafras Street served as a racetrack. By 1761 horse races in Philadelphia were advertised in colonial newspapers, suggesting that its critics had lost the battle to stop the sport.

Quarter horse bred in Chesapeake Horse racing was also a popular sport in the South, and both the quarter race and the quarter horse were developed in the Chesapeake (Maryland and Virginia). Races were run on a straight quarter-mile track rather than an oval course. Horses that ran the quarter mile were called quarter horses and became known for their stamina and ability to release quick bursts of speed. Quarter-horse events operated under a variety of rules, agreed to before the race, that specified handicaps (assessments of the relative winning chances of contestants) for horses and the weight of riders. Increasing wealth and interest in competition and gambling led to better breeding and the importing of thoroughbred horses from England. The first recorded stallion (a male horse kept for breeding), Bulle-Rock, was sired (fathered) by the English horse Darley Arabian and sent to Virginia in 1730. The most famous imported horse was Janus, a grandson of the Godolphin Arabian, that arrived in 1752. English stallions were bred (mated) with local mares, producing fast horses that also had endurance. Their speed and stamina led to the same kind of racing in the Chesapeake as in England and the northern colonies.

Charleston, South Carolina, was the center of horse racing in the lower south. By 1734 racing was a semipublic event advertised in the *South Carolina Gazette,* and the prize was a saddle and bridle (harness). The next year a jockey club (an organization for riders of racehorses) was organized in the city. One-mile races for prizes worth 100 pounds were held at the York course near Charleston. By 1743 monthly races were taking place at York and a new track had opened at Goose Creek. In 1754 a third racecourse opened outside Charleston. Prizes included not only money and trophies but also watches and, in 1744, a finely embroidered jacket.

Board and card games

Colonists knew many board and card games that were popular in Europe. For the most part the games, which involved luck and skill, were held in taverns and clubs or private homes and played for money. Men and women participated in various kinds of games together, usually in homes, since women did not have access to taverns and clubs. During the eighteenth century taverns became larger, offering more rooms and a greater variety of games and other entertainment. Although laws were passed to limit such recreation, especially on the Sabbath, people simply ignored them and spent their Sundays playing cards.

Backgammon Among the oldest known games is backgammon, which involves rolling dice and moving pieces along a board. Records show that versions of the game were played in ancient Egypt, Rome, Greece, Japan, China, and the Near East. By the Middle Ages (A.D. 476–1453) all European nations had a form of backgammon, which was also known as trictrac or

Cards Cause Social Problems

From the earliest days of the colonial period card playing was considered a waste of time that promoted laziness and lack of productivity in workers. Many religious leaders also regarded the pastime as sinful. The Dutch tried to regulate card games on the Sabbath. In Virginia, which was normally did not have overly restrictive laws, card playing—along with dice games—caused so many problems that the government passed harsh laws against idleness. A Massachusetts law ordered citizens to get rid of their playing cards in 1631. Founder of Pennsylvania William Penn's "Great Law" of 1682 prohibited card games and fined or sentenced lawbreakers to five days in jail. None of these efforts was successful, however, and by the end of the seventeenth century card playing was a common form of recreation in all the colonies.

ticktack. The Spanish, French, Dutch, and English all brought the game with them to America. As early as 1656 New Netherland listed "backgammon or ticktack" among a host of other "idle and forbidden exercises and plays" that were banned on Sunday. Like most board games, backgammon was portable and required little equipment. It could be played on a table or on a portable board or box. In taverns and coffeehouses several games would be going at once.

Billiards Played on a special table with a cue (long stick) and balls, billiards was known to nearly all Europeans who settled in America. Because the average billiard table was 12 feet long, the game was played in public houses, taverns, or the homes of the wealthy. Southern plantation owners were drawn to billiards for a variety of reasons. The table itself made a statement about wealth, and the game required only two people. Byrd outfitted Westover, his plantation, with many diversions, including a billiard table. In 1711 he confided to his diary that "Mr. Mumford and I played at billiards till dinner. . . . In the afternoon we played at billiards again and I lost two bits [coins equal to twenty-five cents]." On occasion Byrd also played the game with his wife.

Cards Card playing, like backgammon, is an ancient form of recreation known throughout the world. By the sixteenth century people in every European country played card games. The cards, were often quite beautiful. Card playing came to the New World (a European term for North and South America) with the earliest colonists. Three favorite games were whist, euchre, and piquet. Whist, also called whisk, was especially popular in the eighteenth century (it is an ancestor of modern-day bridge). Using fifty-two cards, two pairs of partners tried to win tricks (cards played in one round of a card game often used as a scoring unit). Euchre was a French game that may have come to America through French Louisiana. Four players, two to a team, used a thirty-two-card deck that had one suit as trump (a card of a suit any of whose cards will win over a card of another suit). Piquet was originally a French game that spread to other parts of Europe. It could be played by two people, so it was suitable for home entertainment. Piquet used a deck like euchre. In piquet both sides declared what cards they held, thus providing room to lie. Byrd and his wife played piquet during quiet afternoons or evenings at Westover, but, as Byrd recorded in his secret diary, his wife could get annoyed with him when she found him cheating.

Blood sports

Sports that resulted in the injury or death of animals were part of European recreational life. Bulls, badgers, and bears were tethered (tied up) so they could not escape in a sport called "baiting." Men on horseback chased foxes with the aid of dogs, which tore the foxes apart once they were caught. In Spain unarmed men ran in the streets with bulls, and at the end the animals were slaughtered.

Animal baits Europeans brought many of their blood sports with them to America. Bullbaiting was apparently confined to New England and the middle colonies. The sport was sponsored by taverns, where it was relatively easy

Slaves, Servants, and Gambling

As children, African slaves in New York engaged in a form of gambling, playing for pennies by shooting marbles, throwing dice, and playing a game called papa. In New York City during the 1740s many male African slaves, like whites, had the leisure and skill to play games that involved gambling. For instance, they gambled at cards at an alehouse owned by a John Hughson. Taverns catered to slaves and to lower-class whites, offering them an outlet for competitive urges and a place away from the eyes of their masters and spouses.

to clear a space for the bull and the dogs. The contests, which catered to the lower classes, took place in the evening hours when workingmen and apprentices could get away from their employers and masters. In Virginia at least one tavern offered bearbaiting, and an early Massachusetts account describes a wolf bait in which hunters trapped a wolf, tied it down, and then set their dogs on it.

Foxhunting Although historical records show that foxhunting became popular in the colonies after 1754, wealthy landowners in the middle colonies seem to have enjoyed the activity during the sixteenth century. For instance, a man known simply as

Although it probably did not gain popularity until late in the colonial period, some wealthy colonists did participate in the sport of foxhunting. *Reproduced by permission of Corbis-Bettmann.*

Butler was the houndskeeper for hunters in Philadelphia. By the mid-1750s, when the city had expanded into the countryside, gentlemen hunters had to move to New Jersey.

Cockfighting

Cockfighting was a contest between two roosters that often had metal spurs, called gaffs, attached to their feet. Money and honor rode on the cocks, so breeders of good birds, like breeders of good horses, gained a reputation. Unlike horses, however, the losing roosters did not live to compete another day. The purpose of a fight was for one cock to kill another.

The fights were held in an enclosed space or cockpit, usually in a tavern. Men of varied social backgrounds—rich and poor, illiterate and well educated—were drawn to cockfighting. In 1711 John Sharpe, a chaplain to soldiers at the fort on New York harbor, spent several February evenings "at ye fighting cocks." In 1741 shoemaker John Romme and his wife ran a tavern that catered to African slaves. There "a negro . . . kept game-fowls . . . and used to come there to bring them victuals [food]." William Shippen, a Philadelphia physician, wrote to a friend in 1735, "I have sent you a young game cock, to be depended upon which I would advise you to put to a walk by himself with the hen I sent you before—I have not sent an old cock—our young cockers have contrived to kill and steal all I had."

In rural areas cockfights were also held in taverns or other places where men gathered. In the South, beginning in the 1750s, cockfights were sometimes advertised in newspapers and people often traveled 40 miles to attend matches featuring as many as sixty birds. Slaves had their own cockfights, in makeshift rings that were easily set up and taken down. Betting on cocks was an essential part of the sport. In the 1760s Robert Wormeley Carter, a Virginia planter [?], confided to his diary that he had lost more than twenty-one pounds at a large event with many birds. This sum of money exceeded the total value of the property owned by an average poor man.

Where to Learn More

The following list focuses on works written for readers of middle school or high school age. Books aimed at adult readers have been included when they are especially important in providing information or analysis that would otherwise be unavailable, or because they have become classics.

Adler, Bill, ed. *The American Indian: The First Victim*. New York: Morrow, 1972.

Armstrong, Joe C. W. *Champlain*. Toronto: Macmillan of Canada, 1987.

Bacon, Margaret Hope. *Mothers of Feminism*. New York: Haper-Collins, 1986.

Bailyn, Bernard. *Voyagers to the West: A Passage in the Peopling of America on the Eve of the Revolution*. New York: Vintage, 1986.

Barbour, Philip L., ed. *The Complete Works of Captain John Smith* *(1580–1631)*. 3 Vols. Chapel Hill, N.C.: University of North Carolina Press, 1986.

Barbour, Philip L. *Pocahontas and Her World*. Boston: Houghton Mifflin, 1969.

Barbour, Philip L. *The Worlds of Captain John Smith*. Boston: Houghton Mifflin, 1964.

Bataiile, Gretchen M., ed. *Native American Women*. New York: Garland Publishing, 1993.

Bergman, Peter M. *The Chronological History of the Negro in America,* New York: Harper & Row, 1969.

Berkeley, Edmund and Dorothy Smith Berkeley. *The Life and Travels of John Bartram from Lake Ontario to the River St. John*. Tallahassee: University Presses of Florida, 1982.

Berkin, Carol. *First Generations: Women in Colonial America*. New York: Hill & Wang, 1996.

Biographical Dictionary of Indians of the Americas, Vol. 1. Newport Beach, Calif.: American Indian Publishers, 1991.

Blackburn, Joyce. *James Edward Oglethorpe*. New York: Dodd, Mead, 1970.

Blodgett, Harold. *Samson Occom*. Hanover, N.H.: Dartmouth College Publications, 1935.

Bolton, Herbert Eugene. *Coronado: Knight of the Pueblos and Plains*. Albuquerque: University of New Mexico Press, 1964.

Bolton, Herbert Eugene. *Kino's Historical Memoir of Primería Alta,* Vol. 1. Cleveland: Arthur H. Clark, 1919.

Bourne, Russell. *The Red King's Rebellion: Racial Politics in New England, 1675–1678*. New York: Atheneum, 1990.

Bradford, William. "Governor William Bradford on the Plymouth Colonists' Relations with the Indians, Early 1620s." In *Major Problems in American Colonial History,* Edited by Karen Ordahl Kupperman. Lexington, Mass.: D. C. Heath, 1993.

Breen, T. H. and Stephen Innes. *"Myne Owne Ground": Race and Freedom on Virginia's Eastern Shore, 1640–1676*. New York: Oxford University Press, 1980.

Brill, Marlene Targ. *Encyclopedia of Presidents: John Adams*. Chicago: Children's Press, 1986.

Burrows, Edwin G., and Mike Wallace. *Gotham: A History of New York City to 1898*. New York: Oxford University Press, 1999.

Cady, Edwin Harrison. *John Woolman*. New York: Washington Square Press, 1965.

Calloway, Colin G., ed. *After King Philip's War: Presence and Persistence in Indian New England*. Hanover, N.H.: Dartmouth College, 1978.

Cameron, Ann. *The Kidnaped Prince: The Life of Olaudah Equiano*. New York: Knopf, 1995.

Campbell, Elizabeth A. *The Carving in the Tree*. New York: Little, Brown and Company, 1968.

Champlain, Samuel de. *Voyages of Samuel de Champlain*. Edited by W. L. Grant. New York: Barnes and Noble, 1952.

Colbert, David, ed. *Eyewitness to America*. New York: Pantheon Books, 1997.

Columbus, Christopher. *The Voyage of Christopher Columbus: Columbus's Own Journal of Discovery*. Translated by John Cummins. New York: St. Martin's Press, 1992.

Connors, Donald Francis. *Thomas Morton*. New York: Twayne Publishers, 1969.

The Correspondence of Jeremias Van Rensselaer, 1651–1674. Edited by A. J. F. Van Laer. Albany: University of the State of New York, 1932.

The Correspondence of Maria Van Rensselaer, 1669–1689. Edited by A. J. F. Van Laer. Albany: University of the State of New York, 1935,

Coulter, Tony. *La Salle and the Explorers of the Mississippi,* New York: Chelsea House, 1991.

Crawford, Deborah. *Four Women in a Violent Time: Anne Hutchinson (1591–1643), Mary Dyer (1591?–1660), Lady Deborah Moody (1660–1659), Penelope Stout (1622–1732).* New York: Crown Publishers, 1970.

Cwiklik, Robert. *King Philip and the War with the Colonists.* Englewood Cliffs, N.J.: Silver Burdett Publishers, 1989.

Dalglish, Doris N. *People Called Quakers.* Freeport, N.Y.: Books for Libraries Press, 1969.

Davis, Natalie Zemon. *Women on the Margins: Three Seventeenth-Century Lives.* Cambridge, Mass.: Harvard University Press, 1995.

De Leeuw, Adéle. *Peter Stuyvesant.* Champaign, Ill.: Garrard Publishing Company, 1970.

Demos, John. *The Tried and the True: Native Amrican Women Confronting Colonization.* New York: Oxford University Press, 1995.

Dockstader, Frederick J. *Great North American Indians.* New York: Van Nostrand Reinhold, 1977.

Dolson, Hildegarde. *William Penn, Quaker Hero.* New York: Random House, 1961.

Dubowski, Cathy East. *The Story of Squanto: First Friend of the Pilgrims.* Milwaukee: Gareth Stevens Publishers, 1997.

Duncan, David Ewing. *Hernando de Soto: A Savage Quest in the Americas.* New York: Crown Publishers, 1995.

Dunham, Montrew. *Anne Bradstreet; Young Puritan Poet.* Indianapolis: Bobbs-Merrill, 1969.

Dunn, Richard S. *Puritans and Yankees: The Winthrop Dynasty of New England 1630–1717.* Princeton, N.J.: Princeton University Press, 1962.

Dupré, Céline. "Réne-Robert Cavelier de La Salle." In *Dictionary of Canadian Biography,* Vol. 1. Toronto: University of Toronto Press, 1967.

Earle, Alice Morse. *Child Life in Colonial Days.* New York: Macmillan, 1899; reprinted Stockbridge, Mass.: Berkshire House Publishers, 1993,

Eccles, W. J. *France in America.* Rev. ed. Markham, Ontario: Fitzhenry & Whiteside, 1990.

Eckert, Allan W. *The Conquerors.* Boston: Little, Brown and Company, 1970.

Eckert, Allan W. *The Frontiersmen.* Boston: Little, Brown and Company 1967.

Eckert, Allan W. *Wilderness Empire: A Narrative.* Boston: Little, Brown and Company, 1969.

Elgin, Kathleen. *The Quakers; The Religious Society of Friends.* New York: D. McKay Company, 1968.

Elliott, Emory, and others, ed. *American Literature: A Prentice Hall Anthology.* Englewood Cliffs, N.J.: Prentice Hall, 1991.

Ellis, Joseph S. *Passionate Sage: The Character and Legacy of John Adams.* New York: Norton, 1994.

Faber, Doris. *Anne Hutchinson.* Champaign, Ill.: Garrard Publishing Co., 1970.

Feest, Christian F. *The Powhatan Tribes.* New York: Chelsea House, 1989.

Ferling, John E. *John Adams: A Life.* New York: Henry Holt & Company, 1996.

Foster, Genevieve. *The World of Captain John Smith.* New York: Scribners, 1959.

Franklin, Benjamin. *Benjamin Franklin: A Biography in His Own Words.* Edited by Thomas Fleming. New York: Newsweek, distributed by Harper & Row, 1972.

Gates, Henry Louis Jr., ed. *The Classic Slave Narratives.* New York: New American Library, 1987.

Gaustad, Edwin S. *Liberty of Conscience: Roger Williams in America.* Grand Rapids, Mich.: Eerdmans, 1991.

Goodfriend, Joyce. *Before the Melting Pot: Society and Culture in Colonial New York City.* Princeton, N.J.: Princeton University Press, 1992.

Grabo, Norman S. *Edward Taylor.* New York: Twayne Publishers, 1962.

Guiterrez, Ramon A. *When Jesus Came, the Corn Mothers Went Away.* Stanford, Calif.: Stanford University Press, 1991.

Gunn, Giles, ed. *Early American Writing.* New York: Penguin Books, 1994,

Haile, Edward Wright, ed. *Jamestown Narratives: Eyewitness Accounts of the Virginia Colony: The First Decade: 1607–1617.* Champlain, Va.: Roundhouse, 1998.

Hamilton, Raphael N. *Father Marquette.* Detroit: William B. Eerdmans Publisher, 1970.

"Hannah Duston." In *The Young Oxford History of Women in the United States: Biographical Supplement and Index.* Edited by Nancy F. Cott. New York: Oxford University Press, 1995.

Harrah, Madge. *My Brother, My Enemy.* New York: Simon & Schuster Books for Young Readers, 1997. (Fiction)

Hays, Wilma Pitchford. *Rebel Pilgrim: A Biography of Governor William Bradford.* Philadelphia: Westminster Press, 1969.

Herbst, Josephine. *New Green World.* New York: Hastings House, 1954.

Innes, Stephen, ed. *Work and Labor in Early America.* Chapel Hill, N.C.: University of North Carolina Press, 1988.

Jacobs, William Jay. *Coronado: Dreamer in Golden Armor,* New York: Franklin Watts, 1994.

James, Edward T., and others, eds. *Notable American Women,* 3 Vols. Cambridge, Massachusets: Belknap Press of Harvard University Press, 1971.

Johnson, Allen, and others, eds. *Dictionary of American Biography.* New York: Scribners, 1946–58.

Johnson, Charles, Patricia Smith, and WGBH Research Team. *Africans in America: America's Journey through Slavery.* New York: Harcourt, Brace & Company, 1998.

Josephy, Alvin M. "The Betrayal of King Philip." In *The Patriot*

Chiefs: A Chronicle of Native American Resistance. New York: Viking, 1969.

Kamensky, Jane *The Colonial Mosaic: American Women, 1600–1760.* New York: Oxford University Press, 1995.

Kelso, William M., Nicholas M. Luccketti, and Beverly A. Straube. *Jamestown Rediscovery IV.* Richmond, Va.: The Association for the Preservation of Virginia Antiquities, 1998.

Kent, Zachary. *Jacques Marquette and Louis Jolliet.* Chicago: Children's Press, 1994.

Knaut, Andrew L. *The Pueblo Revolt of 1980: Conquest and Resistance in Seventeenth-Century New Mexico.* Norman, Okla.: University of Oklahoma Press, 1995.

Krensky, Stephen. *The Printer's Apprentice.* New York: Bantam Doubleday Dell Books for Young Readers, 1996.

Kupperman, Karen Ordahl, ed. *Major Problems in American Colonial History.* Lexington, Mass.: D. C. Heath, 1993.

Lambert, Frank. *Peddlar in Divinity": George Whitefield and the Transatlantic Revivals, 1737–1770.* Princeton, N.J.: Princeton University Press, 1994.

Lee, Susan. *Eliza Pinckney.* Chicago: Children's Press, 1977.

Levin, David. *Cotton Mather: The Young Life of the Lord's Remembrance, 1663–1703.* Cambridge, Mass.: Harvard University Press, 1978.

Lockridge, Kenneth A. *The Diary, and Life, of William Byrd II of Virginia, 1674–1744.* Chapel

Hill, N.C.: University of North Carolina Press, 1987.

"Massasoit." In *Biographical Dictionary of Indians of the Americas.* Vol. 1. Newport Beach, Calif.: American Indian Publishers, 1991.

McCormick, Charles Howard. *Leisler's Rebellion.* New York: Garland Publishers, 1989.

McDaniel, Melissa. *The Powhatan Indians.* New York: Chelsea House, 1995.

McFarland, Philip James. *The Brave Bostonians: Hutchinson, Quincy, and The Coming of the American Revolution.* Boulder, Colo.: Westview Press, 1998.

Middleton, Richard. *Colonial America: A History, 1585–1776.* 2nd ed. Malden, Mass.: Blackwell Publishers, 1996.

Miller, Perry. *Roger Williams: His Contribution to the American Tradition.* New York: Atheneum, 1962.

Montgomery, Elizabeth Rider, *Hernando de Soto.* Champaign, Ill.: Garrard Publishing Company, 1964.

Morgan, Edmund S. *The Puritan Dilemma: The Story of John Winthrop.* Boston: Little, Brown and Company, 1958.

Morison, Samuel Eliot. *The Great Explorers: The European Discovery of America.* New York: Oxford University Press, 1986.

Morison, Samuel Eliot. *Samuel de Champlain, Father of New France.* Boston, Mass.: Little, Brown and Company, 1972.

Nagel, Paul C. *Descent from Glory: Four Generations of the John*

Adams Family. Cambridge, Mass.: Harvard University Press, 1999.

National Geographic Society. *The World of the American Indian.* Rev. ed. Washington, D.C.: National Geographic Society. 1993.

Osler, E. B. *La Salle.* Toronto: Longmans Canada, 1967.

Parish, Helen Rand. *Estebanico.* New York: Viking Press, 1974. (Fiction)

Pinckney, Eliza, ed. *The Letterbook of Eliza Lucas Pinckney.* Columbia, S.C.: University of South Carolina Press, 1997.

Pollock, John Charles. *George Whitefiled and the Great Awakening.* Garden City, N.Y.: Doubleday, 1972.

Putnam, William Lowell. *John Peter Zenger and the Fundamental Freedom.* Jefferson, N.C.: McFarland and Co., 1997.

Quinn, David Beers. *Set Fair for Roanoke: Voyages and Colonies, 1584–1606.* Chapel Hill, N.C.: University of North Carolina Press, 1985.

Rachlis, Eugene. *The Voyages of Henry Hudson.* New York: Random House, 1962.

Reich, Jerome R. *Leisler's Rebellion.* Chicago: University of Chicago Press, 1953.

Riforgiato, Leonard R. *Missionary of Moderation: Henry Melchior Mühlenberg and the Lutheran Church in English America.* Lewisburg, Pa.: Bucknell University Press, 1980.

Ritchie, Robert C. *Captain Kidd and the War against the Pirates.* Cambridge, Mass.: Harvard University Press, 1986.

Rountree, Helen C. *The Powhatan Indians of Virginia: Their Traditional Culture.* Norman: University of Oklahoma Press, 1989.

Rowlandson, Mary. *The Narrative of the Captivity and Restoration of Mrs. Mary Rowlandson.* Excerpted in *American Literature: A Prentice Hall Anthology.* Edited by Emory Elliott and others. Englewood Cliffs, N.J.: Prentice Hall, 1991.

Rudy, Lisa Jo, ed. *The Benjamin Franklin Book of Easy and Incredible Experiments.* New York: Wiley, 1995.

Sale, Kirkpatrick. *The Conquest of Paradise: Christopher Columbus and the Columbian Legacy.* New York: Knopf, 1990.

Salisbury, Neal, ed. *Soveraignty and Goodness of God.* Boston: Bedford Books, 1997.

Sando, Joe S. *Pueblo Profiles: Cultural Identity through Centuries of Change.* Santa Fe: Clear Light, 1995.

Saunders, Richard H. *John Smibert: Colonial America's First Portrait Painter.* New Haven, Conn.: Yale University Press, 1995.

Sewall, Marcia. *Thunder from the Sky.* New York: Antheneum Books for Young Readers, 1995.

Sherman, Josepha. *The First Americans: Spirit of the Land and People.* New York: Smithmark, 1996.

Sigerman, Harriet, ed. *Young Oxford History of Women in the United States: Biographical Supplement and Index.* New York: Oxford University Press, 1994.

Silverman, Kenneth, ed. *Colonial American Poetry.* New York: Hafner, 1968.

Smith, Carter, ed. *The Arts and Sciences: A Sourcebook on Colonial America.* Brookfield, Conn.: Millbrook Press, 1991.

Smith, Carter, ed. *Battles in a New Land: A Sourcebook on Colonial America.* Brookfield, Conn.: Millbrook Press, 1991

Smith, Carter, ed. *Daily Life: A Sourcebook on Colonial America.* Brookfield, Conn.: Millbrook Press, 1991.

Smith, Carter, ed. *The Explorers and Settlers: A Sourcebook on Colonial America.* Brookfield, Conn.: Millbrook Press, 1991.

Smith, Carter, ed. *Governing and Teaching: A Sourcebook on Colonial America.* Brookfield, Conn.: Millbrook Press, 1991.

Smith, Carter, ed. *The Puritan Family.* New York: Harper & Row, 1966.

Spaulding, Phinizy. *Oglethorpe in America.* Athens, Ga.: University of Georgia Press, 1984.

Stanford, Donald E. *Edward Taylor.* Minneapolis, Minn.: University of Minnesota Press, 1965.

Stephen, Leslie, and Sidney Lee, eds. *The Dictionary of National Biography.* London, England: Oxford University Press.

Stevenson, Augusta. *Squanto: Young Indian Hunter.* Indianapolis: Bobbs-Merrill. 1962.

Steven, William K. "Drought May Have Doomed the Lost Colony." In *The New York Times.* April 14, 1998, pp. A1, A14.

Stiles, T. J., ed. *In Their Own Words: The Colonizers.* New York: Berkeley Publishing, 1998.

Stout, Harry S. *The Divine Dramatist: George Whitefield and the Rise of Modern Evangelism.* Grand Rapids, Mich.: Eerdmans, 1991.

Syme, Ronald. *Francisco Coronado and the Seven Cities of Gold.* New York: Morrow, 1965.

Terrell, John Upton. *The Life and Times of an Explorer.* London, England: Weybright and Talley, 1968.

Tracy, Patricia J. *Jonathan Edwards, Pastor: Religion and Society in Eighteenth-Century* Northampton, N.Y.: Hill & Wang, 1979.

Trudel, Marcel. "Jacques Cartier." In *Dictionary of Canadian Biography,* Vol. 1. Toronto: University of Toronto Press, 1967.

Vachon, André. "Louis Jolliet." In *Dictionary of Canadian Biography,* Vol. 1. Toronto: University of Toronto, 1967.

Wainwright, Nicholas B. *George Croghan: Wilderness Diplomat.* Chapel Hill, N.C.: The University of North Carolina Press, 1959.

Waldman, Carl. *Who Was Who in Native American History.* New York: Facts on File, 1990.

Wallace, Paul A. W. *The Muhlenbergs of Pennsylvania.* Philadelphia: University of Pennsylvania Press, 1950.

Warfel, Harry R., and others, editors. *The American Mind.* 2nd ed. Vol. 1. New York: American Book Company, 1963.

Webb, Stephen Saunders. *1676: The End of American Independence.* New York: Knopf, 1984.

Wendell, Barrett. *Cotton Mather.* New York: Chelsea House, 1980.

White, Elizabeth Wade. *Anne Bradstreet, "The Tenth Muse."* New York: Oxford University Press, 1971.

Whitman, Sylvia. *Hernando de Soto and the Explorers of the American South.* New York: Chelsea House, 1991.

Wildes, Harry Emerson. *William Penn.* New York: Macmillan, 1974.

Wilford, John Noble. *The Mysterious History of Columbus: An Exploration of the Man, the Myth, the Legacy.* New York: Knopf, distributed by Random House, 1991.

Williams, Selma R. *Divine Rebel: The Life of Anne Marbury Hutchinson.* New York: Holt, Rinehart, and Winston, 1981.

Winslow, Ola Elizabeth. *John Eliot: Apostle to the Indians.* Boston: Houghton Mifflin, 1968.

Winslow, Ola Elizabeth. *Jonathan Edwards: 1703–1758.* New York: Collier Books, 1961.

Winslow, Ola Elizabeth. *Master Roger Williams.* New York: Macmillan, 1957.

Winslow, Ola Elizabeth. *Samuel Sewall of Boston.* New York: Macmillan, 1964.

Wood, Peter H. *Strange New Land: African Americans, 1617–1776.* New York: Oxford University Press, 1995.

Wroth, Lawrence C. *The Voyages of Giovanni da Verranzzano, 1524–1528.* New Haven, Conn.: Yale University Press, 1970.

Yewell, John, and others, eds. *Confronting Columbus: An Anthology.* Jefferson, N.C.: McFarland and Co., 1992.

Ziff, Larzer. *The Career of John Cotton: Puritanism and the American Experience.* Princeton, N.J.: Princeton University Press, 1962.

Videocassettes

Benjamin Franklin Citizen of the World. A&E Home Video, 1994. Videocassette recording.

Benjamin Franklin Scientist and Inventor. Living History Productions, 1993. Videocassette recording.

Web sites

Africans in America. http://www.pbs.org/wgbh/aia old/part1/1i2992.html Available December 6, 1999.

"The American Colonies— New England" in *Documents Relevant to the United States Before 1700.* http:www.msstate.edu/ Archives/History/USA/ colonial/bef1700.html Available September 30, 1999.

"Anne Hutchinson." http://www.gale.com/gale/ cwh/hutchin.html Available December 6, 1999.

Bacon's Castle. http://www.sightsmag.com/ usa/va/surr/sights/bacon/ bacon.htm Available September 30, 1999.

"Bacon's Declaration in the Name of the People" (30 July 1676) in *Documents Relevant to the United States Before 1700.* http:www.msstate.edu/ Archives/History/USA/ colonial/bef1700.html Available September 30, 1999.

Bacon's Rebellion.
http://www.infoplease.com/
ce5/CE00404.5.html Available December 6, 1999.

Benjamin Franklin: An Enlightened American, http://library.advanced.org/
22254.htm Available December 6, 1999.

"The Cabot Dilemma: John Cabot's 1497 Voyage & the Limits of Historiography" in *Documents Relevant to the United States Before 1700.* http:www.msstate.edu/
Archives/History/USA/
colonial/bef1700.html Available September 30, 1999.

"Charter of the Dutch West India Company (1621)" in *Documents Relevant to the United States Before 1700.* http:www.msstate.edu/
Archives/History/USA/
colonial/bef1700.html Available December 6, 1999.

"Charter to Sir Walter Raleigh (1584)" in *Documents Relevant to the United States Before 1700.* http:www.msstate.edu/
Archives/History/USA/
colonial/bef1700.html Available December 6, 1999.

"Charter of Massachusetts Bay (1629)" in *Documents Relevant to the United States Before 1700.* http:www.msstate.edu/
Archives/History/USA/
colonial/bef1700.html Available December 6, 1999.

Christopher Columbus and his Voyages. http://deil.lang.uiuc.edu/
web.pages/holidays/
Columbus.html Available December 6, 1999.

Columbus and the Age of Discovery. http://www.millersv.edu/
~columbus/mainmenu.html Available December 6, 1999.

Columbus and the Native Americans. http://www.geocities.com/
CapitolHill/8533/columbus.
html Available September 30, 1999.

De Soto's Trail thru the Southeast. http://www.conquestchannel.
com/inset9.html Available December 6, 1999.

Eliza Lucas Pinckney. http://wwwnetsrq.com/~
dbois/pinckney.html Available December 6, 1999.

Estevanico the Moor. http://www.thehistorynet.
com/AmericanHistory/
articles/1997/0897_cover.
html Available December 6, 1999.

The Estevanico Society. http://www.estevanico.org/
Available December 6, 1999.

Father Jacques Marquette National Memorial and Museum. http://www.uptravel.com/
uptravel/attractions/
3.htm Available September 30, 1999.

"The First Thanksgiving Proclamation (1676)" in *Documents Relevant to the United States Before 1700.* http:www.msstate.edu/
Archives/History/USA/
colonial/bef1700.html Available September 30, 1999.

Francisco López De Mendoza Grajales: "The Founding of St. Augustine, 1565" in *Modern History Sourcebook.* http://www.fordham.edu/
halsall/mod/1565staugustine.
html Available September 30, 1999.

Giovanni Verrazano.
http://www.greencastle.k12.
in.us/stark/verrazano/htm
Available September 30,
1999.

"Gottlieb Mittelberger, On the
Misfortune [of?] indentured
Servants" in *Documents
Relevant to the United States
Before 1700.*
http:www.msstate.edu/
Archives/History/USA/
colonial/bef1700.html Avail-
able December 6, 1999.

"Governor William Berkeley on
Bacon's Rebellion" in *Documents Relevant to the United
States Before 1700.*
http:www.msstate.edu/
Archives/History/USA/
colonial/bef1700.html Available December 6, 1999.

*Henry Melchior Mühlenberg: Patri-
arch of American Lutherans.*
http://www.justus.anglican.
org/resources/bio/261.html
Available December 6, 1999.

Henry Hudson and the Half Moon.
http://www.ulster.net/~hrmm
/halfmoon/halfmoon.htm
Available September 30,
1999.

Historic Bartram's Garden.
http://www.libertynet.org/
bartram Available December
6, 1999.

*Images from the Salem
Witchcraft Trails.*
http://www.law.umkc.edu/
faculty/projects/ftrials/salem/
salem.htm Available December 6, 1999.

*Indentured Servitude: A Culturally
Historical Prospective of West
African and African American.*
http://asu.alasu.edu/
academic/advstudies/4b.html
Available December 6, 1999.

Indian Pueblo Cultural Center.
http://www.indianpueblo.org
Available September 30, 1999.

The Indian Wars.
http://www.geocities.com/
Heartland/Hills/1094/indian.
htm Available December 6,
1999.

"Instructions for the Virginia
Colony (1606)" in *Documents
Relevant to the United States
Before 1700.*
http:www.msstate.edu/
Archives/History/USA/
colonial/bef1700.html Avail-
able December 6, 1999.

Jacques Cartier.
http://www.win.tue.nl/cs/fm/
engels/discovery/cartier.html
Available September 30, 1999.

Jamestown Rediscovery.
http://www.apva.org/ Available December 6, 1999.

John Adams.
http://www.studyworld.com/
John_Adams.htm Available
September 30, 1999.

John Rolfe.
http://www.esd.k12.ca.us/
Cadwallader/Room%2020/
Colonies Available December
6, 1999.

"King Ferdinand's letter to the
Taino/Arawak Indians" in
*Documents Relevant to the
United States Before 1700.*
http:www.msstate.edu/
Archives/History/USA/
colonial/bef1700.html Avail-
able December 6, 1999.

*The Journals of Henry Melchior
Mühlenberg.*
http://www.midcoast.com/~
picton/public_html.BASK/
catalog/books/1469.htm
Available December 6, 1999.

La Salle Ship Sighted.
http://www.he.net/~archaeol
/9601/newsbriefs/lasalle.html
Available September 30, 1999.

The Life and Times of Henry Hudson, Explorer and Adventurer.
http://www.georgian.net/
rally/hudson/ Available
September 30, 1999.

Louis Jolliet: Professional Explorer.
http://www.mvnf.muse.
digital.ca/Explor/jolli_el.htm
Available December 6, 1999.

"The Massachusetts Body of Liberties, Numbers 1–49 (1641)";
"The Body of Liberties
50–98 (1641)" in *Documents
Relevant to the United States
Before 1700.*
http:www.msstate.edu/
Archives/History/USA/
colonial/bef1700.html Available December 6, 1999.

The Mayas.
http://www.indians.org/
welker/mayamenu.htm Available September 30, 1999.

"Mayflower Documents" in *Documents Relevant to the United
States Before 1700.*
http:www.msstate.edu/
Archives/History/USA/
colonial/bef1700.html Available December 6, 1999.

"Mayflower Genealogy and History" in *Documents Relevant to
the United States Before 1700.*
http:www.msstate.edu/
Archives/History/USA/
colonial/bef1700.html Available December 6, 1999.

*Motion: A Travel Journal—Time
Travelers: Sarah Kemble Knight
(1666–1727).* (Contains the
only known portrait of Sarah
Kemble Knight)
http://www.nearbycafe.com/
motion/motionmenu/

timetravel/knight.html Available September 30, 1999.

The New England Pirate Museum.
http://www.piratemuseum.
com/pirate.htm Available
December 6, 1999.

Olaudah Equiano.
http://www.atomicage.com/
equiano/life.html Available
December 6, 1999.

"Penn's Plan for a Union" in *Documents Relevant to the United
States Before 1700.*
http:www.msstate.edu/
Archives/History/USA/
colonial/bef1700.html Available September 30, 1999.

Pocahontas: Jamestown Rediscovery.
http://www.apva.org/history/
pocahont.html Available
December 6, 1999.

Pocahontas: Savior or Savage?
http://theweboftime.com/
Poca/POCAHO~l.html Available December 6, 1999.

Popé.
http://www.pbs.org/weta/
thewest/wpages/wpgs400/
w4pope.htm Available September 30, 1999.

*Quakers in Brief: An Overview of the
Quaker Movement From 1650
to 1990.*
http://www.cryst.bbk.ac.uk/
~ubcg09q/dmr/intro.htm
Available September 30,
1999.

*René-Robert Cavelier, sieur
de La Salle.*
http://www.knight.org/
advent/cathen/09009b.htm
Available September 30, 1999.

"Richard Haluyt, Discourse on
Western Planting (1584)" in
*Documents Relevant to the
United States Before 1700.*
http:www.msstate.edu/

Archives/History/USA/colonial/bef1700.html Available December 6, 1999.

"Robert Beverley On Bacon's Rebellion (1704)" in *Documents Relevant to the United States Before 1700.* http:www.msstate.edu/Archives/History/USA/colonial/bef1700.html Available December 6, 1999.

Roger Williams National Memorial. http://www.nps.gov/rowi/ Available December 6, 1999.

Salem witchcraft hysteria. http://www.nationalgeographic.com/features/97/salem/ Available September 30, 1999.

Samuel Champlain. http://www.blupete.com/Hist/BiosNS/1600-00/Champlain.htm Available December 6, 1999.

Samuel de Champlain's 1607 Map. http://lcweb.loc.gov/exhibits/treasures/trr009.html Available December 6, 1999.

Samuel de Champlain's Voyages. http://www.ccukans.edu/carrie/docs/texts/champlai.html Available December 6, 1999.

"Sarah Kemble Knight" in *The Puritans: American Literature Colonial Period (1608–1700).* http://falcon.jmu.edu/-ramseyil/amlitcol.htm Available December 6, 1999.

The South Carolina Business Hall of Fame. [Eliza Pinckney] http://theweb.badm.sc.edu/ja/jaelp.htm Available December 6, 1999.

"Spanish Conquest of Native Americans during the Sixteenth Century" in *Documents Relevant to the United States Before 1700.* http:www.msstate.edu/Archives/History/USA/colonial/bef1700.html Available December 6, 1999.

Spanish Exploration and Conquest of Native Americans. http://www.conquestchannel.com/ Available September 30, 1999.

Susanna North Martin. http:www.rootsweb.com/~nwg/sm.html Available September 30, 1999.

Tlingit Culture. http:www.geocities.com/Athens/Atlantis/4513/ Available September 30, 1999.

"William Bradford" in *The Puritans: American Literature Colonial Period (1608–1700).* http://falcon.jmu.edu/-ramseyil/amlitcol.htm Available December 6, 1999.

William Byrd II. http://marist.chi.il.us/~amlit/laurph2.html Available December 6, 1999.

Index

Italic type indicates
volume numbers.

Illustrations are marked
by (ill.)

Charles Town *1:* 117–18

Charlevoix, Pierre François Xavier de *2:* 356

Chartier de la Lotbiniére, René-Louis *2:* 356

Cheever, Ezekiel *2:* 332

Cherokees *1:* 4, 25; *2:* 257, 323

Chesapeake Bay *1:* 113

Chickasaws *1:* 18, 20

Choctaws *1:* 18

A Chronological History of New-England 2: 358

Church of England *1:* 99, 112

Claiborne Rebellion *1:* 114

Claiborne, William *1:* 114

Clayton, John *2:* 385

Clement, Augustine *2:* 344

Clement, Samuel *2:* 344

Cochiti Pueblo *1:* 6

Coddington, William *1:* 101

Colbert, Jean-Baptiste *2:* 340

Colden, Cadwallader *2:* 361, 380, 385

Colden, Jane *2:* 380

Coligny, Gaspar de Châtillon, comte de *1:* 62

College of William and Mary *2:* 323, 338

Collinson, Peter *2:* 388

Colonial America, map of *1:* 187 (ill.)

Columbus, Bartholomew *1:* 36

Columbus, Christopher *1:* 1, 13–14, 32–36, 33 (ill.), 34 (ill.), 44; *2:* 288

Columbus, Diego *1:* 36

Columbus, Fernando *1:* 34

Comanches *2:* 320

Company of Comedians *2:* 366

Company of the Indies *1:* 76

The Compleat Housewife 2: 390

Congregationalism *2:* 317–18

Connecticut *1:* 99, 100, 164, 209; *2:* 212, 250, 324, 339

The Conscious Lovers 2: 366

Cook, Ebenezer *2:* 364

Cooper, Anthony Ashley *1:* 116

Cooper, Susannah *2:* 281

Copernicus, Nicholas *2:* 383, 385

Copley, John Singleton *2:* 347

Coronado, Francisco Vásquez de *1:* 15, 47–50, 49 (ill.); *2:* 355

Cortés, Hernán *1:* 37

Cosby, William *1:* 175

Cotton, John *1:* 151–54; *2:* 276

Council for New England *1:* 95

Courcelle, Rémy de *2:* 356

Couturier, Henri *2:* 343

Covenant Chain *1:* 22–23

Covenant of grace *1:* 152; *2:* 299

Covenant of works *1:* 151

Creeks *1:* 17, 18

Crèvecouer, J. Hector St. John *2:* 283

Cross, Martha *2:* 272

Crusades *1:* 31

Cuentos 2: 355

Cushman, Robert *1:* 94

D

Daganowedah *1:* 21–22

Danckaerts, Jasper *2:* 338

The Daniel Catcher 2: 362

Darby, William *2:* 365

Dartmouth College *2:* 324

Davenport, John *1:* 100

Davenport, Rachel *2:* 274

Delawares *1:* 19, 23, 164, 181; *2:* 212, 277

De La Warr, Thomas West *1:* 87

Delisle, Guillaume *2:* 379

Dellius, Godfriedus *2:* 324

A Description of the New Netherland 2: 361

Deshon, Moses *2:* 349

Díaz, Melchor *1:* 48

Diseases, Native American *1:* 26 (ill.)

Distilleries *1:* 195

Doctors, colonial *2:* 391 (ill.)

Doeg *1:* 135

Dominion of New England *1:* 169–70

Donnacona *1:* 59, 61

Douglas, David *2:* 364

Douglass, William *2:* 362, 392–93

Drake, Francis *1:* 81, 115

Drayton Hall *2:* 373

Drisius, Samuel *2:* 322

"Dunkers" *2:* 316

Duodecennium Luctuosum 2: 358

Du Pont, François Gravé *1:* 63

Duston, Hannah *2:* 282

Dutch *1:* 163, 181; *2:* 213 (ill.)

Dutch colonial house *2:* 371

Wesley, John *1:* 122; *2:* 360
West, Benjamin *2:* 347
Westminster Assembly *2:* 305
Weston, Thomas *1:* 94, 116
Westover plantation *2:* 372
Whales *1:* 196
Wheatley, Phillis *2:* 363
Wheelock, Eleazor *2:* 324, 324 (ill.)
Wheelwright, John *1:* 153–54
Whipple House *2:* 370
Whitaker, Alexander *2:* 323
Whitefield, George *1:* 122, 206;
    2: 304, 316–18, 318 (ill.)
Whitehall *2:* 373
White, John *1:* 81–82
Wigglesworth *2:* 360
Williamsburg, Virginia *2:* 211, 338
Williams, Eunice *2:* 283
Williams, Hannah *2:* 380
Williams, Roger *1:* 56, 97, 100,
    100 (ill.); *2:* 306
William III *1:* 98, 108, 114, 184;
    2: 293
Wilson, John *1:* 152; *2:* 358
Winnebagos *1:* 24, 68
Winthrop, John *1:* 94–98, 95 (ill.),
    100, 154; *2:* 215, 220, 358, 403
Winthrop Jr., John *2:* 385
Winthrop IV, John *2:* 385

Witch trials *1:* 148 (ill.), 150
Wolfe, James *1:* 78
Women, colonial *2:* 264 (ill.)
Women, Native American
    2: 262 (ill.)
Wonders of the Invisible World
    1: 149
Woolen Act of 1699 *1:* 198
Woolman, John *1:* 141,
    141 (ill.), 174
Wren, Christopher *2:* 373

Y

Yale College *2:* 339
Yale, Elihu *2:* 339
Yamasee War *1:* 17
Yeamans, John *1:* 118
Yumas *1:* 52

Z

Zenger, John Peter *1:* 175–76,
    176 (ill.)
Zinzendorf, Nikolaus von
    2: 309, 315
Zunis *1:* 46–47